The Politics of Sacred Places

Bloomsbury Studies in Religion, Space and Place

Series editors: Paul-François Tremlett, John Eade, and Katy Soar

Religions, spiritualities, and mysticisms are deeply implicated in processes of place-making. These include political and geopolitical spaces, local and national spaces, urban spaces, global and virtual spaces, contested spaces, spaces of performance, spaces of memory, and spaces of confinement. At the leading edge of theoretical, methodological, and interdisciplinary innovation in the study of religion, Bloomsbury Studies in Religion, Space and Place brings together and gives shape to the study of such processes.

These places are not defined simply by the material or the physical but also by the sensual and the psychological, by the ways in which spaces are gendered, classified, stratified, moved through, seen, touched, heard, interpreted, and occupied. Places are constituted through embodied practices that direct critical and analytical attention to the spatial production of insides, outsides, bodies, landscapes, cities, sovereignties, publics, and interiorities.

Christianity in Brazil
Sílvia Fernandes

Global Trajectories of Brazilian Religion
Edited by Martijn Oosterbaan, Linda van de Kamp, and Joana Bahia

Ideologies and Infrastructures of Religious Urbanization in Africa
Edited by David Garbin, Simon Coleman, and Gareth Millington

Migration and the Global Landscapes of Religion
David Garbin

Religion and the Global City
Edited by David Garbin and Anna Strhan

Religious Pluralism and the City
Edited by Helmuth Berking, Silke Steets, and Jochen Schwenk

Singapore, Spirituality, and the Space of the State
Joanne Punzo Waghorne

Struggles for Hindu Sacred Space in the Netherlands
Priya Swamy

Towards a New Theory of Religion and Social Change
Paul-François Tremlett

Urban Religious Events
Edited by Paul Bramadat, Mar Griera, Julia Martinez-Ariño, and Marian Burchardt

The Politics of Sacred Places

A View from Israel-Palestine

Nimrod Luz

BLOOMSBURY ACADEMIC
LONDON • NEW YORK • OXFORD • NEW DELHI • SYDNEY

BLOOMSBURY ACADEMIC

Bloomsbury Publishing Plc, 50 Bedford Square, London, WC1B 3DP, UK
Bloomsbury Publishing Inc, 1385 Broadway, New York, NY 10018, USA
Bloomsbury Publishing Ireland, 29 Earlsfort Terrace, Dublin 2, D02 AY28, Ireland

BLOOMSBURY, BLOOMSBURY ACADEMIC and the Diana logo
are trademarks of Bloomsbury Publishing Plc

First published in Great Britain 2023
This paperback edition published 2025

Copyright © Nimrod Luz, 2023

Nimrod Luz has asserted his right under the Copyright, Designs and Patents Act, 1988, to be identified as Author of this work.

For legal purposes the Acknowledgments on pp. xiii–xv constitute an extension of this copyright page.

Cover image © Thomas M. Scheer / EyeEm / gettyimages.co.uk

All rights reserved. No part of this publication may be: i) reproduced or transmitted in any form, electronic or mechanical, including photocopying, recording or by means of any information storage or retrieval system without prior permission in writing from the publishers; or ii) used or reproduced in any way for the training, development or operation of artificial intelligence (AI) technologies, including generative AI technologies. The rights holders expressly reserve this publication from the text and data mining exception as per Article 4(3) of the Digital Single Market Directive (EU) 2019/790.

Bloomsbury Publishing Plc does not have any control over, or responsibility for, any third-party websites referred to or in this book. All internet addresses given in this book were correct at the time of going to press. The author and publisher regret any inconvenience caused if addresses have changed or sites have ceased to exist, but can accept no responsibility for any such changes.

A catalogue record for this book is available from the British Library.

Library of Congress Control Number: 2023934711

ISBN:	HB:	978-1-3502-9572-8
	PB:	978-1-3502-9576-6
	ePDF:	978-1-3502-9573-5
	eBook:	978-1-3502-9574-2

Series: Bloomsbury Studies in Religion, Space and Place

Typeset by Integra Software Services Pvt. Ltd.

For product safety related questions contact productsafety@bloomsbury.com.

To find out more about our authors and books visit www.bloomsbury.com and sign up for our newsletters

In Loving Memory of My Mothers and Father

Contents

List of Figures ... ix
Preface ... x
Acknowledgments ... xiii

Introduction ... 1
   Places and the Contested Nature of Sacred Places ... 7
   Scale and Sacred Places: Problematizing the Field ... 11
   A Note on Methodology ... 14
   Book Structure ... 17

1 Ethnocratizing the Holy Land: Contextualizing Sacred Places in Israel/Palestine ... 21
   Constructing the Holy Land ... 24
   Ethnocracy and the Religious/Sacred Field ... 36

2 Embodying the Sacred and the Body in Sacred Places ... 47
   Body and Embodiment: A Few Theoretical Clarifications ... 47
   Bodies, Individuals, and Embodying the Sacred ... 54
   Embodying the Nation through Sacred Places ... 60

3 Sacred Sites in Rural Communities ... 69
   Ethnographic Snippets: Entering a Community's Sacred Places ... 69
   The History and Mythology of Maqam Abu al-Hijja and Its Saint ... 73
   The Changing Landscape of the Maqam: A Socio-Spatial Analysis ... 76
   The Politics of Maqam Abu al-Hijja: Dynamics of a Sacred Place ... 81
   The History and Mythology of Mariam Bawardy of I'bbelin ... 84
   The Changing Landscape of the Shrine: A Socio—Spatial Analysis ... 86
   The Politics of the Shrine of Mariam Bawardy: Dynamics of a Sacred Place ... 90

4 Sacred Sites and the Right to the City ... 97
   Lefebvre, Materiality, and Urban Sacred Places ... 97
   The Grand Mosque of Ottoman Bi'r al-Sabʿ in Contemporary Beersheba ... 103

	From Mosque to Museum: The Unsuccessful Struggle of the Local Muslim-Palestinian Community	105
	The Hassan Bek Mosque Conflict and the Semiotic of a Minaret in a Mixed Israeli City	109
	The Premeditated Erasure of Manshiyya	111
	The Struggle over the Mosque: Early Beginnings	113
	Winning Back the Mosque: The Rabita and the Renovation Process	115
5	*ReligioCity* and Decolonizing Acre through the Sacred	123
	Urban Religion and the Urban Sphere	123
	ReligioCity Introduced: Toward a Theory of Urban Religion and Materiality	125
	Contextualizing Acre: "Mixing" Religion into Urban Ethnocracy	129
	ReligioCity in Acre: Voices, Materialities, Religious Infrastructures	136
	De-Colonizing Acre: Exploring the Lababidi Mosque	146
6	Glocalizing the Sacred: The Haram al-Sharif/Temple Mount as the Hypocenter of Israel/Palestine	153
	Entering Jerusalem: The Ultimate and Most Conflictual Sacred	153
	Glocalization as Overthrowing the State: Local to Global Flows of Sanctity	157
	Jerusalem and Its Sacred Center under the Yoke of Nationalism	160
	The Israeli Islamic Movement and the Glocalization of the Haram al-Sharif	166
7	Epilogue	177
	Notes	188
	References	193
	Index	217

List of Figures

1.1	Map of Palestine in 1941 (with permission of Eran Laor Maps Collection, National Library of Israel)	35
1.2	Map of Israel and Occupied Territories (adapted from Wikimedia)	45
3.1	The temporary altar in the renovated shrine	71
3.2	The Bawardy complex (courtesy of Assad Daoud)	88
4.1	Mosque of Beersheba 2022 (courtesy of Dr. Mansour Nasasra)	105
4.2	The proposed plan for the Hassan Bek tourist compound	115
4.3	Mosque of Hassan Bek against the David Intercontinental Hotel	119
5.1	Demographic maps of Acre, 1995 and 2008	134
6.1	The Underground Marwani Mosque (courtesy of Mr. Ron Peled)	169

Preface

This book has its birth in blood, pure and simple. These were my first days as a post-doc at the Department of Geography in UW-Madison in late September 2000. I was just getting used to my windowless no. 480 office at Science Hall when news began to arrive from back home about Palestinian demonstrations, (armed) confrontations with Israeli security forces, casualties, and riots spreading throughout Israel/Palestine following Ariel Sharon's provocative visit at the al-Aqsa Mosque. These intense and traumatic days were the first salvo of what came to be known as the Second Intifada, during which thousands of Palestinians and Israelis were killed and tens of thousands wounded. Contemporary life and research plans became intertwined and inseparable in ways I surely could not have foreseen when I wrote my post-doc proposal earlier that year.

My initial proposed project was titled "The Politics of Palestinian Sacred Places: Past and Present," and it aimed to explore places in the region through a *longue durée* approach, that is, a multi-disciplinary exploration of my chosen sites from the Muslim conquest of the seventh century to the present. This rather ambitious plan was based on previous engagements I had with the realm of the sacred in different periods within the region. But events as they were unfolding on the ground were just too compelling; I simply could not ignore them in my work, nor was I able to distance myself from them. So, I abandoned my previous work plan and started with the contemporary period, while assuring myself that I would delve back into the past of the places explored as the project evolved. This never happened, at least not in the fashion I initially aimed for.

When I returned home—incidentally, a day before 9/11/2001—I continued this voyage among contemporary sacred places, mostly of Palestinian and minority communities in Israel/Palestine—places I addressed under the heading of "on the margins of the state." I certainly had no idea that this would amount to a voyage of more than two decades, indeed, an enriching and inspiring journey which has taken me to numerous sites, hundreds of meetings and interviews with individuals of all walks of life within Israeli and Palestinian societies, and becoming acquainted with several communities in different geographical settings. This move also facilitated a deeper engagement with critical theories, qualitative methods, and expanded both my personal and professional horizons with a growing involvement in the contemporary socio-political aspects of my research.

So why a book? And more importantly, what are the main claims and arguments which inform this study and shape the structure of the book? At the beginning of the third millennium, not only is religion not privatized, neither has it become less influential in the public sphere, as early theorists had predicted. Religion seems to be far from disappearing and continues to define and legitimate both social and political reality. Geographers of religion have followed these developments closely, particularly since the 1990s, along with the critical turn in cultural geography. As the most iconic and common manifestation of religion, sacred places were, and still are, a prime focus within these endeavors. Indeed, one might argue that creating sacred places and assigning sanctity to specific spatialities is a common and a crucial feature of religion(s). In this book I follow socio-political processes as they transpire within and without sacred places in Israel/Palestine. I look at these spatialities through various critical lenses and engage with them through a scalar reading that is from the body scale to the global.

The aim of this book, then, is to offer a critical-analytical study of the socio-political aspects of sacred places in contemporary societies. The book's overarching argument is that sacred places and the ample socio-religious-political practices they entail provide a space which is less scrutinized by the state, and by hegemonic powers within it, where alternative visions of the socio-political may be envisioned, contested, and produced. This argument emerges from an understanding that these spatialities, which are evolving at the intersection of religion and politics, are lenses through which we may further explore society-space reflexive relations. My inclination is usually toward exploring the contested nature of sacred places and the ways they emerge as conflictual and as battlegrounds. This is particularly relevant to the region I have been engaged with for a few decades now, and yet it is surely not endemic to Israel/Palestine alone.

During the time that elapsed since I started harvesting data and exploring sacred places, I was fortunate to engage with different theoretical approaches which enriched my research and allowed me a better understanding of "my" sites. This was an inspiring experience, as I delved into a variety of qualitative methods (interviews, participant observations, text analysis of current affairs, and more). It was also a humbling one, at times of surprising encounters with people of different religious backgrounds and ethnicities. This was also a continuously challenging process as, along the lines of the main argument of the book, sacred places are indeed found at the forefront of socio-political contestations and my positionality was not always easy to negotiate in the field, particularly as most of my time was devoted to studying ethnic minority sites in the region. These encounters, at times highly conflictual, were critical to the development of my understanding of the sacred as it is narrated throughout this book. And now, as I move on to other projects—among them *ReligioCity*, which also features in this book—I invite the reader to a voyage among cutting-edge approaches to the study of sacred places, seasoned with rich ethnography and data analysis. I can only hope that the methodology I developed over the years and the theoretical approach and engagement presented in this study will be helpful for those studying the enchanting field of sacred places elsewhere.

Acknowledgments

It takes a village to raise a book! It certainly takes a global village of friends, of colleagues, and of intellectual mentors, some of whom I have never met but who inspired me deeply, to accomplish the task. Perhaps even more importantly, it necessitates the goodwill of many individuals, most of whom will remain forever anonymous. These people, who we in the business call interlocutors, interviewees, or informants, who so generously shared with me their lives, worldviews, struggles, frustrations, and food, have all won my admiration and awe, and I cherish their precious gift to me and all that they have taught me. I feel so grateful, honored, and humbled, as I think now about the thousands of such encounters over more than twenty years of fieldwork.

Naturally, over such a long period one acquires many debts, and now it is not only my duty, but mostly my pleasure to acknowledge them all, and the readers will have to forgive me (or skip this part) for such a detailed and lengthy string of thanks. I remember fondly my bi-weekly lunches and talks with Prof. Yi Fu Tuan while I was a hopeful young post-doc in Madison, Wisconsin, in 2000–1. Yi Fu was an intellectual pillar, an inspirational cultural geographer, and a kind and a rare soul. Now that he is no longer with us, I can only hope that this book is worthy of his memory. It was in Madison that my friend Prof. Kris Olds suggested contacting Prof. Lily Kong. For the very few who might not have heard of her, she is a powerhouse in the fields of cultural geography and of geography of religion and has been nothing but encouraging since my very first steps on this path. Lily, I cherish your good advice and support over many a year. Prof. Oren Yiftachel has been a constant guide and a staunch supporter of my project(s), even when I did not understand fully where I was going. Oren, I cannot thank you enough for the countless times you were there with a good word, golden advice, and always supplying me with brilliant analysis and critique of my work. I am sure many of the things you told me found their way into this book and my work. I thank my friend and colleague, Prof. Nurit Stadler, who not only shared with me her uncanny intellectual depth and wit but also walked with me part of this way in our joint project of "Enchanted Places," which allowed me to expand my horizons in the field of anthropology of religion. Prof. Valentina Napolitano, Prof. Simon Coleman, Prof. Veronica della

Dora, Prof. Marian Burckhardt, Prof. Mar Greira, Prof. Paul Bramadat, Prof. Irene Becci, and Prof. Mariachiara Giorda have all been so kind and helpful, and I thank you all for being there for me, for your friendship, and surely for your contribution to my work. Special thanks are due to Prof. Susanne Rau and Prof. Jorg Rupke, who invited me to be a fellow in their wonderful project on Religion and Urbanity. My six months with you in Erfurt as a fellow at the Max-Weber-Kolleg were truly an intellectual heaven, which tremendously helped me to think this book through.

While writing this book I benefitted greatly from the knowledge, experience, and kindness of friends and colleagues from across the globe. I thank them all and owe them for their wonderful comments and suggestions, and especially for saving me from many embarrassing moments. Before I name them, I wish to thank and acknowledge the amazing work of my language editor, Dr. Leigh Chipman, who so professionally worked on my initial humble manuscript and rescued me from so many pitfalls. Thank you so much Leigh!! I am grateful to Prof. John Eade, who I am proud to have as a close friend and who has been there for me from the first embryonic proposal that was sent to Bloomsbury through the book's various stages and progress to the last phase of its publication. There are very few scholars of his caliber, but even more than that: of his openness, keen interest, and kindness to others. John, you never cease to amaze me with your big heart and caring for other humans, and I am honored to have you in my corner. Prof. Oren Yiftachel was kind enough to read and comment on Chapter 1, and his influence is surely to be found in other chapters as well. Prof. Haim Ben David and Prof. Jacob Ashkenazi (from back home) lent me their invaluable knowledge on the Holy Land and gave such wonderful notes on both Judaism and Christianity, which are dealt with in Chapter 1. Prof. Anna Secor allowed me to benefit from her expertise and gave me such insightful comments and support while treating body and embodiment in Chapter 2. Dr. Mori Ram and Dr. Hila Zaban, two brilliant young scholars who keep me on my toes, were kind enough to read through and comment on Chapters 4 and 5. Dr. Mansour Nasasra, whose work on Beersheba and the Islamic Movement was so beneficial to me—thank you for answering all my questions and correcting me when needed. Dr. Craig Larkin donated his expertise on Jerusalem and the Islamic Movement in Israel and helped me greatly to improve Chapter 6. I owe special thanks to my friend Prof. Itzhak Reiter, whose voluminous and erudite work and multitude of publications on sacred places in the region proved to be vital to this book.

Over these years I greatly benefited from the immense contribution of wonderful research assistants. I remember you all fondly, and I thank you for bringing such joy and vivacity to the field: Ms. Najwan Khatib, Ms. Hila Raz, Ms. Ranna Musa, Mr. Chen Reuveni, Ms. Yael Amit, Dr. Orit Hirsch-Matsioulas, Dr. Lior Chen, Mr. (soon to be Dr.) Omer Hacker, Ms. Haia Abu-Asaad, Ms. Abir Idlebi, Mr. Idan Edut, and Ms. Maisoon Hamdan.

Last, but surely not least, my family. To Ofri and Ido, whose childhood years also included following daddy to all sorts of strange places. And to Nitsan, my better half, who enabled me this intellectual indulgence over so many years. If I had known then, what I have learned by now, who knows what shape or form this book would have taken. I am so grateful for having you all in my life and for giving them true meaning.

And when all said and done—all the errors and shortcomings of this book are mine and mine alone.

Nimrod Luz

Introduction

The aim of this book is to offer a critical-analytical study of the socio-political aspects of sacred places in contemporary societies. As a cultural-political geographer, I read sacred places' spatialities within the broader understanding of scale and the spatial turn in the study of religion. I focus on contemporary sacred sites and their socio-political meanings for minorities within a hegemonic and secularizing state-system. The overarching argument of the book is that sacred places and the ample socio-religious-political practices they entail provide a space which is less scrutinized by the state, and by hegemonic powers within it, where alternative visions of the socio-political may be envisioned, contested, and produced.

This argument emerges from an understanding that these spatialities, which are evolving at the intersection of religion and politics (in the widest possible definition), are lenses through which we may further explore society-space reflexive relations. Following the likes of Lefebvre and De Certeau and the retheorizing of place within critical cultural geography, the plethora of activities within these places are understood as the appropriation of a symbolic place and an embodied experience which is increasingly liberated from prevailing socio-political constraints (Lefebvre 1991). In this spatially oriented inquiry, places are explicitly understood as always in flux, and constantly being produced, contested, and in a perpetual dynamic process among forces entangled in a complex scalar matrix. The production of scale is perceived as integral to the production of space, as found in the wide-ranging scalar dimensions of social spatiality. Allowing for an expansive approach to scale as both an ontological and an epistemological concept, I explore sacred places in various scalar contexts from the body to the global.

Through a scalar exploration of sacred places and the exploration of the scalar production of these places, this study avails itself of the various forces working conjointly, if not always harmoniously, within the different realms of the sacred.

The empirical data is drawn from over two decades of exploring sacred sites, and the struggles and conflicts revolving around them, in the Israeli-Palestinian context. Admittedly, this opening salvo is highly condensed and for some might verge on the cryptic. The following three short vignettes will hopefully facilitate a clearer view of what the politics of the sacred entails and provide a short introduction to scales in the current endeavor.

Politics of the sacred take 1: May 10, 2021, was destined to be an ominous day in Jerusalem and the aftershocks were to shake (and not for the first time) the entire Israel/Palestine region. There were just too many events and conflicting processes culminating and converging at the same time and at the same (sacred) place. On the Palestinian/Muslim liturgical clock this was the end of the holy month of Ramadan and immediately after *Laylat al-Qadr* (the "Night of Power"), which is the most revered day of the month and arguably the most sacred date in the Islamic calendar, marking the beginning of the Prophet Muhammad's revelations. Palestinian-Muslims streamed in large numbers to the al-Aqsa Mosque atop al-Haram al-Sharif for prayers, while on the Israeli/Jewish national clock this was Jerusalem Day. On this day, official Israel commemorates the reunification of the city after Israeli forces captured East Jerusalem, including the Old City and its holy sites, in the 1967 War. As an aside, I want to suggest that like most things in this contested and conflicted region, one needs to choose one's terminology rather carefully. What would be the proper term in this case? Captured? Liberated? Reunited? And surely no matter what term one chooses, one is bound to fail someone's standards of political correctness or point of view, certainly among fellow critical academics. This is especially true regarding Jerusalem, where every inch is fought over and serves as a major bone of contention between the two ethno-national opposing groups (Luz 2021a).

I decided to flesh out this matter at the outset of the book, as this is a burden and a hurdle one is constantly facing when writing about Israel/Palestine, where everything is highly political, politicized, and contested. Alas, these conundrums do not become any easier even after years of trying to accommodate those sensitivities among different audience. Certainly, I do not delude myself that by doing so I will be able to tone down discussions on my positionality, but hopefully it may assist focusing on the issues at hand better.

Let us go back then to the tension mounting in Jerusalem throughout May 2021. The apex of Jerusalem Day is the annual March of Flags, during which thousands of Israeli-Jews arrive in the city to mark Israeli control over "indivisible" Jerusalem. Upon reaching the Old City, the parade enters through Damascus Gate, a well-known Palestinian urban center of activities, and then crisscrosses the Muslim Quarter and onward to the Jewish Quarter. The participants carry Israeli flags and wave them as they march through the alleys of the Old City while chanting slogans and singing songs usually associated with religious-nationalist Jewish groups and extreme right circles. The parade is heavily guarded by police forces, as it usually elicits heated responses from Palestinians in East Jerusalem.

Be that as it may, in 2021 the parade was never completed. Dead on cue as Hamas' ultimatum, warning Israel to cease all hostile actions against Palestinians in Jerusalem and especially the heavy-handed policing of the Haram al-Sharif compound, expired at 6 p.m. on May 10, a barrage of long-range rockets was fired toward Jerusalem. Consequently, the participants of the parade scattered, and it was effectively dispersed. Israel responded quickly to this transgression and launched Operation "Guardian of the Walls," during which the Gaza Strip was heavily attacked by Israeli forces and Hamas retaliated with consistent shelling of numerous sites throughout Israel.

This is, alas, but one episode that demonstrates the pivotal role of the Haram al-Sharif/Temple Mount in contemporary politics at the national scale in Israel/Palestine. This is surely not the first time this iconic landmark has stood at the epicenter (pun intended) of the ethno-national Israeli-Palestinian conflict (Luz 2004; Dumper 2014; Shlay and Rosen 2015). The power of the sacred as a mobilizing force is precisely what lured Hamas to present the organization as the defender of the nation's most important religio-political landmark (Wallach 2021). This role was previously held by various charismatic Palestinian leaders, among them the Mufti Hajj Amin al-Husayni during the Mandate period (1920–48) and recently by Shaykh Ra'id Salah, the leader of the northern faction of the Israeli Islamic Movement (Kupferschmidt 1989; Larkin and Dumper 2012). What surely exacerbates matters in this volatile spatiality are the mirror projects occurring in both groups, claiming this sacred ground as essential to the nation's future and its irreplaceable heart.

Politics of the sacred take 2: During a visit to the deserted and dilapidating Ottoman mosque in Beersheba, I notice an inscription sprayed on one of its closed external gates stating in Arabic: *Jami' Bir al-Sab'a* ("The Beersheba Mosque"; fieldnotes, August 19, 2004).[1] This ephemeral and insignificant inscription was nothing short of a political statement issued during the decades-long struggle over the ownership and control of this mosque. The mosque was inaugurated in 1906 as part of the Ottoman Empire's project of constructing a modern capital for the southern region of Palestine. The mosque was built in the urban center, next to other symbols of power such as the governor's house and the *saraya* (government building). The construction of the new town was the outcome of a new Ottoman administrative approach to this by-and-large, neglected province, instigated in response to the rising British supremacy in Egypt following the opening of the Suez Canal. The construction of modern Beersheba was also a concerted and highly sophisticated project of establishing the empire's authority over the hitherto unruly Bedouin tribes of the region (Luz 2008b).

The mosque functioned until 1948, when as part of the geopolitical changes and the establishment of the State of Israel, it was confiscated and utilized as a temporary prison and a tribunal for the remaining local Arab population. By 1953 it was handed over to the municipality, which turned it into a museum. In 1974 the Committee for Bedouin Rights began a public campaign to re-establish the place as a Muslim house of prayer. After over twenty years of failing to achieve its goals through the court of public opinion, the Committee appealed to the Israeli judicial system, arguing for its right to religious freedom and reclaiming the mosque. In 2011 the Supreme Court of Israel made its final ruling on the matter and reaffirmed the status of the place as a museum (HCJ 2011). The court, however, suggested that the museum should pay homage to the compound's origin and function as a center for Islamic culture.

When asked about his take on the struggle over the mosque and the official ban on Muslim prayers therein, lawyer Shchada ibn Bari, a Muslim resident of Beersheba who defines himself as secular and a communist, supplied the following rejoinder: "It is like seeing one's father's grave or someone from the family [dead/injured?], which makes you understand what has been done to you and you are helpless ... this is part of you, part of your religion, whether you consider yourself religious or not you feel like your feelings are betrayed, your soul is being hurt" (interviewed by Reiter and Lehrs 2013: 22). For ibn Bari, as for others who were part of the struggle, mainly from among local Bedouins, the mosque became a material symbol of their excluded position as an ethno-national minority in Israel—hence the attachment to a religious landmark even for the likes of ibn Bari, who define themselves as secularists.

In this political situation and against the ethnocratic logic of the state, the mosque transcends its obvious religious/sacred function and is produced and understood (by some) as part of their Palestinian heritage. This is a rather intriguing position regarding a mosque, which was constructed as part of a concerted effort by the Ottomans to strengthen their control and discipline over the Bedouin population. The Beersheba urban project was designed to convey a strong hegemonic message to local Bedouin tribes and constantly to remind them of their subaltern position (Luz 2005b). As Israel assumed control and the mosque ceased to function as an Islamic institution, so its symbolic message altered, certainly among local Muslims.

The past of places, as so astutely suggested by Doreen Massey, is always open to a multiplicity of readings which represent the claims and counterclaims of different, at times opposing, groups in the present (1995: 185). These different narratives and competing histories of places, and the alternative memories they invoke, are more often than not ways to serve the battles of the present. Along with the changing geopolitics and the transformation of local Muslims' status, so did their perception of the mosque, indeed their memories of it, alter. Once an iconic landmark symbolizing their subaltern position vis-à-vis the Ottoman administration, it was transformed under Israeli rule and changed into a place of yearning and a symbol of resistance to the secularizing-cum-modern Jewish state. In the case of the Beersheba Mosque, the struggle was conducted on the urban-regional scale; as the next case, Nabi Illiya (Arabic for the prophet Elijah), would suggest, the production of place can also take place and remain on a very personal and embodied scale, yet entail a highly political claim all the same.

Politics of the sacred take 3: As part of my journey among sacred places, I was fortunate to walk part of the way with Prof. Nurit Stadler, an anthropologist of religion. Following Weber's theorization of the enchanted, we explored what we defined as enchanted places in Israel/Palestine. The gist of the project was to study socio-political processes in fledgling or recently revived sacred places at their charismatic-initial (as opposed to routinized) phase. This will be further elaborated throughout the book as it bears directly on the development of my work, but at this introductory stage, I wish to narrate but one encounter with an enchanted place which clearly demonstrates the importance of the individual/body scale in the politics of the sacred. The following is based mostly on an ethnography conducted on December 27, 2012.

It is a freezing day typical of late December in the Golan Heights and we are on our way to meet with Shaykh Hassan, the impresario behind recent changes in Nabi Illiya. The site is not entirely new, as local Druze traditions already hold this site as a sacred one connected with the biblical prophet Elijah. And yet, it is going through a new surge of activity, and spatial changes are apparent, such as a recently paved road, the construction of new lavatories, and new signs and billboards narrating the story of the place.

We sit with Shaykh Hassan in the main hall of the site as he narrates the (hi)story of the place. In an all-too-familiar fashion that one often encounters in sacred places, his narrative has very little to do with any known linear historical account. Snippets of biblical mythologies are mixed with local traditions, and thus Elijah came to this site where he spent twenty-one years in what was at that time the "Kingdom of Nimrod," according to Shaykh Hassan. As with other sacred sites the mythology is strengthened by stories of miracles that occurred to pilgrims and visitors, and which serve to validate the "true" sanctity of the place (Luz 2020). Shaykh Hassan recounts a few of them, including a story about the contractor who was assigned with the recent renovations, who was scheduled for emergency orthopedic surgery due to some (obscure) leg problem. Upon learning of his predicament, the Shaykh gave him olive oil and wheat that grew on the site to rub on his problematic leg. The healing powers of the sacred site worked, and due to the miraculous cure, the surgery was canceled. As the interview unfolded, so Shaykh Hassan's covert personal motivations to develop this site were revealed.

As he recounts, the initial motivation to construct the site was to protect it from the might of the Israeli Antiquity Authorities' attempts to perform a wide-ranging excavation on his property, of which the sacred site is part, in the late 1990s.[2] In order to obtain a permit to build and halt the excavations, he met privately with none other than Ariel Sharon, a well-known public figure in Israel. As the details and the timetable of events are rather vague, it is impossible to ascertain what public capacity Sharon had at the time which would make such an audience worthwhile. However, the fact that this public figure, who is known for his military career and later served as the Israeli prime minister, is mentioned is highly significant.

To understand the sensitivity and political implications of such a statement by a Druze from the Golan Heights, one needs to hark back to the geopolitical changes brought forth by the 1967 War. Following the war, the Golan Heights, formerly ruled by Syria, became a part of the Israeli occupied territories which was later annexed by the Israeli government in 1981 (Mara'i and Halabi 1992). Once the Golan Heights were annexed, the Israeli government offered all non-Israelis occupants' citizenship, but very few of the Druze accepted it, and most of them retained their Syrian citizenship. For most, the reasons for maintaining their loyalty to Syria were pragmatic rather than ideological. Israeli rule was understood as ephemeral, and in the likelihood that Israel would return the Golan to Syria (as it did with the Sinai to Egypt) any signs of disloyalty to the totalitarian Syrian regime might be regrettable in the future. So, most of the Druze remained on the fence and were not quick to apply for Israeli citizenship (at least not up to 2012, when civil war in Syria began).

Returning to Shaykh Hassan's statement about his alleged intimate connections to Sharon, it may be inferred to be an indication of collaborating with Israeli authorities when such actions were deemed detrimental to the Druze communities of the Golan. This might also explain some of the hostile remarks about him that we encountered while discussing the site with people from his village, Majdal Shams (interview with J. December 27, 2012). This plausible collaboration with Israeli security forces might also explain the silence on the part of the state when all these new construction activities took place without permits or in compliance with state planning regulations. While looking at the personal scale, it seems rather obvious that promoting the site as a sacred place and serving as its main impresario have ample economic benefits for the Shaykh and the members of his family who are also on the board of trustees of the place in various capacities. This may also explain his relentless efforts and blatant attempts to convince us to leave a "substantial donation" in the coffers of the site: "people usually donate five hundred to one thousand NIS," Shaykh Hassan assured us as we were parting ways (fieldnotes, December 27, 2012).

These three takes on the socio-politics of sacred places illustrate some of the different aspects of my forays into the sacred and clearly emphasize the importance of scale when one explores these spatialities. Simultaneously, they reaffirm what scholars of religion have already acknowledged as the contested nature of sacred places. In what follows I further theorize these two topics. First, I will address the contested nature of sacred places as an integral part of their spatiality and then focus on the geographical notion of scale and its relevancy to the current endeavor, as to any geographic discussion of religion(s).

Places and the Contested Nature of Sacred Places

Places are essential to any human activity—humans simply cannot operate without places, and one of the main characteristics of humans is place-making (Sack 1980). The necessity of a spatial language for any human activity may be demonstrated, for example, in the deployment of spatial terms such as sites and domains even when we moved to virtual realities. As such, place and space loom large in theories of human geography and certainly since the spatial turn in the social sciences (Creswell 2014). Geographical definitions of place since the 1970s have focused on the combination of location and meaning and the human subject's crucial importance in the construction of place (Tuan 1977; Agnew 1987; Creswell 2004). This was partially motivated by the overly mechanistic and quantified approach to places which dominated the field until the late 1960s.

Leading theorists such as Tuan and Relph promoted the idea that geographers need to pay attention to people's subjective experience in a world of places (Relph 1976; Tuan 1977). To make human geography fully human, they argued, geographers needed to be more aware of the ways in which we bring a particularly human range of emotions and beliefs to our interactions with the physical world. Central to this awareness is the geographical concept of place. Place is certainly a phenomenon, a location, but at the same time it is a concept, a product, and a process in which humans are involved. The following is a rather useful definition for understanding place as a socially constructed entity: "place is space to which meaning has been ascribed" (Carter, Donald, and Squires 1993: xii). As a product, place cannot be reduced to its mere physical qualities. It is the outcome and process of human endeavors.

The making of places necessitates, then, a variety of human efforts: interactions, politics, design of memory, myth, and more. Places are socially constructed locales, but at the same time they are processes, in which a plethora of forces are constantly working and therefore in a perpetual possibility of change. This understanding entails an acknowledgment of power as a crucial component in the way places are constructed, promoted, understood, and—surely—contested.

Owing mostly to the seminal work of Foucault (1980), Lefebvre (1991), and de Certeau (1984), which prioritized space as critical to the modernist and capitalist (and postmodernist) project, conceptualizations of spatialities emerged, mostly among human (Marxist and cultural) geographers (della Dora 2016). In his invariably persuasive manner, Foucault observed that place is fundamental in any exercise of power (Foucault 1980: 63). Put differently, places are by their very nature political entities, or at least are politicized through various human agencies. These understandings have inspired mostly Marxist geographers, who argue that place is not merely socially constructed and influenced by an array of human feelings such as attachment (sense of place) but also bound up with power (Harvey 1990; Keith and Pile 1993; Rose 1993). If this is the case, then surely place is the outcome and process of construction which therefore implies that it is invested with meaning, with ideology, and certainly with politics.

By its very nature, place is replete with power and symbolism. It is a complex web of relations, of domination and subordination, of solidarities, and of cooperation (Massey 1993: 144). At the same time, place is inexorably linked with controversies, conflicts, struggles over control, and debates (as well as actual physical conflict) over meaning and symbolism. Being a "web of signification" (Ley and Olds 1988: 195) inevitably transforms place into a site where that significance and its "true" nature are up for grabs by those already in power or in search of it. Places are spatial metaphors through which people (singular and plural) can represent themselves and thus concretize their culture: through places, cultural ideas and the abstract become concrete. Therefore, the struggle over the ownership of places and their control must also be seen as a cultural struggle for autonomy and self-determination (Escobar 2001: 162).

Place provides both the real, concrete settings from which culture[3] emanates to enmesh people in webs of activities and meanings, and the physical expression of those cultures in the form of landscapes (Agnew and Duncan 1989: preface). Additionally, we must consider that places are not only spatially constructed but also have a temporal dimension. In other words, the articulation of social relations that we are naming as a particular place has a history (Massey 1995: 188). Furthermore, any claim to establish the identity of a place depends upon presenting a certain reading of history. Thus, in various conflicts over the contemporary meaning of place, the past as memory, or at times a mythology of a certain past, is involved (Luz 2011). The ongoing conflict over the ownership of the Temple Mount/Haram al-Sharif between Israelis and Palestinians is a pertinent case in point. Current claims from both sides rest on a very specific, fragmented, and surely political, reading of the past of the place.

Thus far I have established that places are always on the "way of becoming" (Pred 1984); that is, they are always in the process (or possibility) of changing, and that conflict and competition are inherent to spatiality, along with collaboration, negotiation, and indeed, production of understanding and meaning. Sacred places make for a rather intriguing example of the socio-political and constructed character of place. Chidester and Linenthal (1995) suggested a binary approach of substantial and situational. While the "substantial" relates to the insider's perspective and focuses on the poetics of place, the situational operates from an outsider perspective and locates the sacred at the nexus of human practices and social projects and focuses on the politics of place. The *situational approach* follows the Durkheimian tradition, which theorizes the sacred as an empty signifier and therefore susceptible to any form of interpretation and assigned meaning (Durkheim 1995).

I will address the substantial through the work of the famous historian of religion Mircea Eliade. His structuralist approach promotes binaries of sacred and profane. For him, "man becomes aware of the sacred because it manifests itself as something wholly different from the profane" (1959: 11). Thus, space is not homogenous and the sacred is an interruption into the heterogenous profane space of the everyday. This manifestation of the sacred—hierophany in his vocabulary, that is, the breach of sanctity into the profane space—is often to be found in the Axis Mundi. Think if you will of the sacred center in Jerusalem where the Rock of Foundation in Jewish tradition connects, among other things, heaven and earth. This is echoed in the Muslim tradition by the concept of the Mi'raj, which refers to the Prophet Muhammad's ascent from Jerusalem to the heavens. The sacred emerges as an ontological given, a known and fixed local around an *axis mundi* which interrupts into the mundane landscape, thus creating an almost out-of-world spatiality. When believers encounter it, they are faced with the omnipotence of God which amounts to what Otto defined as the numinous: being in the awesome presence of divinity (1958).

In such ways, a certain spatiality is carved out and recognized as sacred: this is geopiety, as defined by Wright (1966). However, as a geographer who looks at places as ways of understanding the world (Creswell 2014) and imbued with power, my general approach prioritizes and focuses on the situational, through an engagement mostly with socio-political processes as they unfold and are spatialized in sacred places. In what follows, I will elaborate further on this approach under the heading of the contested nature of sacred places.

Following the spatial turn in the social sciences (Warf and Arias 2009), scholars increasingly criticized Eliade's concept of the sacred as an ontological given. Along with the retheorized approach to place, a new wave of explorations emerged, accounting for a variety of spatial issues (place, landscape, and materiality) within religious studies (Knott 2010; Kong 2010). Starting with Durkheim, who emphasized the centrality of the sacred in a variety of human projects, and surely following the likes of Lefebvre, who prioritized place as crucial to any exercise of power, a critical re-evaluation of the sacred emerged in social theories, beginning with Harvey and other critical Marxist scholars (Harvey 1990, 2003, 2008; Massey 1993, 1999, 2005). Following conflict theory and Foucault more implicitly, Eade and Sallnow focus our attention on the highly contested nature of the sacred: "The power of a shrine, therefore, derives in large part from its character almost as a religious void, a ritual space capable of accommodating diverse meanings and practices" (Eade and Sallnow 1991: 15). Geographers dealing with religion have also pointed to the presence of conflict and contestation involved in the production of sacred sites (Kong 1993a, 1993b, 2001; Chivallon 2001; Naylor and Ryan 2002). Indeed, the very word "production," when applied to the allegedly transcendent external quality[4] of the spatiality of a sacred site, immediately grounds the place and locates it within the realm of everyday life.

Chidester and Linenthal present us with an understanding of the multivalence of sacred sites and their inherent contested nature. They claim that "a sacred place is not merely discovered, or founded, or constructed; it is claimed, owned, and operated by people advancing specific interests" (Chidester and Linenthal 1995: 17). Therefore, becoming a sacred place involves a process of production, but is also inescapably linked to cultural-political contests regarding the multiple meanings assigned to the place. The conflict is not just over the production, Chidester and Linenthal continue to argue, but also over the "symbolic surpluses that are abundantly available for appropriation" (1995: 18). Therefore, sacred sites are arenas where resources are transformed into surplus of meaning. They are heavily invested with symbolism, emotions, and indeed, mystification. This also explains why sacred sites are the location of competing discourses! Too much is at stake and there is too much to lose for contesting groups or influential actors. Taking over and controlling the sacred involves various forms of politics (van der Leeuw 1933/1986). Thus, the sacred is always to be found intertwined with political power, agency, and rather profane[5] social forces. The very concept of production of space necessitates human agency and activity, and therefore implies politics in various manifestations.

As one moves away from the substantial approach to situational theory, sacred places become more and more central to any exploration of sociopolitical processes and the growing impact of religion in contemporary societies (Casanova 1994; Berger 1999). Adhering to this school of thought, the boundaries between the profane and the sacred are becoming extremely fuzzy. More importantly, it locates sacred places squarely within mundane and daily life and a plethora of socio-political processes. This leads me to address the concept of scale, its ample geographical meanings, and the ways it facilitates my analysis of sacred places.

Scale and Sacred Places: Problematizing the Field

Scale is a highly charged geographical concept. Until relatively recently, the notion of scale was usually understood as a form of spatial hierarchy (Herod 2011). In its traditional, predominantly cartographic meaning, scale is defined as the ratio of the distance on a map relative to that same distance on the earth's surface. For geographers, scale as size has been a matter of central importance—consideration of appropriate map scales for forms of analysis and presentation. Surely, scale as size is of central importance for geographical analysis and presentations (Hagget 1965). As a measurement for the size of fixed *a priori* phenomenon which informs the ways we understand the world, it originates initially with Kantian philosophy. His idealist and binary approach to time and space are at the very core of how scale was conceived as part of a pre-given spatio-temporal ordering system (Dikec 2012).

However, following the spatial turn and the emergence of a re-theorized human geography during the 1980s, geographers questioned this notion of scale as an unproblematic fixed hierarchy of bounded spaces (Passi 2004). Growing attention has been drawn to the relations between processes operating at different geographical scales (from the local to the global) and the ways they inform each other. Geographers question the validity of scale as a concept that facilitates an analysis at one geographical scale to other scales or within a different spatial frame at the same scale (Marston et al. 2005).

The idea of scale as level, often conflated with scale as size, with a common implication of a nested hierarchical ordering of space has been put to more and more scrutiny. Along with the growing influence of post-structuralists such as Deleuze and Guattari, the scaffolding upon which scale was initially theorized was challenged by non-hierarchical theories (1987). Within geography it was Taylor's seminal work (1982), aiming at setting an agenda for a relevant political geography, that charged scale with new meanings and launched a heated debate about its very nature. Taylor diverted the discussion towards a deeper understanding and better theorization of the social construction of scale (Smith 1997). His most important contribution was that alterations of geographical scale mattered. Specifically, he argued that there were two types of geographical scale: the vertical and the horizontal. He suggested that people's experiences of everyday life were mediated by the nation-state, the global economy, and the local environment and, on the other hand, that different places could be categorized on the basis of their relative positions within the world economy. Taylor argued that scale is intimately tied to political economic processes.

Following him, it was Smith who revolutionized the field by introducing an innovative conceptualization of scale (Jones et al. 2017). Scale was understood at times as a metaphor, rather than a result of social and material activities (Jonas 1994). Smith profoundly changed the way we look at scale by arguing that scale is a non-fixed entity constituted within broader capitalist processes (1993). He introduced what is now a common currency, that is, scalar politics, alternatively known as "politics of scale" (Smith 1984). This take on scale is a way to grasp the complex interplay of existing power structures and political struggles, in which scale is used not only as a mechanism of constraint and exclusion but also as a weapon of expansion and inclusion (Smith 1992). These endeavors include what he referred to as scalar jumping or jump scale. To give but one concrete example, consider, if you will, the role of the most sacred and highly contested

Islamic site in Israel/Palestine, namely the Haram al-Sharif in contemporary politics. The Israeli Islamic movement (as well as other actors) established its position and strengthened its role as a relevant player by deploying a scalar politics and constantly pushing toward the global scale. Jumping scale in this case seems a highly efficient way to challenge prevailing power structures at the national level.[6]

Following these two important developments, the discipline was heavily engaged in theorizing and in attempts at refining the concept of scale. These took several interrelated lines of analysis. The first was a focus on the "politics of scale." The second line was the broadening and loosening of understandings of strict scalar boundaries (e.g., urban, nation-state, global) and the increased integration of vertical scalar productions with horizontally conceived social networks (Jones 2017). Marston argued for a scalar exploration which entails an understanding of scale from the urban downward to the home, the street, and more importantly in the current context, the body. This, she claimed, would allow to "engage in the ways power relations and power structures, outside the main purview of the field which tended to concentrate on relations of capital and labor" (Marston 2000: 238). In tandem with the growing body of works engaging with scale, critique of certain aspects of scale which were deemed problematic arrived. Jones (1998) questioned its ontological nature and suggested that we should understand it as a representational trope. For her, scale was epistemological—a way of classifying the world—and not a fundamental given of the world (Blakey 2021). This intervention proved to be highly significant, and scholars indeed began to conceptualize scale as a discursive or representational device (Mansfield 2005; Moore 2008). This debate over the very nature of scale and its validity or utility as a geographical trope spiraled into one of the most lengthy and heated debates in the field. Arguing against its validity as an epistemological construct, Marston, Jones, and Woodward went as far as to suggest "a human geography without scale" (2005), in which they implied expunging scale altogether. This suggestion to eradicate scale within geography was challenged by those such as Jonas, who argues that to reject scale altogether would be to miss out on an important dimension of thinking about and acting upon contemporary economic, political, social, and environmental changes (2007).

Admittedly, it is also true that geographers have sometimes appeared to offer rather crude scalar frameworks, which appear to act as pre-given spaces or domains of social and economic life. And yet, issues of scale continue to permeate not just geography but also the broader social sciences and, with the advent of the spatial humanities, the humanities as well. I study sacred places through scale, as I think it is conducive to any critical discussion of the spatialities (and other aspects) of the politics of scared places. Against previous calls to expunge scale altogether, geographers continue to do so simply because it is a commonsense idea (Blakey 2021), and it is also the way the people we study understand their world. Scale is understood throughout this book as a process that involves politics; therefore, it is constantly being fought over by contesting forces. Scale is the spatial configuration where sociopolitical relations are contested (Swyngedouw 1997). Scalar configurations are not pre-given platforms upon which social life simply takes place. They are constantly being remade through sociopolitical struggles. Scale and the production of scale (scaling) are indeed political and social projects. Scale is socially constructed, which implies that in each and every level of analysis—that is, from the personal to the global—our understanding of scale is the outcome of social processes and political struggles. The question of scale and the setting of scale is a matter of political struggle and involves power relations and the change or the contestation of existing power-geometries (Smith 1993).

Scale and scaling are not politically neutral. They are both the result and the outcome of struggles for power and control. Scale is a constitutive dimension of sociopolitical processes. It demarcates the site of social or political contest. It is also about setting a context to the struggle. Scale is an active progenitor of specific social processes; it sets the boundaries for struggles over identity, and control over places. Jumping scales, for example, allows the subordinate or the controlled to dissolve spatial boundaries that are largely imposed from above and that contain, rather than facilitate, their production and reproduction of everyday life. By discussing challenges to, and political contestations over, specific scales I hope to indicate and elucidate the invariable ways sacred places are constructed in different levels, by different actors and in relational ways. Harnessing scales to the current endeavor will enable an understanding of how places are constructed at each level and between them from the body scale to the global.

A Note on Methodology

This book is the product of a myriad of multidisciplinary and intradisciplinary approaches and qualitative research methos. My intradisciplinary training as a cultural geographer and a historian of Muslim societies has enabled me to start my research in each of my chosen sites with a critical text analysis and a survey of historical as well as cartographical and visual sources. This was a crucial step that allowed me to understand the ways the past of places is used, utilized, and interpreted by contemporary individuals and communities. That is, I was able to conflate the data harvested in the field with a more grounded past of places to understand the impacts of their socio-cultural-political perspectives, needs, and sure enough frustrations on the part of my interlocutors. This was a critical phase while engaging with places that have a rich and a lengthy (and contested) history such as the sacred places in Jerusalem (al-Haram al-Sharif to state the obvious), or Maqam abu al-Hijja which was initially constructed circa early fourteenth century CE. A case in point is an Islamic literary genre called *Fada'il Bayt al-Maqdis* (namely, "Literature in Praise of Jerusalem") which is considered the earliest Islamic source on the city. In this amalgam of early traditions, a certain history of the city is narrated and as such it is rather clear that the Islamic building project of the late seventh century CE was constructed on the site of the ruined Jewish temple (Elad 1995).

Be that as it may, in my ongoing work on the Islamic Movement as an agent of change in Jerusalem (see Chapter 6) many of my interlocutors narrated a completely different historical narrative, essentially dismissing any Jewish heritage therein. One may question if these historical documentations are relevant to the subjects in question. And yet they are crucially important for whomever wants to understand the contemporary construction of places and how the past of places is produced and perceived against current socio-political processes.

Archival research complemented with news, social, and web media survey were the initial step while working on recently built sites such as the Hassan Bek Mosque in Jaffa, Mosque of Beersheba, or the Lababidi Mosque in Acre. As such before entering the field in Jaffa and conducting my ethnographic work, a comprehensive survey of archival material to be found at Tel-Aviv-Jaffa municipal archive was undertaken. Thus, I was able to locate the current struggle in conjunction with urban development plans, became privy to relevant news material of the time of the struggle, and surely was able to draw a web of relevant actors which were later approached and duly interviewed.

An essential part of my research was undertaken through an array of methodologies that can be loosely defined as anthropological. Rich and lengthy ethnographies were conducted at each of the places concerned. I found open-ended interviews particularly useful as they not only allowed me to harvest invaluable and, in many cases, informal (but crucial) data but proved vital in navigating and interpreting the contestation at hand as they were informing the sites in question. Although I cannot supply an accurate number because some of these interviews were taking place on site and were less formal in nature, but it would be safe to estimate them in the hundreds over two decades of research. For example, during the many years I have explored the Haram al-Sharif I have undertaken more than sixty open-ended interviews. Furthermore, during the twenty and more years I conducted an ongoing weekly ethnography of Maqam abu al-Hijja I have met and subsequently interviewed dozens of village residents as well as pilgrims who arrived at the site. In my *ReligioCity* project, where I was supported by a group of research assistants, we were able to conduct numerous interviews with members of different communities. Additionally, I was engaged in participant observation at most sites. Accordingly, I attended prayers, ceremonies, processions, and special gatherings such as the annual gala evening conducted in Acre in commemoration of Rabbi Yitzhak Kadduri, an iconic Qabala leader. I participated in religious processions be it the annual one for Mariam Bawardy of 'Ibbelin or the Ramadan nights' festival of light in Acre. I firmly believe that this array of research methods and my interdisciplinary expertise have provided me with a unique position from which to narrate, explain, and interpret the sites explored and present a balanced, highly informed, and theoretically sound research on the politics of the sacred. My approach may also help scholars who are engaged with similar projects.

However, as I conclude this section, I also think it is vital to highlight the methodological challenges I have encountered while working in the field. Ethnography, participant observation, and interviews were essential to my project. They are a powerful tool for "really" knowing what a group or individuals think and how they perceive their world. Nevertheless, as with any human encounter, they are concerned with (and influenced by) language, power structures, misunderstandings, and contingencies. Given the continuation of the Israeli-Palestinian ethno-national conflict and the predicament of the Palestinian minority in Israel—a state that despite defining itself as Jewish and democratic should be regarded as an ethnocracy—one need not be surprised why a Jewish-Israeli researcher, who is focusing mostly on Palestinian sacred places, would attract remarks concerning his personal position and the validity and merit of his work. Throughout my work I have had to reflect on my positionality in the field. During the many years of research, I had surely wonderful and heartwarming encounters and at the same time had to negotiate more challenging encounters. Indeed, while conducting my Haram al-Sharif research I was referred to as a Jew, an Israeli, a Zionist, an orientalist, a second-rate Middle Eastern scholar, and even a suspected collaborator or informer of Israel security forces. I was not deterred as I felt that I could triangulate and work the differences and still produce valid ethnographies.

Against the backdrop of the current political situation in Israel/Palestine it is not surprising that a Jewish-Israeli researcher analyzing the production of the sacred places would attract such remarks. That said, and anthropologists have exhausted those issues in surges of papers and books, it is unlikely to halt academic endeavors on the ground of positionality. We need not accept that only people of the same class, race, gender, social and economic status can conduct research on their respective group. I have welcomed the challenges that confronted me in the field, and I hope this approach has enabled me to present a sound, culturally sensitive and respectful picture of the worldview of the people and groups I present herewith.

Having delivered what to my mind is the main scaffolding of this book, in the remaining part of the introduction I present both the structure and a short synopsis of the chapters of the book.

Book Structure

Chapter 1: Ethnocratizing the Holy Land—This chapter begins with a short survey of the emergence of the sacred map and geography of Israel/Palestine. This is followed by an introductory analysis of the complexity and problematics of sacred sites in the region and then moves to explaining the changes in and around them since 1948 and against the construction of Israel as a modernist-Jewish-ethnocratic state. This involves an explanation of ethnocracy and a few examples of state versus sacred, mostly when appropriation and control of formerly non-Jewish sites are concerned. The chapter will also entail a discussion of state mechanisms to control and confiscate sacred places of absentee or fractured communities.

Chapter 2: Embodying the Sacred—This chapter engages with the study of activities and performances in sacred sites on the individual-personal scale. Embodiment takes many forms, and this chapter delves into the personal take within and without sacred sites. It therefore looks at activities performed in those places and, at times, regarding those places, that are manifestations of faith, habitus, and identity politics. As such, it narrates encounters with my interlocutors, be they Muslims, Christians, or Jews from mostly marginal groups.

Chapter 3: Sacred Sites in Rural Communities—This chapter looks at the role of rural sacred places and engages with the ample meanings they entail for their respective communities. It follows current transformations of local sacred sites and the micro-politics surrounding them in their communities. The chapter focuses mostly on two case studies. The first is a Muslim site by the name of Maqam Abu al-Hijja and the second is the emerging Christian site of Sitt Mariam Bawardy, a recently canonized Palestinian nun. Set against the changes of their respective communities and the Jewish majority group and the state, these sites mirror fundamental changes not only in their communities, but also in the ongoing engagement with the secular-ethnocratic state.

Chapter 4: Sacred Sites and the Right to the City—This chapter engages with Lefebvre's notion of the right to the city and his general post-Marxist approach, to examine the ways in which different actors in the urban sphere are conversing about—and surely contesting—the sacred. It centers around the struggles of subordinate communities in Israeli cities to reclaim the city through the sacred. This chapter explores struggles over sacred sites, the ways they have shaped the urban sphere, and the outcomes of these conflicts on urban communities and dialogues. The chapter narrates those issues while focusing on the urban conflicts over the Mosque of Beersheba and the Hassan Bey Mosque in Tel-Aviv-Jaffa.

Chapter 5: ReligioCity and Decolonizing Acre through the Sacred—This chapter offers the concept of *ReligioCity* as an umbrella term to understand both the tangible and intangible aspects of the religion in urban scale and the reciprocal relations between religion(s) and city. Following a theoretical introduction to *ReligioCity*, the chapter takes Acre, a multi-religious and multi-ethnic mixed city in the north of Israel, as a case in point to study the intricate connections between religion and the urban sphere through religious infrastructures. As such it will allow a myriad of voices of religious actants and their personal readings of Acre. This will be complemented with an analysis of the struggle over the Lababidi Mosque under what I frame as the decolonization of the city. This engagement with colonization/decolonization theories permits a deeper insight into the role of urban religion(s) as a site of converging and conflicting visions and voices, practices, and orientations, which arise out of the complex desires, needs, and fears of many different people.

Chapter 6: Glocalizing the Sacred—This chapter presents the complexities of sacred places as they emerge as national and supra-national icons/landmarks in the global sphere. Taking the extremely complex sacred compound in Jerusalem, al-Haram al-Sharif/the Temple Mount, as a point of departure, this chapter portrays an intricate and highly nuanced picture of the ways this site is assuming a unique and unparalleled position in the ethno-national conflict as it becomes crucial to both the Jewish majority and the Muslim minority in Israel. The chapter will focus mostly on the Muslim-Palestinian struggle to control the site and involves a discussion of the unique role of the Israeli Islamic Movement therein. This will serve to allow an analysis of the ways this sacred place is upscaled and becomes a highly sensitive global problem involving states, religious leaders, and diplomatic-cum-political activities worldwide.

Epilogue—The concluding part of the book serves to weave together the different threads which were brought forth through the analysis of the changing scalar setting of the sacred. The conclusion firstly reiterates the main themes and theoretical outcomes of the discussions of the sacred in its various levels, as narrated throughout the book. Furthermore, it launches an analysis of sacred places in contemporary societies in the context of the modern secularizing state. This concluding part highlights the overarching argument of the book, which emphasizes the socio-political role of the sacred in contemporary societies, focusing our attention on its fascinating spatiality and the myriad social-cultural-political meanings to be found at the intersection of religion and politics under the title of sacred places.

1

Ethnocratizing the Holy Land: Contextualizing Sacred Places in Israel/Palestine

This chapter offers both an introduction and a contextualization of the highly complex and variegated hagio-geography of Israel/Palestine. To that end, I focus on two seemingly separated concepts: the Holy Land and ethnocracy. Consequently, the goal of this introductory salvo is twofold: First, to narrate the emergence of the Holy Land sacred landscape which serves as the blueprint for perceptions of contemporary sacred places among actants in the field. This will entail a discussion of both spatial and theological changes through a longue durée analysis of the spatialization of different religions' sacred perceptions upon this sliver of land between the Eastern shores of the Mediterranean and the Jordan river. Second, to explain how contemporary spatialization processes within sacred places are inexorably linked to the State of Israel's ethnocratic logic. This will allow for the necessary background to understand the move from using a fundamentally theological concept as the Holy Land, to Israel/Palestine, a highly contested geopolitical term. The shift from using the concept of the Holy Land to Israel/Palestine corresponds with the dramatic changes that have transpired in the region as winds of modernity began to arrive at its shores. It is indeed a move from a theological-cum-religious lens of inquiry to a geopolitical one. This also follows the change that took place as the Ottoman Empire was faltering to its demise in the late nineteenth century and the people(s) of the region began to adopt a different vision of their future and certainly of their political status.

During the four hundred years of Ottoman rule over the region (1571–1917), its population enjoyed relative religious freedom under the *Millet* system. This concept refers to an organizing mechanism that classified all Ottoman subjects according to their religious affiliation. The *Millet* system allowed the Ottoman regime and its rulers efficiently to organize the empire's highly diverse population into ethno-religious communities and to delegate power to trusted intermediaries, mostly religious leaders (Barkey and Gavrilis 2016). This also enabled them to thwart, as they often did, local initiatives which aspired to break free from under their yoke. This political arrangement and logic were increasingly challenged toward the end of the nineteenth century. No longer satisfied with their status as mere "subjects of the Sultan," local groups began to promote nationalism as the preferred political system. This change is commonly known as the Arab national awakening, which manifested itself throughout the Middle East in a growing demand for self-rule and nation-states (Antonius 1938). More specifically, in *fin de siècle* Palestine, the Jewish and the Palestinian national movements began to take shape. As these movements each aspired for a nation-state on the same geography, they found themselves on an inevitable course of collision. Arguably, this became the most lingering and septic ethnic-cum-national conflict. This was also the main challenge the British Mandate (1917–48) had to confront while controlling the region (Cohen 2015).

And thus, Palestine, as it was officially named and demarcated in 1921 by the British Mandate, became the battleground for these two opposing national movements. As the conflict escalated, international forces strived to find a solution which amounted on November 29, 1947, to a United Nations resolution which sought to divide Mandatory Palestine into Arab and Jewish states. While the Jews agreed to the proposal, the Palestinians rejected it and hence on May 15, 1948, following the declaration of the State of Israel an all-out war broke out between Israel and its Arab neighbors. In the aftermath of the war, Israel controlled roughly 78 percent of Mandatory Palestine, circa 750,000 Palestinians had become refugees and over 400 Palestinian villages were demolished (Morris 1987; Khalidi 1992). The territory of Mandatory Palestine was divided into three parts: the State of Israel; the West Bank (of the Jordan River) which was in the hands of the Hashemite Kingdom of Jordan; and the Gaza Strip under Egyptian rule. This was the first and most devastating phase of the Palestinian Nakba (Arabic: disaster, ruin, catastrophe) which was extended further following the 1967 war, during which Israel gained direct control of both the West Bank and the Gaza Strip and their Palestinian population. This had direct bearing on numerous processes, such as the nationalization (i.e., Palestinization) of Islamic sacred sites, that are to be found at the core of this book regarding sacred places, as later chapters will discuss in detail.

As suggested by its founders and heralded in its Declaration of Independence, Israel's *raison d'être* was to build a modern democratic state, which would be a safe haven for Jewish people in their "promised land," namely, the Land of Israel

(Kimmerling 2001). To that end, Israel defines itself as a democratic regime but in parallel initiated a concerted project of Judaizing the land. This type of regime is characterized as an ethnocracy (Yiftachel 2006). This concept indicates a political regime that facilitates expansion and control by a dominant ethnicity within a modern national state. In the Israeli case, rights and access to common goods and state resources are allocated primarily based on ethnic origin. In proposing this concept, Yiftachel presents a critical theory and a framework that enables a better understanding of the unfolding of spatial and socio-political processes in Israel/Palestine. This is the core and most essential logic which dictates and permeates all aspects of life. Ethnocracy involves a certain spatiality and is certainly a progenitor of spatial dynamics and changes which had, and still have, enormous influences on the processes I address in this book along a scalar hierarchy.

After introducing the logic that stands behind wedding the two concepts of the Holy Land and ethnocracy, in what follows I offer an analysis of the emergence of the complex sacred geography of this region. The analysis starts with the early manifestations of sanctity in Judaism and moves on to include both Christianity's and Islam's contributions to this complex and multi-layered canvas. The analysis highlights the role of Jerusalem as the epicenter of the Holy Land. It also entails a discussion of interfaith conflicts over sacred grounds until 1948. Following this watershed year in the region, with the emergence of Israel as a nation-sate and the dramatic geopolitical changes it entailed, new meanings and dynamics permeated sacred grounds. This will be dealt with under the heading of "ethnocratizing the Holy Land," which means to suggest an engagement with the spatialization of this logic unto the realm of the sacred. This will also include a discussion of state mechanisms of controlling and confiscating sacred places of absentee or fractured communities.

Before I delve into this analysis, which aims to demonstrate the ways the Holy Land was understood and conceptualized in the three Abrahamic religions, I deem it necessary to offer a word of caution. As much as I try to be both inclusive and critical in this analysis, it stands to reason that this ambitious undertaking cannot cover, in all honesty, all the nuances within the intellectual and theological constructions and understandings of this highly complex concept, particularly regarding internal debates within each religion. Certainly, I tried to the best of my (poor) ability to present a well-balanced and informative study of what seemed to me pertinent to the understanding of the multifaceted and constantly changing notion of the Holy Land as it is played out and implemented in modern Israel/Palestine.

Constructing the Holy Land

The idea of the Holy Land has been with us for over two millennia and yet remains rather obscure, at least concerning its origins and spatialities. It is certainly not a clearly demarcated geographical unit; yet it is unequivocally accepted among Abrahamic religions that regardless of what it may include, Jerusalem stands at its sacred epicenter. This understanding is clearly demonstrated in the first time that the notion of the Holy Land appears in a biblical text. The following excerpt is to be found in the prophetic book of Zechariah, written most likely at the beginning of the sixth century BCE:

> Sing and rejoice, O daughter of Zion
> For, lo, I come, and I will dwell in the midst of thee saith the Lord
> And many nations shall join themselves to the Lord in that day, and
> Know that the Lord of hosts hath send me unto thee.
> And the Lord shall inherit Judah as his portion in the holy land, and
> Shall choose Jerusalem again.
>
> (Zech. 2: 14–16)

The Lord shall choose Jerusalem again, Zechariah promises in this prophecy to diasporic Jews, and offers them crumbs of comfort against their contemporary dire situation of exile from their land of origin and religious center. Given that the earliest construction of Jerusalem's holiness among the Israelite tribes starts circa 1000 BCE according to the accepted chronology (but see Finkelstein and Silberman 2001), and the fact that for hundreds of years there existed other central sacred locations for the Israelite tribes, it was a rather long process until the city achieved its unrivaled sacred-cum-religious status. As one cannot understand the notion of the Holy Land separately from Jerusalem, let us now explore the emergence of Jerusalem as its religious (at times political) center among the three major religious groups that lay claim to this imaginative-cum-spiritual territory. This is not a mere intellectual or scholarly endeavor, but an essential component that is crucial to understanding the contemporary disputes, conflicts, and politics of sacred places in Israel/Palestine. The move from Jerusalem to the entire region will complement this analysis.

Urshalimu, Shalem, or Jebus, as it was called prior to becoming the Israelite capital, was never more than a lesser settlement confined to a barren hill of circa sixty square dunums for the better part of its first four millennia (Maeir 2000). It was certainly not on par with contemporary established Israelite urban centers, such as Hebron or Bethel. So how and why did this unlikely candidate come to play such a pivotal role in religious history and among various belief systems? The simple answer is that its lack of prior "Israelite" history and its tribal geopolitical neutrality suited the Davidic dynasty's ambitions to consolidate the Israelite confederation under its rule. A crucial component of this project was to enhance Jerusalem's political centrality for the Israelites by establishing it and its temple as the ultimate and exclusive site for the Israelite religion. As the sacred is indeed an empty signifier (Durkheim 1995) and its surplus meaning is up for grabs, establishing Jebus as the City of David and constructing a temple therein were indeed efficient steps in this direction. The sacred center that was built on the hill above former Jebus, now the City of David, was the outcome of the political necessity and prerogative of the royal house (Smith 1987). Consistent with these efforts is the association, gradually becoming rock-solid (pun intended) connections, between the Land of Moriah as the binding place of Isaac ('Aqeda), David's altar at the threshing floor of Araunah the Jebusite where a plague was stopped, and later on the site for the Solomonic Temple Mount, ultimately becoming Mount Moriah—the site in which all these traditions converge (Kalimi 1990). These are summed up neatly only in the belated Books of Chronicles: "Then Solomon began to build the temple of the LORD in Jerusalem on Mount Moriah, where the LORD had appeared to his father David. It was on the threshing floor of Araunah the Jebusite, the place provided by David" (2 Chr. 3:1). These connections stand at the very center of the idea of the Holy Land, which also inspired both Christian and Islamic traditions and their actions in Jerusalem. The concerted efforts by the Davidic dynasty to transform Jerusalem into a political-cum-religious capital were accepted neither quickly nor without contest by a variety of disgruntled political adversaries, who opposed the production process of sacralizing Jerusalem. This was manifested, for example, in the construction of rival religious centers by the first king of the northern Kingdom of Israel, which seceded following a revolt against the Davidic dynasty and its Judean kingdom:

> And Jeroboam said in his heart, now shall the kingdom return to the house of David: If this people go up to do sacrifice in the house of the LORD at Jerusalem, then shall the heart of this people turn again unto their lord, even unto Rehoboam king of Judah, and they shall kill me, and go again to Rehoboam king of Judah.
> (1 Kings 12, 26–7)

Jeroboam felt compelled to respond to the religious materialities constructed in Jerusalem by his political rivals. However, this was but one (minor) setback in the protracted and meandering process which ultimately transformed Jerusalem and its temple into the most significant political, religious, and symbolic site for the Israelite tribes. This process is well attested in situating the rather vague biblical directive regarding pilgrimage to "wherever the Lord will command" to the temple in Jerusalem:

> Three times a year all your men must appear before the Lord your God at the place he will choose: at the Festival of Unleavened Bread, the Festival of Weeks and the Festival of Tabernacles. No one should appear before the Lord empty-handed: Each of you must bring a gift in proportion to the way the Lord your God has blessed you.
>
> (Deut. 16, 16–17)

Hand in hand with the ascendancy of the Davidic traditions and the durability of the Judean kingdom (until its demise in 586 BCE), Jerusalem and its religious center (Solomon's Temple) surmounted and shunned all other existing pilgrimage centers and plausible destinations for the three Jewish annual pilgrimage festivals. According to the prevailing Jewish narrative, constructed by canonized texts that largely follow Judean literature, after its inauguration by King Solomon in 970 BCE, the Jerusalem Temple became the most important and revered Jewish pilgrimage site. Although this narrative has come under increasing scrutiny (Finkelstein and Silberman 2001; Eliav 2005, 2008), there is ample evidence to support the growing role of the Jerusalemite temple as the focal point of Jewish pilgrimage ('aliyah la-regel) during the Second Temple period (Eliav 2005). This construction would inform the modern Israeli national understanding of Jerusalem as the heart of the nation and the "eternal" capital of the Jewish national homeland.

The continuation and persistency of rituals therein elevated Jerusalem and its temple to their special status and were conducive to their growing importance (Smith 1987). These shifts notwithstanding, the dramatic physical and material changes brought forth by a gargantuan Herodian building project are what transformed the temple into a distinct compound and a separate mountain within the city (Eliav 2005). This new materiality, which made the temple and its "mountain" into a bounded compound, was largely responsible for the growing use of the term Temple Mount, which is the main frame of reference for the site among Jews to the present. The demise of Jewish autonomy, symbolized mainly by the destruction of this sacred site in 70 CE by the Romans, transformed this physical earthly compound into the most meaningful sacred geography for Jewish communities worldwide.

While the Jewish temple in Jerusalem was, at the end of the day, built at an arbitrary location based on political needs, the Christian understanding rested on religious narratives that connected the city and its temple to meaningful events in the Passion of Jesus. Therefore, Christianity from its onset was tied to Jerusalem's sacred biography, history, and religious materiality, and connected mostly to its sacred center, the Temple Mount. Put simply, the Church of the Holy Sepulcher could ultimately not have been built anywhere but in Jerusalem (Smith 1987). However, much like in Judaism, Jerusalem's revered status (as part of the Holy Land) in Christian theology and practice was in flux for centuries and knew fundamental changes ranging from total rejection to full embrace (Wilken 1992). The initial Christian attitude to Jerusalem, as reflected in the New Testament, was that the Holy Land and Jerusalem were to be avoided and rejected, as they disallowed Jesus' messages and served as the location for His crucifixion (Prawer 1987). Earthly Jerusalem was destined to make way for and be replaced by a heavenly Jerusalem, as suggested in the book of Revelation: "And I John saw the holy city, new Jerusalem, coming down from God out of heaven, prepared as a bride adorned for her husband" (Rev. 21: 2). However, the lure of the land and the yearning for a concrete and direct connection to the landscapes upon which Jesus lived and walked proved to be too tempting to be ignored. By the fourth century CE, it was none other than the Roman emperor Constantine who stood at the forefront of this transformation and was heavily invested in the construction of sacred places throughout the Holy Land. Surely, the inauguration of the Church of the Holy Sepulcher in 324 CE was the apex of these endeavors (Ashkenazi 2009). This transformation, which completely altered Jerusalem's religious landscape, was too dramatic and tempting to be ignored by leading Christian theologians, who until then had stood firmly against pilgrimages and visitations of the Holy Land. One notable case in point was historian and bishop Eusebius of Caesarea (d. 340 CE), who in his "Life of Constantine" failed to maintain his famously reserved (and usually negative) approach to pilgrimage to Jerusalem against the might of this new materiality, constructed by the emperor in the holy city: "Perhaps this was that strange and new Jerusalem, proclaimed by the oracles of the prophets to which long passages prophesying by the aid of the divine spirit make countless allusions in song" (cited in Peters 1985: 132–4). This exegetical interpretation was intended to praise Constantine for his building project in Jerusalem, which transformed the city into a major pilgrimage site. The Temple Mount was left in ruins to commemorate Jewish sin and punishment. This Constantinian initiative was but one of many new Christian compounds constructed in Jerusalem from the fourth century onward. As late as the fifth century CE, Christian theologians still found it difficult to accept the idea of the land of Israel as holy, as this was linked to the ongoing disputes with the Jews over the biblical prophecies of latter days and the apocalypse (Ezekiel as a case in point). In a letter responding to a Roman general from Gaul asking for assistance regarding the concept of the Holy Land, Jerome (347–420), writing from his residence in Palestine, is still hesitant to accept the holy status of the land: "The Jews assert that it is this land is the land of promise. They believe that *terra repromissionis* is the land which the Jews possessed when they returned from Egypt, which had been possessed by their ancestors previously, and is therefore not promised but restored" (cited in Wilken 1986: 307). Nevertheless, this reluctance gradually dwindled against the building spree which engulfed Palestine and the growing stream of pilgrims, including imperial figures like Empress Eudocia (Ashkenazi forthcoming). By the late sixth century CE, Jerusalem's landscape held a plethora of Christian compounds, as demonstrated in the mosaic map of Madaba (Donner 1992). This Christian landscape (hagio-geography) and heavily saturated religious materiality confronted the third religion that was to enter the scene in the early- to mid-seventh century CE: Islam. By then, many of the traditions previously assigned in Jewish theology to the Temple Mount were redirected toward the new holy Christian Mountain that was constructed in Jerusalem, in the form of Golgotha and the compounds surrounding it (Bitton-Ashkelony 2005: 59–61).

Islam arrived at the gates of Jerusalem in the 630s CE (Gil 1987). However, the city had already received a special status in Islam by then, as it served as the first direction of the prayers (*qibla*) for the young Muslim community while still in its embryonic phase in the city of Medina (Rubin 2008). The changes brought forth by the new rulers and religion in the city were slow to arrive. Muslim rulers were bound by strict conditions, as stipulated in the peace treaty (*amān*) signed with the people of Jerusalem, which prevented them, among other things, from confiscating non-Muslim religious buildings. If we are to believe the testimony of a Christian pilgrim by the name of Arculfus who visited the city circa 679 CE, a rudimentary mosque was constructed on the platform of the ruined Temple Mount shortly after the conquest (Creswell 1969: 33–4). This location is rather intriguing, for several reasons. First, it set a precedent which would be followed by later Muslim rulers, who constructed the Muslim religious center therein. Second, it suggests that from its earliest encounters in Jerusalem, Islam preferred the old Jewish mountain to the newly constructed Christian one. Third and most importantly, as well attested in early Islamic traditions, the initial Islamic attachment to Jerusalem was the already well-established Jewish sanctity. This sets the proper background for understanding the flamboyant undertaking of the Umayyad caliph 'Abd al-Malik ibn Marwan, which transformed the deserted temple area into an impressive Islamic compound consisting initially of an administrative center to its south, an expansive Friday Mosque (later to be known as al-Aqsa) and an exquisite concentric shrine named the Dome of the Rock (Arabic: *Qubbat al-Sahra*). It should be noted that the rock in question was the mythologized Jewish Stone of Foundation from which, as traditions have it, creation began, and which served as the site of Isaac's sacrifice and numerous other Jewish traditions (Smith 1987: 84). This was part of a intensive effort made by the Umayyads to exalt both the religious and political status of Jerusalem (Elad 1995). However, the Umayyads' initial intent to elevate Jerusalem's sacred role in Islam vis-à-vis Mecca (which was at the time in the hands of a political rival) was short-lived, and thus alternative myths began to circulate regarding this new religious materiality. The most prominent one, which today is largely accepted by Muslims worldwide, connects the compound to the Prophet's night journey and ascendance to heaven (*isra'* and *mi'raj* respectively) (Luz 2004).

Let us go back to Zechariah's verses, mentioned above, consisting of the only time the notion of the Holy Land (rather than a holy place) is mentioned in the biblical text, as they allow us to appreciate how the growing sanctity assigned to Jerusalem radiated to the land surrounding it. In Jewish understanding the land of the Israelites gradually becomes God's land, a sacred land, a promised land, and in post-Second Temple period rabbinical literature, the Holy Land. It is not a clearly demarcated geographical unit and yet it is accepted as "a land which the Lord thy God cared for: the eyes of the Lord thy God are always upon it" (Deut. 22:12). It becomes God's favorite land and what solidifies this position is the emergence of a multiplicity of sacred places and the performances of a variety of rites and ceremonies therein, which turns it into the "holiest of all countries" (Mishnah, Kelim 1, 6). Surely, as other groups developed claims to this geography, transforming the entire land into a sacred Jewish one served also to bolster Jewish counterclaims of ownership (Reiner 2014). Hence from Late Antiquity (fourth-sixth centuries CE) and onward, new Jewish sacred places which ultimately serve as pilgrimage destinations emerged throughout the land. By the nineteenth century and the eve of the national struggle between the Jewish and Palestinian national movements, a highly variegated sacred map had emerged. This map became the blueprint against which dramatic changes took place with the creation of the Jewish state of Israel (Luz and Collins-Kreiner 2015). Some of these sites, mostly major and well-known historical pilgrimage sites (the Tomb of David in Jerusalem, the Cave of Elijah in Haifa, etc.) were nationalized and are supervised under the auspices of the state (Bar 2007). However, before I move on chronologically to narrate the Christian understanding of the Holy Land, I think it is pertinent at this stage to allow a critical reflection on the seemingly smooth development from a biblical promised land to the idea of the Holy Land and the emergence of the modern (mostly Zionist) construction of the Holy Land as a Jewish homeland.

This narrative has won growing criticism in recent years, which merits further discussion here as it is ultimately highly relevant to the development of a Zionist ethnocratic logic. The concept of the promised land was part and parcel of Jewish collective memory for centuries, and yet the traditional Jewish perception of this ancestral land was not centered around the idea of ownership, let alone as an essential place for a national homeland (Sand 2014). The ambiguity of this concept is also attested in the lack of clear demarcation and accepted borders of this territorial unit among both past and present Jewish scholars (Biger 2004). Certainly, one may find several indications in the Hebrew Bible where a solid connection is made between the Jews and the (even if geographically obscure) promised land by virtue of a divine promise (Tadmor-Shimony 2013). Notwithstanding, the yearning for the lost promised land that features heavily in Jewish prayers and rituals for centuries has never amounted to an operative plan, nor was it inferred as a call to arms to own it until the emergence of Zionism as a secular movement of national awakening (Ohana 2008). The traditional Jewish perception of the land never entailed an aspiration for collective tenure of a national homeland. Rather, this much revered land was perceived as awaiting the Jewish people in that utopic time when God would send the Messiah, a king from the line of David, to rule the Jewish people from Jerusalem. Put simply, not only were all political aspirations deferred until that latter day, but the very thought of redemption (i.e., messianic hopes to be implemented in the here and now) was considered sinful. Following the destruction of the Jerusalem Temple in 70 CE and the obliteration of Jewish autonomy in then Roman *Palaestina*, rabbinic Judaism was mostly concerned with the survival of Jewish life as the ultimate goal, rather than cultivating pipe dreams about Jewish political freedom within the boundaries of the rather general biblical borders. One may even argue that a Jewish political tradition is a contradiction in terms because rabbinic Judaism constitutes an accommodation to the absence of sovereignty, which is tantamount to the absence of politics (Weiler 1976; Cooper 2016). Exile was deemed an outcome of God's will, inflicted as punishment for Israel's sins (Scholem 1971). Therefore, it was regarded as sinful to try to hasten the appearance of the Messiah; Jews must wait patiently for God's supernatural intervention to send the Messiah, ingather the exiles, rebuild the Temple, restore the Jewish kingdom, and bring about final redemption. Hastening the Messiah's return in any active way was strictly forbidden (Shahak and Mezvinsky 1999).

Only upon the arrival of the savior would the living and the dead gather together in eternal Jerusalem. For most Jewish scholars, the hurrying of collective salvation was considered a transgression to be severely punished; for others, the Holy Land was largely an allegorical, intangible notion—not a concrete territorial site but an internal spiritual state. This reality was perhaps best reflected in the hesitant reaction of most of the Jewish rabbinate to the birth of the Zionist movement (Sand 2014). The passive redemption approach is evident in the words of Rabbi Samson Raphael Hirsch, who is considered the "father of modern Orthodoxy." In a letter to Rabbi Kalisher, one of the first religious figures who suggested a more active approach to redemption, he writes: "And we have never taken upon ourselves the path of redemption through enhancement and rectification of the holy land, rather through enhancement and rectification of our hearts" (Hirsch 1951: 12, cited in Mashiach 2021). It was only the Zionists who constructed a new understanding of redemption through the owning of the land and charging it with manifold meanings through a concerted effort of daily reification and banal nationalism, which included the construction of historical narratives and perpetually working toward the establishment of a new collective memory (Raz-Karkotzkin 2007). The initially secular Zionist movement based its claim of ownership to the "Land of Israel" based on the unbroken Jewish spiritual-cum-religious linkage to this very territory. This understanding was ironically conceptualized by Raz-Karkoztkin as "there is no God, but he promised us this land" (2005). The Zionists constructed a new vision of redemption of the Jewish people in its historical homeland and formulated new ways of trying to give this redemption tangible, political, cultural, and social expressions. The ties between Jews and their homeland were based on a firm theological conviction and the secular Zionist project embraced this theological myth while negating the existence of a God. Its ideology was the fulfillment of Jewish history and the realization of Jewish messianic expectations through a very specific secular interpretation and an innovative modernistic understanding of the scriptures (Raz-Karkotzkin 2002). In its initial stages, Zionism was a modernist secular movement that nationalized the age-old rabbinical-messianic Jewish texts and implemented them in the Holy Land. That said, the Zionist movement asserted its claims of ownership in Ottoman Palestine based on Jewish linkage to and mythology about that territory, while formulating their perceptions and actions based on a rather Christian conceptualization of the Holy Land (Saposnik 2021). The Zionist movement ultimately settled Jews in the Holy Land, not only because it was intellectualized as their ancestral land but also because it adopted a lingering Christian perception of the Holy Land as a place where people can be educated, reshaped—indeed, indoctrinated—as new liberated subjects (Eliaz

2008). With this in mind, let us now follow the ways Christianity and Islam conceptualized the Holy Land.

While the Jewish understanding of the Holy Land developed through the daily deeds and performances of religious rituals and the emerging sacred landscape(s) in the "Promised Land," Christianity followed a different path altogether, at least in its earliest stages. Initially, early Christian theologians rejected the notion of the Holy Land (Wilken 1992). And yet the uniqueness of the land where Biblical events took place, and especially its association with Jesus' life, mission, death, and resurrection, could not be ignored. From early on, Christian pilgrims and travelers visited the Holy Land to familiarize themselves with the biblical sacred places and to experience direct contact with sacred places, events, and objects within the Holy Land (MacCormack 1990). Until the fourth century CE, the importance of Christian sacred sites in Palestine/the Land of Israel relied solely on the authority of the scriptures. Places were considered sacred not because of the rituals performed therein, as in the Jewish precedents, but because they were mentioned in the sacred texts. The "textualizing" of the Holy Land was an integral part of the process by which Christianity was transformed into a universal religion embraced by peoples throughout the world. However, during the fourth century CE Christianity underwent a fundamental change in its attitude toward sacred places (Markus 1994). This change is manifested in the spree of constructions of religious-cum-sacred sites in Palestine under the patronage of the emperor Constantine and some of his imperial successors and contemporaries. The hallmark of this new trend is surely the Church of the Holy Sepulcher in Jerusalem, but it was duly followed by the emergence of a plethora of sacred sites across the Holy Land. Against others (such as Smith, who see this as a move to the locative pole) Markus pins this change to a fundamental transformation of fourth-century Christianity's perception of sacred time. Thus, he argues that the emergence of sacred places and a sacred Christian topography in Palestine were an indirect consequence and outcome of this theological and teleological change (Markus 1994). These discussions notwithstanding, post-Constantine Christianity was heavily engaged in constructions of sacred places in Palestine and transforming it into a highly Christianized Holy Land. This is clearly manifested in the late-sixth-century floor mosaic of a church in today's Hashemite Kingdom of Jordan, commonly known as the Madaba Map, which contains the oldest cartographic depiction of the Christian Holy Land. And so, the change was completed and Christianity, which initially rejected the concept of Palestine/the Land of Israel as holy, embraced it and fully adopted the very notion it had previously scorned. The change, argues Wilken, is part and parcel of Christians becoming the "owners" of the region and so he sees it not only as a religious concept but also as, and just as much, a political one (Wilken 1986). This would change dramatically following the arrival of Islam in the region. While the concept of the Holy Land would remain a constant component in Christian perception, Christian sacred places were to undergo changes over the years and would serve time and again as bones of contentions between Muslim rulers and communities, and Christendom and local Christian communities (Luz 2013c). The importance of the Holy Land in Christian theology would fuel the endeavors of European powers and American Christian communities to strengthen their positions in the declining Ottoman Empire during the nineteenth century and later. This manifested itself, among other things, in intense activities of purchasing and renovation of sacred places and promoting Christian pilgrimage and travel to the Holy Land (Rogers 2011).

Unlike its monotheistic predecessors, the concept of the Holy Land was embraced rather smoothly in early Islamic understanding. The Prophet Muhammad acknowledged the holiness of the area as might be inferred from his setting the first direction of the prayer (Ar.: *qibla*) for the embryonic Muslim community in Medina toward Jerusalem (Rubin 2008). This understanding emerges also in the Qur'an, albeit only once, while utilizing the term *al-ard al-muqaddasa* namely, the Holy Land. The sole Quranic verse that mentions this term appears in relation to the Prophet Moses' command the Israelites to enter the land north of them as they walk in the Sinai Peninsula:

> Remember when Moses said to his people: "My people, remember Allah's favor upon you when He raised Prophets amongst you and appointed you rulers, and granted to you what He had not granted to anyone else in the world. My people! Enter the Holy Land which Allah has ordained for you; and do not turn back for then you will turn about losers."
>
> (Qur'an 5, 20–1)

What, then, is the Holy Land according to Islamic understanding? A fifteenth-century Islamic source sheds some light on this otherwise rather obscure concept. In a manual destined to serve as a bureaucratic road map for administrative staff, the Egyptian writer al-Qalqashandi (1355–1418) states: "the province of Palestine (Ar.: Jund Filastin) which is the Holy Land that houses al-Aqsa Mosque ... the mosque and tomb of Abraham, as well as the birthplace of the Messiah" (al-Qalqashandi 1987, 7:13). According to early Islamic interpretations, the borders of the Holy Land are equivalent to the biblical Land of Israel which lies between the Euphrates in the north to Wadi al-'Arish in the south (Goitein 1950).

The term itself is far from being clear geographically and cannot be separated from the political position of the beholder (Luz 2004). Shaykh Ra'id Salah, who headed a faction of the Islamic Movement in Israel until it was outlawed in 2015 by the Israeli government, promotes the idea of Palestine in its entirety not only as a holy land but also as a *waqf* (endowed) land, which, therefore, according to Islamic jurisprudence cannot be divided or shared, let alone relinquished, in any future Israeli-Palestinian negotiations (Luz 2013a). Certainly, he is not alone and was preceded by numerous actants in the field in harnessing the Holy Land to their political interests. A case in point was mentioned earlier while discussing the European powers' conduct in reasserting their control over parts of the Holy Land during the nineteenth and twentieth centuries.

The Islamic conquest of the seventh century initiated a few processes which effected changes in the sacred map of the Holy Land. With the growing of Islamic communities in the area along with general acceptance of former traditions, both Jewish and Christian, new Muslim sacred places began to appear. Some of these places emerged as part of the growing rivalry with Christian and Jewish communities (Luz 2002). With the increasing importance of the area in Islamic theology, particularly the revered status of Jerusalem, Islamic rulers felt compelled to express their piety by constructing and taking care of sacred places in this otherwise insignificant region. This trend was exacerbated following Salah al-Din's (Saladin) victory at the Battle of Hattin in 1187 (Talmon-Heller 2006; Petersen 2018). This was also an effective way to establish legitimacy among local Muslim communities. Accordingly, Mamluk and Ottoman sultans, as well as other dignitaries, were engaged in various activities in the Holy Land, mostly through constructing and renovating sacred places. By the beginning of the twentieth century and the eve of the British Mandate in Palestine, the Islamic Holy Land consisted of circa 800 sacred places (Canaan 1927). Some of these sites were solely Muslim; others were shared with other religious communities (Barkan and Berkey 2014). Unlike the Christian sacred map of the Holy Land that remained mostly intact, the ethno-national Israeli-Palestinian conflict and the establishment of the State of Israel effected dramatic changes in the Islamic Holy Land and its perceptions. The most significant change is surely the highly politicized character of those sites and map (Luz 2021b). These will be further elaborated in the following chapters and consists of a significant part of the empirical data which furnish this book. The changes brought forth by the emergence of the State of Israel and the implementations of specific policies will be discussed herewith through the notion of ethnocracy and its manifold impacts on sacred places.

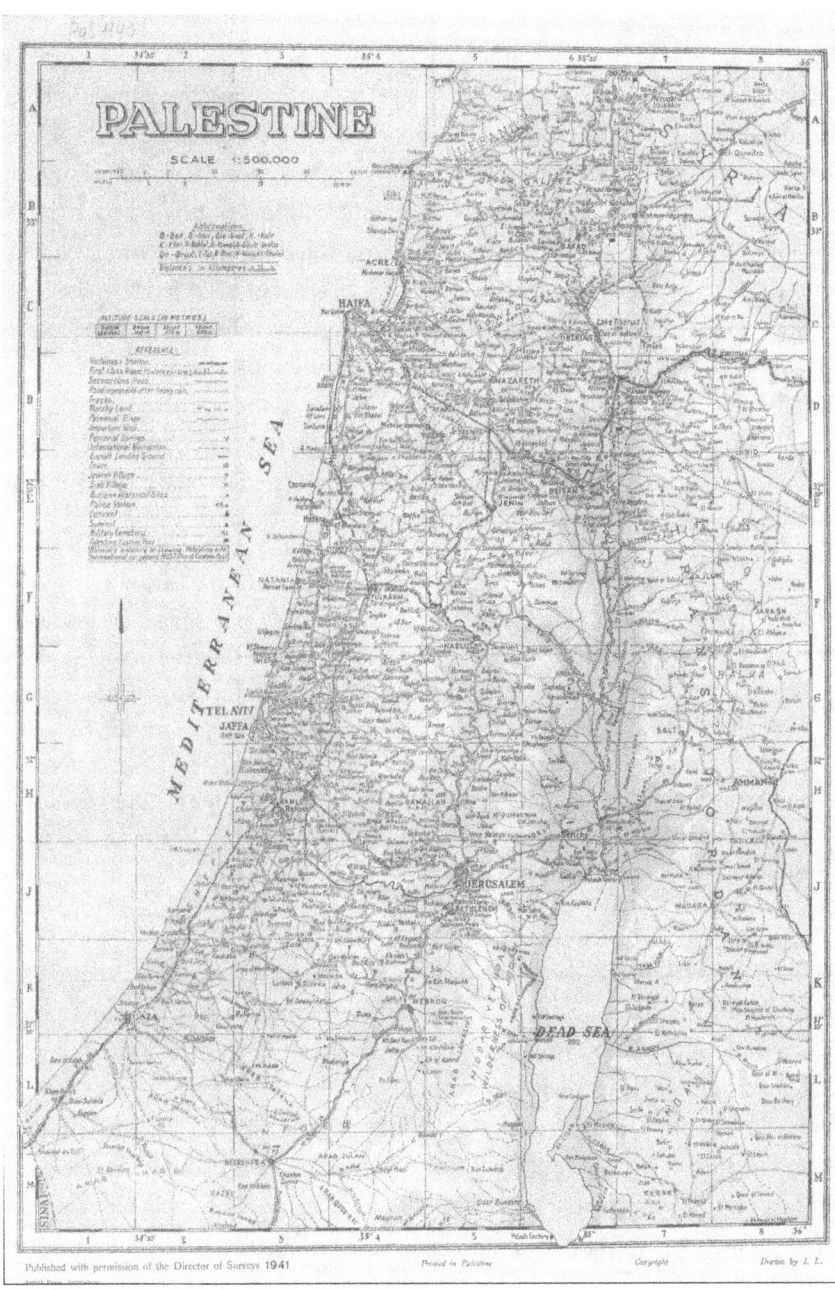

Figure 1.1 Map of Palestine in 1941 (with permission of Eran Laor Maps Collection, National Library of Israel).

Ethnocracy and the Religious/Sacred Field

On July 14, 1948, IDF forces conquered the village of Ma'lul, located in the lower Galilee (Morris 1987: 199–200). The village population, which comprised both Muslims and Christians estimated at about eight hundred people, fled (or was driven away with the arrival of the Israeli troops) in its entirety and was never allowed to come back. Ma'lul is surely not alone and shares its fate with roughly 400–600 other villages which were destroyed and their population evicted, following the 1948 war (Morris 1987; Khalidi 1992). The emergence of the State of Israel and its obtaining supremacy in the region was translated on the ground to assuming control over vast tracts of Palestinian lands, and the expulsion of over 700,000 people. These events, which amount to the complete destruction of Palestinian society, are known as *al-Nakba*, that is, the Catastrophe. The following is a description of what has transpired in the village since it was captured by the Israeli army in July 1948:

> The village site is now covered with a pine forest planted by the Jewish National Fund and dedicated to the memory of prominent Jews and some non-Jewish Americans and Europeans. A military base is also on the site. The mosque and two churches still stand and are used intermittently as cow sheds by the residents of Kibbutz Kefar ha-Choresh. Overlooking Wadi al-Halabi, between the village site and the site of al-Mujaydil, is an Israeli plastics factory. Cactus, olive trees, and fig trees grow on the site, which is strewn with piles of stones. A few tombs in the Muslim cemetery across from the mosque can be seen. The main village site also contains the remains of houses.
>
> (Khalidi 1992: 348)

Ma'lul's fate was shared by hundreds of Palestinian villages and urban areas throughout the land. This was consistent with the Zionist movement's overarching goal since its early beginnings, assuming control over the area which comprised by its own understanding of the "Promised Land." This was manifested in the idea of the Judaization of Palestine and the elimination of its Arab Palestinian heritage and built environment. This is demonstrated clearly in the case of Ma'lul as well as in many other villages, which included the mass expropriation of Arab land in Israel (Kedar 1998). The erasure of the Palestinian past which ensued from the 1948 war and the emergence of the State of Israel was achieved in many forms but mostly by constructing around seven hundred new Jewish settlements, often on sites which were formerly Arab villages. And yet, even within the massive and efficient deployment of this policy, as in the case of Ma'lul, sacred and religious sites usually enjoyed a different destiny and were left unscathed. It is as if their revered status and unique spatiality served as a shield against the initial onslaught of Israeli's ethnocratic conduct and spatial logic. But with time, many of these places were either confiscated, reused for non-religious purposes, or left to their own devices and gradually deteriorated with no community to protect them. It would seem that under the guise of democracy, Israel has (and still is) implemented an ethnocratic logic which among other fields has dramatically changed the role and significance of sacred places among non-Jewish communities under Israeli rule. How did this come about? How did Israel achieve these goals, which ultimately amounted to what I have termed above the ethnocratizing of the Holy Land? This was accomplished by adopting a rather efficient legislation mechanism which ultimately enabled Israel to conclude the circuitous route from previously Arab land to Israeli lands, begun by the appropriation of Arab land in 1948. Israel accomplished that by enforcing a spatial logic and a set of laws which ensured the erasure, confiscation, and reuse of former Palestinian lands (Benvenisti 2000; Yiftachel and Kedar 2000). As these had a profound and all-encompassing impact on the unfolding of events within and without sacred places, I will now narrate them briefly, focusing mostly on the mechanisms that enabled these changes, following the logic of ethnocracy.

As suggested above, Ethnocracy is a concept that implies a political regime that facilitates expansion and control by a dominant ethnicity within a modern national state. Under the heading of democracy, rights and access to common goods and state resources are allocated primarily based on ethnic origin. This theoretical construction was launched by Yiftachel, who presents a critical theory and a framework to account for the political geographies of ethnocratic societies and regimes (2006). In Israel/Palestine, the primary manifestation of ethnocracy has been a concerted strategy by the state through its various agencies and manifestations to Judaize the region, that is, to assume control over the land by the Jewish state and for the Jewish ethnic group. This is the core and most essential logic which dictates and permeates all aspects of life. Ethnocracy involves a certain spatiality and is certainly a progenitor of spatial dynamics and changes which had and still have enormous influences on the processes which are to be found at the core of this book.

The most notable feature of ethnocratic regimes is the collaborative effort to obtain ethno-national control over a territory perceived as the nation's homeland. The regime is, therefore, operating in accordance with a collective feeling of entitlement among the majority group to control its state and its homeland as part and parcel of what is conceived as a natural right to self-determination. The imposition of this political logic over a heterogeneous territory composed of different groups (which do not share the majority group's understanding, nor do they have the inclination to do so) is likely to cause conflicts (Yiftachel 2002). Claims and counterclaims to the same territory amount to conflictual views and hence contestations over allocation of resources, power, and prestige (Akenson 1992). Since ethno-nationalism is enmeshed in the definition of the state and its prevailing logic, marginalized minorities are usually barred from, or extremely limited in access to land and common goods, as well as representations in the public sphere. Following this logic, ethnocratic regimes are designed to exclude minorities from fully integrating and accepts as a norm partial citizenship for them. Hence, for example, in Israel historically non-Jews have been practically barred from purchasing residences within Jewish municipalities, especially in rural and border areas. Ultimately, over a thin layer of democratic veneer, ethnocracy imposes rather elaborate and sophisticated limitations on minority rights and capabilities. This is all the more apparent in Israel's land policy and the legal dispossession of the Palestinians displaced by Israel in the wake of the 1948 war and the ensuing emergence of Israeli statehood. One of the direct and more meaningful outcomes of the war was the transfer of vast tracts of land, including religious institutions, religious endowments (Ar.: *awqaf*), and sacred places, into the direct control of the new state. This was executed by a series of laws known generally as the Israeli Absentee Property Act (1950), and was complemented by the formation of the state's regulatory institutions. Together, these laws created the legal framework through which a newly established authority by the name of "the Custodian of Absentee Property" consolidated its control over millions of dunums of refugee land, as well as movable property (Fischbach 2003). According to article 19/A of the said law, absentees' land and movable property could only be sold to the Israeli Development Authority (Israel Book of Laws 37 20.3.1950, 86–101). This restricting article ensured the sale or transfer of absentee lands solely for purposes which were approved by state authorities. This restriction hindered any would-be legal claim to return land or property to its former Arab owner(s).

In 1965 the Absentee Property Act was amended with a new article (29/b). This was yet another turn in the state policy toward its Arab citizens' property, which was about to directly change the municipal status of urban religious endowments. The amendment to the 1950 law called for the establishment of a new legal entity, by the name of the Muslim Charitable Trust, in seven mixed cities in Israel. Before I move on to discuss these trusts, a short clarification on the mixed Israeli city is needed. Surely, modern cities are by definition mixed entities (Monterescu and Rabinowitz 2007). Since early on urban sociologists have acknowledged that cities were always mixed and presented the sites of meeting with the "other" (Simmel 1903). In Israel, the term usually implies an urban situation in which Jewish and Arab communities share the same urban space. However, what is concealed by the rather neutral description as "mixed" are the conflicts, inequalities, and the general recoil from the sharing of the same urban space, by the two ethno-national communities. In Israeli mixed cities, reality is generally controversial and when possible, clear spatial division exists between ethnic groups (Yacobi 2003). In Israel/Palestine, the concept originally related to the emergence of Jewish neighborhoods within existing Arab-Palestinian cities where Jews were also an urban minority. Following 1948, these cities have undergone considerable changes, among them a demographic inversion upon which the Jewish population became the majority as part of the ethnocratic logic of Judaization (Monterescu and Rabinowitz 2007). In contemporary Israel, even though many cities are slowly becoming ethnically mixed, the term usually refers to the original seven cities defined as mixed during the Mandate period. The term is laden with negative connotations, such that municipalities go to great lengths to deny the very existence of mixed population under their jurisdiction. In these (original) seven municipalities, the State enforced the establishment of trusts that were officially authorized with the management of Muslim endowments. However, the state made sure that the appointed members of this new regulatory mechanism were approved by a special governmental committee that was to ensure their collaboration and cooperation. Under these circumstances, it is hardly surprising that those trusts became mere rubber stamps that facilitated an easy transformation of Muslim property into agents that were deemed supportive of the state's goals. Under the guise of an amendment that allegedly enabled Muslim communities to manage their own religious heritage, the foundation of these trusts facilitated (at least during the 1960s and 1970s) the transfer of more religious properties into the hands of mainly Jewish entrepreneurs. This will be further elaborated through the case studies that furnish my discussion of the sacred in the urban scale. However, at this stage, I will allow but one comment that illustrates the reality on the ground following the foundation of the trusts. This comment derives from an interview with an activist from Jaffa, who was part of a local initiative to frustrate the cooperative nature of the trust in his city:

> The trusts were founded during the 1960s. What is a charitable trust? This is a sovereign body that, like the Vatican, answers to no one. And yet, those who were appointed did not know their rights and were always bowing their heads before their master.
> (interview with Aḥmad ʿAṣfur, November 27, 2003)[1]

Control of the land was indeed central to the Israeli ethnocracy project. To achieve this supreme goal, the State of Israel applied and modified an array of legal instruments, some of which followed earlier Ottoman and British legal precedents and mechanisms (Forman and Kedar 2004). To date, Israel claims circa 93 percent of its territory as public domain, which is by and large geared to serve, mainly, the Jewish majority. The Palestinian communities within Israel have experienced, time and again, confiscation of lands which have had disastrous outcomes in various aspects of their daily life. Following the 1967 war, Palestinian communities in the West Bank and Gaza (at least until the 2005 disengagement from Gaza) have been under the yoke of Israeli military occupation and experience gradual encroachment on their lands under the massive Israeli settlement project (Home 2003; Lecoquierre 2019).

As with other ethnocratic regimes, the main mobilizer of socio-political processes in Israel is the logic of ethno-nationalism, and yet the national question is intimately involved with an institutionalized and politicized religion (Yiftachel and Roded 2010). Judaization still looms large in the Israeli ethnocratic regime. Furthermore, even though nationalism is deemed fundamentally (pun intended) a secular project (Anderson 1991), the histories, identities, and boundaries of groups within ethnocratic societies are inescapably linked to their religious affiliations. The religious logic is paramount in Israel/Palestine as it essentializes a discourse of rigid political and social boundaries that serves the interests of the majority group. This is manifested throughout Israel in Palestinians' land that was confiscated and physically fenced off by the Israeli state. This repeated action is usually justified on behalf of a religious community that includes Jews of all kinds but excludes non-Jews, especially those Palestinians who had occupied the territory before the foundation of the State of Israel. Following the same ethnocratic logic, the religious affairs of Jewish communities are administered by the Ministry of Religious Affairs. At the same time, all non-Jewish communities' religious needs within Israel are catered for by a special department that operates within the Ministry of the Interior. While the needs and the management of

Jewish religious sites are mostly funded by the state, non-Jewish communities are time and again left to their own devices and are forced to generate the funds through donations or external sources. This proved greatly detrimental to the preservation of the religious and sacred places of the non-Jewish minorities in Israel. In the introductory part of the *Encyclopedia of Sacred Places in Palestine*, a project that was initiated by the Al-Aqsa Association for the Upkeep of Sacred Places (an off-shoot of the Islamic Movement in Israel), the then head of the association confronts us with the way these policies are perceived by a member of the Muslim minority in Israel:

> The Israeli government has not ceased its efforts, since 1948, to ruin everything that is under its hands: cemeteries, mosques, churches in villages and in cities that it conquered in 1948. The regime is working according to an organized plan to alter the role of sacred places and the original purposes for which they were initially constructed and to obliterate and conceal every sign and memory left of the Arab and Islamic existence in this land.
>
> (Abu 'Amar et al. 2014)

Abu 'Amar narrates a disastrous dynamic that has taken place in many Palestinian sacred places since 1948. However, it is not solely the policies of Israel that effected dramatic changes within those sites. As early as the British Mandate, there are indications of changes and a general decline in interest and attendance at these places (Canaan 1927; Frantzman and Bar 2013). Winds of modernity bringing to these shores the notion of secularization were also responsible for this direction, and likewise the growing influence of fundamentalist Salafi ideas that advocate severe restriction on visitations to graves and sacred sites (Weismann 2001). A recent survey of sacred places under the Palestinian Authority revealed that many of them have become heritage sites in which the religious-cum-Islamic component may no longer be the dominant one (Lecoqierre 2019). However, Abu 'Amar's analysis is still valid within the context of the Israeli ethnocratic impact on Israel/Palestine. Despite its origins within European secular-democratic philosophy, Zionism was quintessentially an ethnocratic movement that called to establish a "Jewish" state in Palestine (Abulof 2014). Jewish religion and ethnicity were increasingly entwined with Zionism's legitimation of its statehood project (Gans 2008). From early on, Zionist leaders sought political legitimacy from within and without the Jewish world to elicit support for the founding of the Jewish state and thus ensuring its survival (Abulof 2009; Bar-Tal 2013). Religious symbols, ideas, principles, customs, and figures drawn from the nation's imagined past were thus heavily used in early Zionist rhetoric and actions to justify the nation and its goals (Shoham 2014). The ascendancy of religious elements within the Jewish state and society adds an additional theological dimension in the ongoing battle to eliminate the natives, that is, the existing Palestinian communities. Weaving religion into the ethnonational vision was perceived as beneficial for the establishment of the state, and certainly for its upkeep. The ethnocratic logic harnessed religion to the national Jewish project as can be seen, for example, in targeting the infrastructures of Islamic endowments (*awqaf*). But it goes far deeper than that, as from the birth of Zionism mundane, rather secular activities were assigned with sanctity and conceived as sacred and surely of spiritual importance. This is all the more apparent in the early Zionists' approach to the land as a desired goal, illustrated in calling the purchase of new lands "redemption of the land" (Neuman 2015). This desire is epitomized in Aaron David Gordon, arguably the exemplar of the early Jewish pioneers (Hebrew: *ḥalutz*). God, according to his view, is to be found in the land and through the cultivation of the land. Gordon represented a new type of Jew who is diametrically opposed to Jewish life in the diaspora, which means a Jew who is connected to the land and of the land. He advocated agriculture and the tilling of the soil as the best remedy for the Jewish people's plight. In the following excerpt from his voluminous philosophical writing, he explains his spiritual (even religious) approach to the land:

> And when, O Man, you will return to Nature—on that day your eyes will open, you will gaze straight into the eyes of Nature, and in its mirror, you will see your own image. You will know that you have returned to yourself. When you return you will see that from you, from your hands and from your feet, from your body and from your soul, heavy, hard, oppressive fragments will fall, and you will begin to stand erect. You will understand that these were fragments of the shell into which you had shrunk in the bewilderment of your heart and out of which you had finally emerged. On that day you will know that your former life did not befit you, that you must renew all things: your food and your drink, your dress and your home, your manner of work and your mode of study—everything.
> (Hertzberg 1997)

These are the early beginnings of the Israeli ethnocratic policy of controlling (as much as possible) the land. It is the fusion of this political stance with a religious understanding that allows it a very exclusionary and segregative approach to the original native society, which, as it so happens, adheres to a competing religious creed. This also explains the growing encroachment on lands and properties, and on non-Jewish sacred sites that were also either eliminated, banned from use, or transferred into Jewish hands, as the case may be, either with the help or the silence of the state authorities. Indeed, since 1948 time and again compounds that served for religious purposes, such as mosques and Sufi lodges, were utilized by their new owners for mundane and highly secular purposes. The converting of mostly Islamic institutions into pubs and restaurants, as well as other functions, became a theme and a constant concern for the Islamic Movement in Israel, often becoming a high-profile public campaign to contest the legitimacy of such confiscations (Luz 2013a). Some of the case studies discussed herewith emerged exactly from these confrontations with state authorities or municipal agencies over the right of ownership, and certainly the proper use, of these compounds. Such is the case of the conflict over Hassan Bey Mosque in Tel-Aviv-Jaffa which was destined to become a touristic attraction and part of the growing central business district (CBD) during the 1970s (Luz 2008a). The conversion of a Muslim shrine in Tiberias into a Jewish pilgrimage site is also part of this ongoing battle (Luz 2020). The former Ottoman Mosque in Beersheba was a bone of contention for decades between the local municipality and a group of activists that struggled to restore its former functions as a mosque for the urban and regional Muslim communities (Reiter and Lerhs 2013). At the epicenter of Israeli ethnocracy project stands the city which symbolizes the heart of the Jewish Holy Land, Jerusalem. Since early on Jerusalem became paramount in Zionist theory, and when the time arrived to choose a capital for the new State of Israel, it was Jerusalem that was chosen, even though it was under siege and only partially in Jewish hands. If anything, this step clarifies the religious aspects in the seemingly secular Israeli ethnocracy. This understanding is met with a mirror project of sacralization on the Palestinian part, which explains the ceaseless conflicts over ownership, control, and indeed, the right to its religious history, since the budding of the two opposing national projects. The sacred landmarks of the city will serve us to explore further religion and urbanity and the globalization of a sacred place in the final chapter of this book. These are but a few examples, central though they are, of the ongoing conflict between the ethnocratic state and its ethno-religious minorities regarding their heritage, right of ownership, and especially the utilization of these sites.

The foray into the realm of the sacred confronts us with the limitations of the ethnocratic logic. In the Israeli case, complementing the ethnocratic logic with the transcendental and cosmic dimension giving growing legitimation to the latter has surely proved to be a double-edged sword. Time and again, and in growing numbers in recent years, the State of Israel finds itself involved in conflicts and contestations over the ownership and control of sacred sites. As the religious component is heavily enmeshed into the Israeli ethnocratic logic, it is more often than not impossible to exclude religious justifications and logic from allegedly mundane-political issues. The right of ownership of a deserted mosque, obtaining a permit to renovate a dilapidated church, the infiltration of a Jewish group into a ruined Muslim pilgrimage site, and in particular, the ongoing contestations in Jerusalem's holy basin have become a constant threat to the very legitimation of the ethnocratic Israeli regime. The cosmic-transcendental-religious logic challenges and ruptures the ethnocratic logic, as will be further elaborated throughout the many case studies discussed hereinafter. The increasingly political component within sacred sites in Israel/Palestine cannot be understood in isolation from the logic of ethnocracy. Hence, since 1948 we are witness to the lasting and increasing ethnocratization of the Holy Land. The centrality of Israel and its control of the entire Israel/Palestine region affected changes in the spatialities of sacred sites of all religious groups. Furthermore, against the ongoing process of the Judaization of the region, we witness a plethora of socio-political processes within sacred places framed as land-claiming, anti-hegemonic rhetoric, and actions, and surely resistance, by minority groups. Israeli ethnocracy harnessed religion or, put differently, had a very strong religious component while promoting and fulfilling its goals. Ethnocratizing the Holy Land was indeed implemented very successfully, as might be inferred from the establishment of the state of Israel as the homeland of the Jewish people. The fusion of religion into this process proved a highly effective mechanism in the short and medium terms for sustaining the Israeli ethnocratic regime. It allowed the construction of legal mechanisms, disproportional allocations of resources for religious activities and indeed sacred places, and general neglect of minorities' religious affairs. Sanctity is heavily used to buttress the Jewish hegemonical position, as will be further discussed hereinafter regarding sacred places in different scalar settings. However, it is rather doubtful that the state can maintain this differential and ethnocratic approach to ethno-religious minorities within the perimeters of the ethnocratized Holy Land.

Figure 1.2 Map of Israel and Occupied Territories (adapted from Wikimedia).

2

Embodying the Sacred and the Body in Sacred Places

Body and Embodiment: A Few Theoretical Clarifications

Let us go back to sacred places and their multifold socio-political meanings in Israel/Palestine. Our foray begins with the individual-body scale. Accordingly, this chapter explores the links between the body scale, embodiment processes, and sacred places. Before I explain more about the importance of the individual scale in the politics of sacred places and surely what is meant by embodiment, it is pertinent to remind ourselves of the relational dynamics of the spatial and the social. The body, as succinctly suggested by the anthropologist Mary Douglas (and others), is a "reflection of society" (1970). Along these lines, Michel Foucault was seminal to the social constructionist understanding of the body. He advanced the notion that the social discourse is what "makes up" the body; that is, the body is the product of particular social practices and networks of meaning (Foucault 1980). And yet, in his inquiry into the nature of space and the ways it is produced, Lefebvre finds his theoretical approach wanting:

> He [Foucault] never explains what space it is that he is referring to, and how it bridges the gap between the theoretical realm and the practical one, between mental and social, between material and social ….
>
> (Lefebvre 1991: 4)

It was Butler who attempted to clarify (some of) the Foucauldian ambiguity regarding the performativity of gender and the social construction of the body. Butler follows Foucault's notion that subject positions are not natural givens, but rather discursive products of power (Butler 1990). She argues that the theoretical division between a socially constructed gender and a presumed biological sex ultimately constitutes the illusion that the subject's gender is grounded in a fixed and binary biological essence. Gender and, hence, body prove to be performance:

> Hence, within the inherited discourse of the metaphysics of substance, gender proves to be performative— that is, constituting the identity it is purported to be. In this sense, gender is always a doing, though not a doing by a subject who might be said to preexist the deed.
>
> (Butler 1990: 25)

Gender, then, is not just a process, but it is a particular type of process! Indeed, one may argue (as some of her critics did) that Butler's initial account of performativity neglects the materiality of the body (Sedgwick 1993). This critique was met by Butler in her later engagement with performativity, as she elaborates on the question of how bodies are made and yet are also material and makes it clear that matter and discourse interact in the production of bodies (Butler 1993).

In his project on space, Lefebvre expanded on Foucault by demonstrating that space was first and foremost socially constructed and that the body was central to its production and always the starting point of inquiry:

> The whole of space proceeds from the body, even though it so metamorphoses the body that it may forget it altogether—even though it may separate itself from the body as to kill it. The genesis of the far-away order can be accounted for only on the basis of the order that is nearest to us—namely the order of the body ... [the body] prefigure[s] the layers of social space and their interconnectedness.
>
> (1991: 405)

Lefebvre treats space not simply as the physical imposition of a concept, or a space, upon the body but rather as a product of the human body, as a perception and as a conception. In his predominantly Marxist project regarding space and its production, the body is the main site of resistance that starts with the human body and its corporeal ability to produce space. This trait, rather than just conceiving space, is how people can take back power in their everyday lives. This resonates, as I will demonstrate in this chapter, in the daily and sometime seemingly mundane activities of individuals in sacred places. Following in Lefebvre's wake, Kim Knott launches a spatial analysis of the location of religion and manages to circumvent the Cartesian dualism which hitherto has been largely responsible for a common approach that severs the body from the mind (Knott 2005). Alongside this understanding, she holds the body as formative for conceptual development, social relations, and the imagination of both in relation to space (2005: 19). This means suggesting that through the body, we may understand better how socio-political processes associated with religion, and certainly systems of belief are spatialized and materialized in sacred places.

Drawing closer to home—home being geographical theories of (sacred) place and politics—it is worth reminding ourselves of Massey's illuminating and concise discussion regarding these reciprocal and co-constitutive relations between the social and the spatial before I discuss the connections among body, embodiment, and embodied religious geographies. Massey, as suggested also in the introductory part of the book, is crucial to my approach to places and their inherent social and contested nature:

> The spatial is socially constituted. Space is created out of the vast intricacies, the incredible complexities, of the interlocking and the non-interlocking, and the network of relations at every scale from local to global. What makes a particular view of these social relations specifically spatial is their simultaneity … but simultaneity is not stasis. Seeing space as a moment in the intersection of configured social relations means that it cannot be seen as static.
>
> (Massey 1993: 155)

Places, therefore, are far from being flat surfaces across which we walk, but rather are dynamic and prone to changes both temporal and spatial. As such, they bear myriads of stories and human interactions. This chapter brings this understanding to the fore by looking at the individual body scale. Musing on the neglected role of the body both as producer of sacred space-time and as a site for signification in and of itself in geographical accounts of religion and spirituality, Julian Holloways makes the importance of looking at the body scale very clear: The body is not "a mere receptacle or 'inscriptive surface' for the work of representation-cum-discourse" of religion, but the body and bodily practices are central to the enactment of sacred space (Holloway 2003: 1963).

Therefore, social, temporal, and spatial aspects of being are co-dependent and intertwined. Being in this respect refers to being-in-place, which is inescapably being-in-time, and being-in-society (Howitt 2002). Following these fundamentals about place, self, and body, we may agree that exploring the body in sacred places in its most private and individual moments offers a window on the wider social and political issues of co-existence and underpinnings of geopolitics and power. Gillian Rose made this abundantly clear when she summed up her analysis of body and embodiment while pioneering an exploration on geography and feminism in the 1990s. She wrote that "far from being natural, bodies are maps of the relation between power and identity" (Rose 1993: 32). The body is a place where social practices happen, and through the body, these practices are marked or embodied. Coming nearer to the role of the body in sacred places, Julian Holloway explains:

> This means, then, allowing the body to signify and make sense of (sacred) space, rather than seeing it as a mere receptacle or "inscriptive surface" for the work of representation-cum-discourse. ... I intend here to foreground a corporeal perception that takes all the senses, as well as the rhythm and comportment of the body in action, as central to the affective making of sacred space. To a degree this is nothing new. That the body and bodily action are fundamental components of the production of sacred space has been recognized in anthropology and ritual studies for some time.
>
> (Holloway 2003: 1963–4)

The body, then, is structured by society's discourse and endless cultural processes and yet individuals are not void of agency to act and be more than mere receptacles of ideologies, norms, and other societal codes and prerequisites. It is through the body that we occupy positions in social space and (may) challenge or change existing power-geometries. This is exactly what Bourdieu defined as a field—a metaphor that serves him to explain the semi-autonomous structure of relations between positions and social statuses endowed with different degrees of capital (of sorts), where actors (individual scale) struggle to proclaim and obtain their right to that capital (Bourdieu 1985). In her extensive ethnographic research on veiling practices among women in Istanbul, Gökriksel approaches veiling as a gendered embodied spatial practice that reveals the intertwined production of bodies and subjectivities (2009). Through a personal decision on veiling, women are negotiating between the wider political contexts and social meanings and their own individual experiences to shape the production of corporeal piety. The embodied practice of veiling allows women to use the body for the formation of the self (Mahmood 2004). While exploring veiling among Turkish women in Istanbul, Anna Secor demonstrates this embodied practice as that which enables women to negotiate the body in space (both spatial and social) and the self between social forces such as secularization and Islamization (Secor 2002). Thus, while exploring what are seemingly the most private and intimate moments such as veiling, crawling, praying, kneeling in sacred places, one may encounter the wider social and political issues of coexistence that underlie geopolitics and power. The tangible body is indeed a social entity which through embodied practices expresses itself, echoes and spatializes social and political processes. As Julian Holloway and Oliver Valins already suggested, while advocating for more rigorous engagement of geographers with religious and spiritual geographies:

> [they] are (re)produced through a variety of embodied acts and bodily practices. Thus, the corporeal enactment and performances involved in, for example, prayer, ritual, and pilgrimage, ... are central to the maintenance and development of religious spaces and landscapes.
>
> (2002: 8)

Embodiment of the subject is a highly effective medium for exploring larger social issues, for as the body moves through space and time, it negotiates and reveals a variety of social developments and in particular, conflicts. Thus, the body is an interface of internal expressions and needs and of external perceptions. Not only do subjects form bodies, but bodies also form social reality. Struggles are fought through the body, as well as enactments of social codes, creeds, and surely the ability to change them, or, at the very least, oppose them. Our bodies are manifestations of ourselves in our everyday worlds. At the same time, embodiment is our way of knowing those worlds and interacting with them (McGuire 1990). To illustrate these arguments, I will conclude the introductory part of this chapter with the personal story of Manal Rimawi or as she is known in her town, Acre, Umm Ahmad.[1] Manal was interviewed as part of my *ReligioCity* project which explores the relations between city and religion(s). I will elaborate further on this project, which is pertinent to the current endeavor, in Chapters 5 and 6. At this stage, suffice it to say that this project looks at Acre, a multi-religious and multi-ethnic city in the north of Israel, and explores these intricate relations through several urban infrastructures. As part of looking at faith-based organization in the city the project followed an Islamic women's group named *Suna' al-Haya* (literally, life makers but may also be understood as acts or creators of moral virtues). Manal is the founder of this group in Acre and for many years has been the leader-cum-organizer of its activities. The women who join in the group's activities accept her as their leader and acknowledge her authoritative position as a religious instructor. Manal, or as she is generally known today, Umm Ahmad, was born in the Old City of Acre. She is married to a local imam and is the mother of five children ("all grown up now") who lives in a modest apartment in the center of Acre. The following are excerpts from the interview, in which Manal often "scale jumps" from the personal to the national, through the urban and back to the personal.[2]

Q: Are you the founder of this group? And why?
A: The purpose was religious … I was with another "sister" who like me learned *shari'a* as part of the *da'wa*. This is where the idea sprang from, at the beginning we managed to obtain rooms in the mosque. … these rooms were kindergartens that belonged to the municipality and when [representatives] from the Islamic movement entered the municipality as aldermen they said: we freed them. However, as a matter of fact, many kindergartens are being closed in Acre. Did you understand? They are trying to close [us] in Acre. So, we took them and used them for *da'wa* … we have turned them [the rooms] through our feminine efforts, even when we collected donations most of them came from women …

Manal is alluding here to a common practice among Islamic movements to engage in *da'wa*, that is, the act of calling people to embrace Islam usually by teaching the *shari'a*, the religious law and conduct that forms the Islamic tradition. The term literally means invitation, but over time it has acquired a much more elaborate meaning and refers to numerous (usually) non-violent efforts aimed to ameliorate Muslim societies through preaching, education, and various social activities of a religious nature to restore Islamic virtues (Canard 1965). As such, Manal considers the claiming of these rooms within the precinct of the mosque as, indeed, *da'wa*.

Q: You talk about the old city with a lot of yearning. Is there something you had there, and you feel you lost it? Do you want to bring it back?
A: … in the past there was much more love, comradery, and cooperation among people. People were simpler … things have changed. There was no violence and corruption like today … and it spreads [these misfortunes]
Q: What is the reason for that?
A: The Zionist policy is the reason. It is the one that supports those bodies [that aim to draw Arab citizens from the old city] and it transforms Acre into Acre of drugs, Acre of illegal weapon. And why? To make people frantic and to make them sell [their houses] and leave intramural Acre for the modern parts …
Q: What was your goal when you established the group?
A: My goal was religious and [to establish] a religious infrastructure, I was with another "sister" who also studied the *shari'a* and it was part of *da'wa*.
Q: And when did you become religious?
A: At the age of sixteen when I was a tenth grader.
Q: Do you come from a religious home?
A: Not at all. I was the second one in Acre who put on [the hijab].[3] When I started to cover my head, there were no young women in Acre who wore

the hijab. I was also the second one who wore the jilbab.... My mom was against it, and I still remember how it happened. We were in Jenin, and I stood in front of a shop that sells jilbab and I said to my mother: I want a jilbab and I will not return home without it.... My mom said I was too young, and this is not the time ... she thought it was just a whim and that soon enough I would say enough is enough and put it down, but I stayed with it—jilbab and head cover.

Q: Did you have any problems with it?

A: Yes, I had, in school the Christian girls used to laugh at me ... when they saw me for the first time with it, they laughed at me ....

(interview with Manal Rimawi, February 2, 2020)

Scales, as the argument goes, do not exist as "things out there" that stabilize or alter political, economic, or cultural relations. Rather, scales are performed by different actants through the scalar positions they hold or adopt in response to and within different socio-spatial contexts as they engage in their daily life. Manal's narration of herself moves back and forth from her body to the community and the urban, but also alludes to the national. This scale jumping is informed first and foremost by her own personal decision of "becoming more religious," which was initially manifested in the embodied practice of wearing the hijab and the jilbab. In forging such an understanding of the interrelations between the body scale, dress, and space, Joanne Entwistle highlights the ways embodied practices are ways of self-presentation performed by individuals as they move into and between everyday spaces of activity:

> [T]he study of dress as situated practice requires moving between, on the one hand, the discursive and representational aspects of dress, and the way the body/dress is caught up in relations of power, and on the other, the embodied experience of dress and the use of dress as a means by which individuals orientate themselves to the social world.
>
> (Entwistle 2000: 39)

For Manal, adopting "Islamic" dress codes seems to empower her not only regarding taking charge of her own personal space. She presents a critical approach toward men from her own Muslim community who were not responsive to her requests early on, when she initiated the group. She is also highly critical and fully aware of the ramifications of the ethnocratic logic for the present state of Muslims in Acre, and surely one may also detect a larger claim toward the State of Israel and its "Zionist" conduct. This is demonstrated not only orally, by what she conveys during the interview, but also spatially, in her choice of residence as near as possible to the historic pre-modern and predominantly Muslim part of Acre, which is the old intramural Acre. In her thought-provoking work on veiling in Istanbul, Anna Secor argues that to understand veiling as an embodied and situated practice, we need to acknowledge space as relational and, therefore, encompassing more than an individual body (Secor 2002). Veiling, she goes on to argue (or for that matter any form of "religious" garment), should be understood as situated and embedded in relations on different scalar levels. One cannot understand such embodied practices in isolation from larger and multi-scalar relational contexts. That said, dress codes are surely not the only embodied practice performed within and without sacred places. In what follows I want to expand on that and explore body in sacred places and various embodied practices preformed therein. Firstly, I will present various ethnographies and encounters with individuals in sacred places and explore through them embodied practices and the body as a constitute of sacred place and constituted by it. Secondly, I will discuss, along the general approach of the book and its emphasis on socio-political processes, cases of "embodying the nation" in sacred places.

Bodies, Individuals, and Embodying the Sacred

As argued above, in his predominantly Marxist project Lefebvre holds the body as pivotal to the production of space. Social space proceeds from the body in the same way that the body is constituted by the "weight of society's demand" (Lefebvre 1991: 195). Lefebvre's articulation of the body in space enables us to see how the body is crucial to construction of space:

> Can the body with its capacity for action, and its various energies, be said to create space? Assuredly, but not in the sense that occupation might be said to manufacture spatiality; rather, there is an immediate relationship between the body and its space, between the body's deployment in space and its occupation of space. Before producing effects in the material realms (tools and objects), before producing itself by drawing nourishment from that realm, and before reproducing itself by generating other bodies, each living body is space and has its space: it produces itself in space and it also produces the space. This is truly a remarkable relationship: the body with the energies at its disposal, the living body, creates or produces its own space; conversely, the laws of space, which is to say the laws of discrimination in space, also govern the living body and the deployment of its energies.
>
> (1991: 170)

These ideas became very vivid during the interview with R., a very articulate woman who frequents the Tomb of Rachel in Tiberias. She originates from a religious family but did not adhere to a religious lifestyle while growing up. She "made a U-turn" (to use her own words) and adopted religion again following her husband, who grew up as a secular person and embraced religion as an adult. Her lengthy and lucid descriptions of her reasoning and experience of visitations of sacred places echo Lefebvre's point about how the place makes the body at the same time the body constructs space. The following is her response when asked why she visits the Tomb of Rachel:

> I am very happy for this opportunity of being able to leave the house on a Friday noon, complete a round of visits to righteous people's graves (Hebrew: *tsaddiqim*), a bit of shopping, [plunging] in the Sea of Galilee, and returning home fulfilled by the places that fulfil me. This [Tomb of Rachel] place certainly fulfils me, that is, a shopping mall would not give me the same spiritual satisfaction and the pleasure of communication [with transcendence] because there is nothing in it save matter and materialism. Here, one may find a kind of distillment and refinement ... I have here in my bag a book about Leonardo da Vinci and it discusses how he feels divinity in everything he does, and divinity is not something you can prove but the world proves it to you.... This place is a place of divinity ... it is a symbol (like da Vinci's Sistine Chapel [*sic*]) for those who do not always understand.... This is a place that tells| you: here lived, acted, created, and died someone whose life was larger than other people's life. And why? Because it is beyond ... when I pray here, I aim at these [inner] places ... [Rachel] left the house of her father, who was one of the richest men of the land, to follow a shepherd who did not know until the age of forty how to read or write.... And he could not become such an eminent scholar [Hebrew: *gedol ha-dor*] if it were not for her belief in him ... when I pray here, I aim at these standards, that I would be able to do the same for my husband ... I try to connect to the essence of this particular place....
>
> (interview with R., March 28, 2014)

R.'s response and explanation of her own personal motivation to visit sacred places in general and the Tomb of Rachel in particular resonate Geertz's approach to religion as a cultural system (1966). While addressing the role of sacred symbols he alludes to the ways sacred materials inform people's perceptions of reality:

> sacred symbols [which] function to synthesize a people's ethos—the tone, character, and quality of their life, its moral and aesthetic style and mood—and their world view—the picture they have of the way things in sheer actuality are, their most comprehensive ideas of order.
>
> (1966: 3)

For R., the sacred place is a spatiality that allows her to transcend daily realities and enables her to connect to what she perceives as a more profound existence as she eloquently states: "I try to connect to the essence of the place." She is certain the site is indeed the tomb of a righteous Jewish woman—a narrative which has only recently begun being promoted by the current director of the site (Luz 2020). This new narrative will be discussed at length in Chapter 4, in which I engage with the sacred and the urban scale. However, it is intriguing to see how the ephemerality and non-routinized character of the place inform corporeal responses in space. This is quite clear from R.'s description of a recent visit to the site accompanied by two friends who do not share her religious belief, as follows:

> People take off their shoes when they enter a sacred place, and it seems obvious and understandable.... But here we are with our shoes on, and I am speaking loudly while you record me ... because there is a different sense of sanctity here, it is a different place and there are also couches here ... incidentally, I arrived here with two friends not long ago, one of them was totally wasted and she just fell asleep on the couch. I, in the meantime, went to the Sea of Galilee [a short walk from the Tomb, N. L.] and later came back and picked her up. And this is cool, she fell asleep on the couch, and nobody told her anything. She was here wearing trousers [and not a long dress which is the custom among religious Jewish women, N. L.] took off her shoes and lay down on the couch ... this is an accommodating space. I think that the north [of Israel] is much more tolerant, open-minded and breathes more freely.
>
> (interview with R., March 28, 2014)

R. is immersed here in a rather critical reading of the map of sacred places in Israel and makes a distinction between the way she experiences the more "official" and hence rigid and routinized sacred places in Jerusalem and its environs, versus the non-routinized and hence less restricting sacred places she encounters in the north of Israel. This feeling of intimacy and of a "different sense of place" that R. relates to, and even more so, the way she experiences the sacred space is exactly what Lefebvre argued about the importance of the body in the construction of space. These feelings of intimacy and closeness are also apparent in the following paragraph, which narrates U.'s experience and narration of her encounters with the Shrine of Mariam Bawardy, located in the village of Ibbelin in the Galilee, Israel.

Mariam Bawardy was an avowed Carmelite nun who according to written and oral traditions endured harsh supernatural adversities, diabolic possessions, and stigmata. According to one tradition, she was born in the village of Ibbelin on January 5, 1846, and died in Bethlehem on August 26, 1878. In 1983 she was beatified by Pope John Paul II and on May 17, 2015, she was canonized by Pope Francis (Nabulsi 2015). As will be further elaborated in Chapter 3, over the years her birthplace in Ibbelin has become a site for veneration and serves as a shrine and a pilgrimage site. Although heavily renovated in recent years, the site remains easily accessible as there are no gates nor any barriers, thus pilgrims can arrive at all hours. For U., this is probably one of the most alluring features of the site, which informs her personal conduct during visitations therein. She expresses her very personal attachment to Mariam's place by making some parallels between her own life and Mariam's:

> I am a forty-one year old woman, unmarried. Both my parents have passed away, so I live with my sister and her husband who is also my boss at my workplace. I belong to the Greek-Catholic church.
>
> Q: How often do you visit the shrine of Mariam?
> A: Our church has a special day for Mariam Bawardy and all the village people attend and light candles, but I, as soon as I feel the need to visit her, I arrive at her shrine. It is more when I am unwell or troubled than when I am in a good mood. Whenever I want to find her, I will, no matter what time it is … Sometimes I visit her at night. When I feel the need I run to her. I walk to her house as this is the easiest place to visit. Should I want to go to church I need to bring the keys, but her house [Mariam's shrine] is always open, I feel that no matter when I need her, I will always find her.
> Q: What does the visit to Mariam's shrine mean to you?
> A: This is something that we got accustomed to since we were kids, that is; going to her place on Saturday evenings and lighting candles. On the face of it, the visit looks like a regular thing to do, a custom. However, as I grew up it dawned on me that prayer is the bond between us and God, between us and the place we visit, and I have begun to visit the site when I feel the need … I go there when I feel the need for her. Sometimes I think to myself: maybe no one visited her today, so I must go [to be with her].
>
> (interview with U., November 6, 2015)

U. finds solace in her visits to the place, as it enables her to be in direct contact with Mariam Bawardy. She feels intimate with her because, as she discloses during the interview, she shares with her the fate of a troubled, childless, and unmarried life and indeed other sorrows which were all part of Mariam's fate according to local legend. Indeed, the capacity of the place to accommodate the body, the personal scale, and surely these feelings of connection and closeness with the sacred site demonstrate clearly how space emerges from the body and constructed by it. Much like R., who firmly believes the Tomb of Rachel is the tomb of a virtuous Jewish woman—even though most indications confirm that it was originally a holy site dedicated to Sukayna bint Husayn ibn Ali ibn Abu Talib (Sukayna, daughter of Hussein, the son of Ali b. Abu Talib), that is, the granddaughter of the fourth Muslim caliph—U. feels attachment to the shrine of Mariam and frequently visits it, although her actual birthplace in still heavily debated among different communities in the Galilee. Space is indeed social space in the sense that one cannot experience it in isolation from one's own societal views and surely constraints. These constraints are beautifully described by Edward Said:

> Just as none of us is outside or beyond geography, none of us is completely free from the struggle over geography. That struggle is complex and interesting because it is not only about soldiers and cannons but also about ideas, about forms, about images and imagining.
>
> (1993: 7)

The way one perceives place is therefore bound up with assertations and imaginings which are inspired, by and large, by one's socio-cultural background and upbringing. I would argue (in the wake of other geographers as Tuan 1977; Mitchell 2001; Massey 2005), even more strongly than Said, that ideas, imaginings, and images are more important to our perceptions and experiences of place than concrete struggles (wars) over geography. For M., whom I meet during a bi-weekly lesson on religious law conducted by Rabbi Raphael Cohen at the Tomb of Rachel in Tiberias, this is surely the case.

M. grew up in an observant Sephardic Jewish family. His parents arrived in Israel during the 1950s following the establishment of the State of Israel and the ensuing war with its neighboring states (Bard 2003). He hails from a small village not far from Tiberias where his parents found their (meager) livelihood as farmers. After his mandatory army service, he became a welder and at the age of twenty-six married and in due time became a father of three. Our encounters at the Tomb of Rachel and subsequent talks, following the meetings of the study group we both attended, have provided me with more information as to his motivations, needs, and goals that ultimately caused him these visits and growing attachment to the site.[4] For most of his adult life and despite his religious background, he drew apart from religion. His recent divorce forced him to move out of the house he shared with his ex-wife. Since then, he suffers from depression which also rendered him unemployed save a few, sporadic, and far between, small private commissions. A friend who saw him in this hour of need invited him to join the study group. As we sit by the tomb in the men's section of the shrine after class, he tells me: "Here with Rachel, I find solace I rarely find nowadays ... I learned from Rabbi Raphael [the director of the site and the person conducting the classes N. L.] about her tribulations and it made me think she can understand me ... I feel good when I come here" (fieldnotes, March 7, 2013). This healing process of the body (and soul) in sacred places is a recurring theme among pilgrims/visitors to many of the places I have explored. This quality assigned to sacred places is paramount in Maqam Abu al-Hijja, a local shrine found near the village Kaukab Abu al-Hijja l in the north of Israel. The following was narrated by N., who I met at one of the inner rooms of the shrine, as she arrived accompanied by her mother. Our conversation started after she came in and sat near me and began a phone conversation. I was half listening to her conversation as I was watching her mother pray and bow by the tomb of Abu al-Hijja. Suddenly, N. started to chant and sing rather loudly to the other party on the phone. When she rang off, we began to talk, and I learned that they are, indeed, a mother and daughter who regularly come to the site from the nearby town of Sakhnin. They also shared with me that they belong to a Sufi group, and the phone call was with the shaykh leading the group, who resided at the time in Nazareth.[5] The chant I heard was relayed in this manner from the sacred place to the shaykh's house for him and other followers, who could not attend the site. Like many other interlocutors I met on site, both N. and her mother recounted the story of Husam al-Din Abu al-Hijja, and the healing powers assigned to this tomb-shrine. Apparently, when someone from their group is taken ill, they convene at the site and spend the night by the graves which are found in the inner room of the shrine:

Q: Yes, we all come here together and if many of us arrive we split up, women in one room and men in the other. And we sleep here until morning. If someone is sick, we get a phone call and then we arrive at Abu al-Hijja and he [the patient] sleeps between the two graves until the next morning. And in the morning, he wakes up completely healed.

Q: And what kinds of diseases are they that this site can heal?

A: Every illness, even the most difficult ones, God willing (*in sha'a Allah*). A daughter of one of the men in our group who arrives here for the *dhikr*[6] was diagnosed with cancer in her face. So, everybody gathered here, and you would not believe what happened, listen to me, she slept between the two tombs while we were in the next room. On one of the tombs someone left a *masbaha* [Muslim prayer beads] and when she (the sick woman) woke up in the morning the *masbaha* flew up in the air and landed on her neck. And since that day, and this happened seven or eight years ago, she is strong as a horse.

(fieldnotes August 28, 2013)

Healing, both physical and spiritual, is arguably one of the most striking embodied practices often associated with sacred places. Religious practitioners, pilgrims, visitors are often engaged in recreating self and body through rituals enacted on site.

Crawford argues that at the heart of all religious traditions are practices of healing, to be enacted within the sacred realm (2006: 30–1). Lourdes, France, is probably the best-known place where healing is the paramount reason that motivates the millions of pilgrims that arrive at the site annually. Here, in 1858, a peasant girl named Bernadette Soubirous reported that the Virgin Mary appeared to her eighteen times, calling the world to prayer and repentance. At Mary's bidding, Bernadette uncovered a spring within a grotto. Lourdes has attracted particular interest, because of its international popularity and its reputation for miraculous healing which rendered it the very name of a "healing shrine" (Gesler 1993, 1996). Harris investigated Lourdes "as a site for the exploration and negotiation of embodied aspirations" and followed the ways pilgrims use the site as a space to negotiate and explore their own bodily and holistic aspirations (2013). Therefore, she argues, their encounters with the site on the personal scale enable them to connect to this "therapeutic landscape" and construct their own understanding and conduct while there. This understanding resonates also in the narratives discussed above, in which we were privy to the ways individuals (singular) make sense of these places and create their own embodied experience. And yet healing, praying, wishing, kneeling, prostrating, and sleeping, as the case may be in sacred places are only part of the embodied practices performed therein. In the final section of this chapter, I will focus on ways in which individuals embody larger political networks (namely the national level) as they negotiate their visits to sacred sites.

Embodying the Nation through Sacred Places

As local traditions would have it, the person interred at Maqam Abu al-Hijja is the amir Husam al-Din Abu al-Hijja. Abu al-Hijja (literally, "the fearless warrior") was an officer (Ar: *amir*) of Kurdish origin in Saladin's army, who gained recognition as a formidable *mujahid* (a person engaged in jihad) while fighting against the Crusader army in Palestine in the late twelfth century CE (Arraf 2008). I discussed his personality and revered status in local Muslim communities' collective memory with Ahmad Hajj. Ahmad served as the mayor of the local municipality of Kaukab Abu al-Hijja from 1989 to 1993. Hajj is, by his own admission, a self-professed Marxist, who was a member of the Israeli communist party. During his time in office, he initiated a project renovating the sacred place and its environs. He defines himself as a secular Palestinian and for him this sacred place is important, not because of any assigned holiness but as part of his heritage as a Palestinian. That is, the site is of importance to him regardless of its religious-cum-spiritual meaning but rather due to its political implications as it challenges the Jewish-Israeli identity of the state. I was rather intrigued by his take and asked him to explain how a secular person, who also identifies as a Marxist, connects with a military man of a different ethnicity who received a grant from the Sultan (Saladin) to exploit the local villagers and who inflicted heavy taxes upon them. Furthermore, the scanty historical data about him indicate also that he never resided in the region (Arraf 1996).

> Q: So, how can you, a communist by your own admission, identify with this military man who did nothing for the local farmers (Arabic: fallahin) save take their money?
> A: I feel close to Abu al-Hijja not because he was a general or a Kurd, but since he was engaged and highly committed to the battle against the Crusaders. His battle against the Crusaders ultimately contributes to the Palestinian struggle for freedom and to the people here.
>   (interview with Ahmad Hajj, December 28, 2015)

Hajj merges in this narrative the twelfth-century battle between the Crusader Kingdom and the Ayyubid Sultanate with the contemporary Palestinian national struggle and the current plight of the Palestinians. The sacred place enables him to embody the national struggle and allows (a certain) history to be concretized therein. The Maqam, like any other place, is a complex and ever-changing spatiality through which dynamics of control, subordination, solidarity, struggle, cooperation, and conflict are manifested. Hajj uses the place's past as a resource for his contemporary socio-political needs (Massey 1995). Therefore, the idea of the nation, be it imagined or concrete, and surely the national struggle, is spatialized through his embodied interpretation of the sacred. This is a common feature in sacred places in Israel/Palestine, as previously indicated, since due to their surplus of meaning they become time and again sites of contestation over meaning or control between the two opposing ethno-national groups. A case in point is Rachel's Tomb, located on the northern outskirts of Bethlehem along and due west of the main road to Jerusalem.

In 1858, Josias Leslie Porter, an Irish Presbyterian minister and missionary-cum-avid traveler, arrived at Rachel's Tomb and made the following observation: "It is one of the few shrines which Muslims, Jews and Christians agree in honoring, and concerning which their traditions are identical" (cited in Strickert 2007: 105). Originally a Christian pilgrimage site of the fourth century CE, it was embraced in following centuries in both Jewish and Islamic traditions as the Tomb of Rachel the Matriarch (Selwyn 2009). Muslim accounts of veneration of the site date from as early as the eleventh century and are consistent with Jewish interpretations and travelers' accounts of the twelfth century and onward (Al-Harawi 1953; Strickert 2007: 87–9). The place is aptly named *Qubbat Rahil* (Rachel's Dome) in Arabic and *Qever Rachel* (Rachel's Tomb) in Hebrew. However, in recent years, a new layer of traditions is being produced by Palestinians, according to which the site is identified as the Bilal ibn Rabah Mosque. Bilal was the Prophet Muhammad's personal companion and former slave, who is also considered Islam's first *mu'adhdhin* (or *muezzin*, a crier who calls the faithful to prayers) (Arafat 2013). This change is directly related to the geopolitical dynamics between Israel and the Palestinians since 1967, which dramatically altered the tomb and its environs and gradually barred Palestinians from visitations within.

Following the 1967 war, Israel gained direct control of Rachel's Tomb as of the entire former territory of the Hashemite Kingdom of Jordan known as the West Bank. In the decades after 1967, the area around the Tomb was not so much the zone of exclusion it would become, but rather an area of connection, notwithstanding the oppressive impact of occupation. In the nearby commercial area along the Hebron Road, Israeli Jews and Palestinians would shop together in a generally relaxed atmosphere (Van Teeffelen 2021). However, from the late 1980s through the 1990s, the years of the first Intifada (Palestinian uprising), there were incidents of shooting between the Israeli army and residents of the nearby A'ida camp, as well as Molotov cocktails being thrown at the Tomb while Jewish pilgrims were performing rituals. This escalation greatly affected the pilgrimage of Israeli Jews to the tomb and completely stopped non-Jews from arriving there. During those tense years, visiting by Israelis was only permitted with special armed buses and was often restricted by the Israeli army. Following the Oslo Accords (the Israeli-Palestinian Interim Agreement) in 1993, Rachel's Tomb was placed under Israeli security control, falling under the designation "Area C." The original plan called for the site to be fully controlled by the

Palestinian Authority (Area A)[7] in due time, as it was considered part of the Bethlehem municipal boundaries. However, following heavy pressure from Israeli religious figures and political parties on the Israeli government, it was ultimately annexed and remained under Israeli control (Shragai 2002). These unilateral geopolitical measures, and the Judaization and nationalization of Rachel's Tomb, which lead to Rachel's depiction as the mother of the Jews' return to the Holy Land, have not gone unchallenged. Since 1996, Palestinians have reinforced their claims to the shrine and its territories. This is manifested among other things in the emergence of a new mythology for the site which ultimately renders it the Mosque of Bilal, and not, as it was commonly known for centuries, as *Qubbat Rahil*.

Thus, the Tomb, which had served as an example of plausible accommodation among the rival religions, became yet another contested sacred place under the yoke of nationalism and the ethno-national conflict. The national conflict was marred by religious claims which ultimately were translated into geopolitical demands, both of which were translated into concrete barriers and border lines that serve to deny Palestinian claims and to exclude Palestinians' access to the site (Stadler and Luz 2015). As the Israeli-built "separation barrier" was extended into Bethlehem to encompass the Tomb, it sealed it off from the West Bank, and access for Israeli Jews and tourists was also severely restricted, when not rendered impossible because of site closure.

These conflicts are, as I argue throughout this chapter, embodied and manifested on the personal-individual scale. I will bring but two examples, one from each side. Smadar is a Jewish-Israeli woman in her forties who was interviewed while visiting Rachel's Tomb. Her answer reveals how the role of Rachel the Matriarch, who was mostly associated with fertility problems, has been transformed into the mother of national return:

> Rachel's life was tragic, but we know that throughout her ordeal she remained absolutely faithful to God. All the sages declared that Jacob buried Rachel on the roadside, so that she could pray for them [i.e., her progeny] as they were being led into exile … Jeremiah reminded us all that "Rachel weeps for her children; she refuses to be comforted for her children who are gone …" God's answer was clear: "Restrain your voice from weeping, your eyes from shedding tears, for there is reward for your labor." Therefore, we know that this place belongs to us today and that the Jews will "return from the lands of their enemies to their own country" [Jeremiah 31: 14-15]. These are God's words to our mother.
>
> (interview with Smadar, 2009, cited in Stadler and Luz 2015)

This transformation and new interpretation of the role of Rachel as mother of the nation are embodied while visiting and praying at the site. The emergence of a new narrative of the Tomb by Israelis, along with the closure of the site to Palestinians' visit, was met with a new narrative among Palestinians, according to which the site is the Mosque of Bilal ibn Jarah. A report from 2015 aired by Al-Aqsa TV, a Palestinian national channel, aptly demonstrates this new emerging mythology/understanding. The correspondent describes the continuous efforts of Israel to Judaize the site, which he refers to as "the dome of the Mosque of Bilal ibn Rabah" (cited in Reuveni 2022). He quotes an unnamed religious scholar (*shaykh*), stating that under the dome one may find a tomb and the person interred inside is unknown and hence one cannot be sure that Rachel the Matriarch is buried there. The report also includes information regarding the ample ways the "Jews have confiscated the place" and their endless efforts to ban Palestinians' processions near the closed enclosure. This emerging narrative is embodied and echoed among Palestinians in recent years. A., a Palestinian from East Jerusalem, explains that this place has been known as the Mosque of Bilal for centuries, and when confronted with the common tradition among the three Abrahamic religions, namely that this is Rachel's Tomb, delivers the following answer:

> The Old Testament [the Bible] conveys that Rachel was buried on the road to Jerusalem close to Bethlehem. And yet, no accurate location is suggested and therefore one cannot be certain that this is indeed the Tomb of Rachel (Arabic: *Qubbat Rahil*).
>
> (fieldnotes May 4, 2014, cited in Reuveni 2022)[8]

Set within the context of a national struggle, the banning of Palestinian pilgrims from visiting the site effected changes in the way individuals imagine the site and make sense of it on a personal scale. But while Rachel's Tomb/Mosque of Bilal remains out of reach, the most holy sacred place, namely the compound of the Haram al-Sharif, remains accessible (most days and pending police instructions). As I will discuss in Chapter 6, the site is now understood as the most venerated religio-national landmark (Luz 2004; Reiter 2008). This is vividly described by Umm Majid, a Muslim Palestinian woman who is a member of a group named *Murabitat al-Aqsa*:

> The Jews want Jerusalem as their capital. They want a capital without Palestinians. So, Jerusalem became like a war zone … we are living under siege, and al-Aqsa is at the center … the heart. Al-Aqsa is more than our religion. It is our sacred space, our love, our home, and our identity as Palestinians.
>
> (cited in Ihmoud 2019: 518)

The Murabitat are a group of Palestinian women who since the 2000s have arrived at the compound of the Haram al-Sharif daily to gather, pray, study together, and mostly, as they proclaim, to defend the holy place from Israeli incursions and the deepening presence of Jewish settlers (Schmit 2020). The name *Murabitat* derives from *murabata* which may be understood as the act of staying in place, usually in frontier areas facing hostile enemy forces and/or defending a sacred place. *Murabitat* is the feminine plural active participle drawn from the root *RaBaTa*, which might be understood as to tie, stationed (troops); to line up, take up positions; to be moored (ship); to move into fighting positions (Wehr 1994). So, adopting this name for their group is rather telling and clearly indicates their vision and ideology as manifested in their steadfastness at the Haram al-Sharif in Jerusalem. These goals are achieved daily and take corporeal shape at the site and its perimeter in the Old City of Jerusalem pending police restrictions. In 2015 the Israeli government outlawed the "Northern Faction" of the Israeli Islamic Movement, an act which rendered the Murabitat lacking any organizational support, having started under its wings. Furthermore, in this new situation they found themselves in growing confrontations and constant risk of incarceration and interrogation by Israeli security forces. Surprisingly, or not, this new phase only strengthened their various activities, as has been manifested time and again since then (Ibrahim 2021). In their actions, they literally place the body at risk for the sake of the nation as the following narrative by Samira, a former activist in the Islamic movement, recounts:

> I am in my land and homeland. I am an Arab-Palestinian, and I do not see myself Muslim and Arab like in any other place. This belonging to the homeland is very important to me. Sometimes, when I travel to Mecca or South Africa, immediately I get homesick for the homeland. It is my country of birth like a hugging mother. It is a waqf land to the Prophet of God and to the Muslims. I see myself in the court of the al-Aqsa Mosque and I want to be in this place which has tremendous importance for praying. …. I see the role a woman has in protecting the al-Aqsa Mosque which is a sacred place. [A woman] has a role in defending the land and the homeland. We women are very active when men are banned from entering the mosque, and for us it is a very important mission.
> (interview with A., cited in Alinat-Abed 2022)

The importance of the body and its physical presence in the compound as part of one's religious-cum-national responsibilities loom large in Umm 'Abdallah, a Murabita who spoke to an al-Jazeera correspondent under a pseudonym, for fear of repercussions and infringement of her freedom by the Israeli authorities:

They want to divide al-Aqsa between us and them. They want to take it away. But al-Aqsa is for us; it is our place … my role in protecting al-Aqsa is my presence. Every time we hear there is a threat, or if al-Aqsa is empty, we come and sit to show them we are here all the time … our presence is protection.

(O'Toole 2016)

In her exploration into the urban religious women's mosque movement in Cairo, Mahmood (2004) challenges the accepted wisdom of feminist theories and secular liberal politics. While trying to grapple with the enormous appeal of these religious compounds for Egyptian Muslim women, she looks at the ways these places offer them agency. In this *tour de force*, she moves on to reformulate agency in a way that avoids analyzing the mosque participants' actions as simply a passive submission to norms. She expands our approach to agency, which she holds as a "modality of action" (157) that includes how norms are "performed, inhabited and experienced" (22). Mahmood demonstrates how the women are engaged in corporeal practices such as prayer or wearing the hijab with the aim to cultivate virtues like humility and modesty: "For the mosque participants, it is the various movements of the body that comprise the material substance of the ethical domain" (Mahmood 2004: 31). Thus, religious rituals and bodily activities are understood as self-fashioning and accomplishing a more virtuous body. For the women participating in the *Murabitat* activities in al-Aqsa, it is not only about obtaining a higher moral and religious ground but also about defending the nation and the mosque through their body. The sacred place indeed offers them agency which allows them to defy the occupation and to gain recognition as pious Muslim women in their respective society.

* * *

In this chapter I set out to explore the links between the body scale, embodiment processes, and sacred places. I focused on what I deem highly important, which is the web of significance individuals weave within and without sacred places and the personal-scale politics which their encounters construct. Embodiment, as explored in its various (but surely not all) manifestations in the realm of the sacred, puts on many shapes and narrates the relational dynamics of the spatial and the social. As such, Umm Ahmad's narration of herself demonstrated clearly how the embodied practice of wearing the hijab and the jilbab is pertinent to her conduct in different scales and informs her approach to the sacred. It is in the body and through the body that sacred places are experienced, and other scales (rural, urban, national, and the global) are enacted and surely become more tangible. The narrative suggested by R. at Rachel's Tomb in Tiberias clearly shows how our encounters with the sacred place invoke numerous responses during which our bodies are not mere receptacles or just a surface of inscription by external forces.

In these numerous encounters the body proves to be (following Douglas) the reflection of society and the product of multiple socio-political processes. The surface of the body, as the common frontier of society, the social self, and the psychobiological individual, becomes the symbolic stage upon which the drama of socialization is enacted, as well as the politicization of the sacred in the Israel/Palestine dynamics. And yet, as shown time and again, it is necessary to acknowledge individual agency. These encounters are always discursive processes in the self-fashioning of the virtuous body, such as to be found in Secor's and Gokariksel's work on Istanbul or in Mahmood's in her analysis of Cairo's religious movements. The individuals discussed throughout this chapter presented their personal, social, and certainly political self in acts of endorsement, resistance, acceptance, and defiance of various forces operating in different scales beyond the individual one, but at the same time being influenced by it and surely printing their influence upon it. The body as explored here in sacred places, then, is structured by society's discourse and endless cultural processes and yet individuals are not void of agency to act and be more than mere receptacles of ideologies, norms, and other societal codes and prerequisites. It is through the body that we occupy positions in social space and (may) challenge or change existing power-geometries.

3

Sacred Sites in Rural Communities

Ethnographic Snippets: Entering a Community's Sacred Places

"You better come quick, the Maqam was set on fire," read the WhatsApp message from Mahmood Qasim, the treasurer of Kawkab Abu al-Hijja local council (personal communication, February 13, 2016). Even despite the gravity of the message, I felt a touch of pride at being considered worthy of notification of this news, terrible as it was. Indeed, it was by then fifteen years since I began my almost weekly ethnographic survey of the Maqam, and early on Mahmood and I had established a very amicable rapport. As per usual, I was in his debt for constantly being kind and accommodating and allowing me access to learn more about the place and the village. So, heeding his call, I promptly went out with my camera and notebook to the Maqam, which is located less than 3 kilometers from my house. As I approached the smoldering shrine, I could smell that rather typical stench of a fire's aftermath. A small group of council officials was already there, surveying the place and assessing the damages. Mahmood greeted me with a sullen face, and we started to walk together, examining the damage within and without the Maqam. The two inner rooms were completely blackened, which gave the site a distinctly bleak atmosphere. All the paraphernalia that had been accumulated over the years through visitors' donations, be it volumes of the Qur'an, embroidery, praying beads, pictures, and other mementos, and most devastating of all, the ornamented green cloth, which covered the two graves that are the main reason for pilgrimage, all were vanquished and consumed by the fire. The only remaining movable object was a small plastic container by the graves, which was immediately suspected by the group of being the can used to carry the inflammable liquid that started the fire. As I saw a new electricity cable that had recently been installed in a very unprofessional manner in the Maqam, and suspecting that if indeed the can was there during the fire, it would not have lasted, I did not join in the throng, and instead asked Mahmood: What do you think happened? Who is motivated enough to harm the Maqam? He was quick on the uptake: "I suspect two possible groups that might be interested in damaging the Maqam. The first is surely the hardcore right-wing religious Jewish groups who have been active in violating Muslim sacred places in recent years." "The second," he claimed, "might well be Salafi Muslims."[1] As we were exiting the Maqam, the police arrived, and following a short interrogation and concealed suspicion toward the only non-Muslim in the group, I was allowed to leave (fieldnotes, February 13, 2016).

During my last visit at the shrine of Mariam Bawardy, J., who resides by the shrine, informed me that the local Catholic priest of I'bbelin, Michel Tu'ama, had initiated a weekly prayer at the site as of Saturday, March 28, 2015. This was done in anticipation of the Pope's much-awaited declaration of Mariam as a saint this coming May in Rome.[2] This is why I set my sights on the said Saturday and arrived at 1650 at the shrine. The first thing I noticed was the presence of the two respective priests of the two local Christian communities in I'bbelin: the Catholic and the Greek-Orthodox. The two of them were standing together and although the Catholic (Father Michel) was the one conducting and leading the ceremony, time and again he motioned to his colleague to take the lead and recite the prayers.

The congregation attending the first ever prayer at the site was mostly composed of women from the village. Approximately fifty people attended, out of whom less than ten were men. Contrary to other events I attended, I could not see any Muslims in the crowd.

A shiny new booklet of prayers just off the press was handed to each of the devotees by volunteers who helped the priest during the ceremony. Among the attendees were also three members of the Greek-Orthodox local community council, while the Catholic members of the council were noticeably absent. A member of the Catholic community who is also very active in the ongoing works at the site lamented to me, expressing his opinion about the shameful and distasteful aspects of this act. Later on, I discovered this had to do with an internal quarrel among leading members of the community and the priest regarding the location of the ceremony celebrating Mariam's sainthood, as we approached her up-coming canonization by the Pope.

The ceremony, which included prayers and chanting, was conducted in a westward direction and not in the common Christian fashion in the region (eastwardly), mainly due to the micro-geography of the shrine's locality. Praying to the east would mean facing the rear of one of the neighbor's houses, while in the current direction the congregation was facing the emerging shrine of Mariam. Two pictures of Mariam were hung on special hangers facing the congregation, which

Sacred Sites in Rural Communities

Figure 3.1 The temporary altar in the renovated shrine.

also signified the rudimentary altar where the priests lead the ceremony.... After fifty minutes the ceremony ended with a very moving speech by Father Michel, who made a special point of acknowledging the reverence of Mariam by both Christian communities of I'bbelin and by thanking his "brother" (Arabic: *al-akh*) Father Saba Khaj and the other Greek-Orthodox members who came to pray with "us" and praised Mariam's virtues excessively. Father Michel also thanked Assad Daoud for his relentless efforts in reconstructing the site over the last few years.[3] Light refreshments were passed among the small congregation that gathered for the ceremony. Some went to pray and kiss the new engraved picture of Mariam, an act that was followed by donating money to the small box near it.

The most remarkable point for me was perhaps the two priests hugging and blessing each other before parting ways, as each of them was to go to a different church to conduct the evening prayers separately. Surely, this has to do with the current predicament of both communities vis-à-vis the growing Muslim community in the village, and the charismatic stage of the site which enables new modes of action and is still flexible and as yet "un-canonized" (fieldnotes, March 28, 2015).

* * *

This chapter looks at rural sacred places and engages with the manifold meanings they entail for their respective communities, as well as at the location-community interactions. It follows current transformations of local sacred places and explores both the micro and macro politics within and without their communities' scale. Arguably, in this discussion of two rural saints' shrines I marry two unlikely bedfellows: Husam al-Din Abu al-Hijja (d. 1196) and Mariam Bawardy (d. 1878). Husam al-Din Abu al-Hijja was a Kurdish Muslim general (Arabic: *amir*) in Saladin's army, who according to local traditions excelled himself in the battles against the armies of the Third Crusade in the plains of Acre (Arraf 1996). Mariam Bawardy was a Carmelite nun who was born in I'bbelin and died at the young age of thirty-three in Bethlehem and canonized (2015) by the Pope (Dallaire 2016). They are joined together here, as they allow us to explore the sacred at the community scale from different perspectives and in different settings. This is readily apparent even against the two short ethnographies which opened this chapter. The engagement of the Kawkab officials with the Maqam, their concern about conflicts with rival Muslim groups, and surely the problematic interactions with Jewish groups (even if unsubstantiated), all attest to a different level of politics and interaction revolving the sacred. The same goes for the shrine of Mariam Bawardy, where internal politics and conflicts at both congregation and village levels were fleshed out during one short ceremony. The feud between the Catholic priest and the local Catholic committee, the interaction between the two Christian communities in the village, and certainly the relationship with the Muslim majority, are all present and revealed during the joint prayer at the shrine. These short forays into the field demonstrated clearly how places are always a part of dynamics and relations which are certainly not confined to their immediate location (Knott 2005). Furthermore, places are conceived and produced in different spheres (spatial, social, some would argue mental) and are the outcome (and, lest we forget, process) of hierarchies and socio-political positions and stances to be found in different scales. In focusing on the community level of rural shrines, I hope to achieve a better understanding of these intricate and reciprocal relations. In doing so, I am reminded of Robert Hertz's pioneering study of the local Alpine cult of St. Besse that in recent years has gained recognition as a classic in the field (Wilson 1985; Isnart 2009). This mythical Christian saint has been venerated since prehistoric times (according to Hertz) by five rural parishes in which the saint takes three different identities: a soldier, a bishop, or a shepherd. While conducting his ethnography, Hertz (at least consciously) does not engage in a scalar analysis and yet when one reads the following paragraph one is bound to acknowledge his profound understanding of the various factors and dynamics that construct a place:

> Before we penetrate inside the shrine of our saint, let us cast a quick glance at the region which surrounds it and at the people who frequented it over many generations. These few scattered traits will perhaps be sufficient to give some idea of the social and mental state associated with the cult which we are studying. Our description will proceed from its fixed and most constant elements to those which are more elusive and variable. We will examine in turn the role played by St. Besse in life today and in the ritual practice of these worshippers—that is, the organization of the cult devoted to him—and then the legend which explains and justifies the modern devotion by reference to past events.
>
> (Hertz 1985: 55–6)

Hertz goes on to provide an expansive description of the site, its geography, history of pilgrimage, and the regional connections and conflicts among the different communities that revere the place. I wish to engage in two separate discussions of the two sites under discussion in this chapter. In both I will address the saint in question and the mythologies concerning him/her and the site. A discussion of the changing landscape of the place through a socio-spatial lens will follow, to be concluded with an analysis of the politics of place and community(s) and larger scales when relevant. The mythology of the place and the changing landscape and materiality are, I argue, manifestations of the politics of the place. The ways a place is constructed, produced, and surely understood among community members and its evolving landscape and materiality are nothing short of the spatialization of politics in different scalar setting. This will be made clear hereinafter as I engage with an analysis of Maqam Abu al-Hijja and of the shrine of Mariam Bawardy.

The History and Mythology of Maqam Abu al-Hijja and Its Saint

The histories of Maqam Abu al-Hijja and the village of Kawkab Abu al-Hijja are closely entwined, and both are tightly connected to amir Husam al-Din Abu al-Hijja. The term *maqām* in Arabic literally means a place, but when applied to a burial place of someone who is considered a righteous or a holy person, it should be understood as a sacred place (Goldziher 1967). So, who is this Abu al-Hijja and what were his virtues that transformed his grave into a local pilgrimage shrine? To be clear: the data from historical sources are rather scarce and most of what is transmitted about him derives from oral traditions that still circulate in the village. The teknonym (Arabic: *kunya*) Abu al-Hijja, which is how he is commonly referred to, may be translated as "the father of war" or better yet, "a fearless warrior." In some of the chronicles he is also known as al-Samin, namely "the fat one," which should be inferred as a status symbol, an indication of good health, and surely of a sound financial situation. He was of Kurdish origin and served as a high-ranking officer (*amir*) in the army of Saladin (Ṣalāḥ al-Dīn). He won recognition as an able and devoted *mujahid* (someone who performs jihad and fights for Islam and the Muslim *umma*) while besieging Crusader Jerusalem following the battle of Hattin in 1187, and later during the siege of Acre in 1191–2 (al-Isfahani 1888: 562). As a reward for his performance on the battlefield, he received, like other senior officers at the time, an *iqta'*: a form of administrative unit granted by the Sultan to members of the elite as taxable lands. The receiver of an *iqta'* (unlike his European counterpart in the feudal system) was but the tax collector and rarely resided therein (Sato 1982). Kawkab was part of Abu al-Hijja's sizeable *iqta'* in the region, but there are no indications that he ever visited it (Arraf 1993). Following the death of his patron Saladin in 1193, his career declined, and he was forced to maneuver between the contending rivals for the Ayyubid Sultanate. In 1196, we are informed, he headed a military mission west of Teheran at the behest of the 'Abbasid Caliph but was soon removed from office. He died shortly after that, on his way back to his hometown of Irbil (currently in Iraq) (Ibn al-Athir 1982, 9:157). It is rather difficult to learn from this meager and scanty historical data how and when he became revered by the villagers of Kawkab. Indeed, the family name Abu al-Hijja is very common in the village and yet none of the people I interviewed claimed they were direct descendants of that officer. Further still, the village people are ethnically Arab while Abu al-Hijja was of Kurdish origin (interview with Ahmad Hajj, December 28, 2005; interview with Mahmood Qasim, May 18, 2015). So how has this improbable candidate for a saint (*wali* in the local parlance) come to be connected to the village, and particularly, to the shrine carrying his name? Against the lacuna of substantiated historical evidence connecting the man and the village, there exists a layer of local traditions which allows for this mythology to flourish. According to these traditions, Abu al-Hijja launched numerous attacks against the Crusader army in the vicinity of the village, during one of which he also met with his death. The local landscape consists of a few sites which all commemorate this period of Islamic versus Crusaders encounters. One such site is the Cave of the Forty Heroes, which is located near the peak of the mountain overshadowing the village. The common narrative is that from this cave these warriors, commanded by Abu al-Hijja, launched their attacks on Crusader forces. It is almost superfluous to explain that forty is a highly charged number in Islam and the myth of the forty heroes is assigned sometimes to the period of the Prophet Muhammad and the early Islamic conquests. Forty is also the age of the Prophet when he began to receive the divine revelations according to Islamic traditions. Within the village boundaries one may still find the graves (*maqam*) of Shaykh Sa'id and Shaykh al-'Ajami. Both are considered sacred, and both are regarded as close friends of Abu al-Hijja. Until 1948, the locals used to conduct a procession which connected all these sacred places. The annual procession took place prior to the rainy season and while visiting the sites *en route*, special prayers beseeching Allah to grant this rural-agricultural community the much-needed rain (these prayers are called *istisqa*) were recited (interview with Mustafa 'Abd al-Fattah, April 28, 2005). The religious ceremony facilitated an ad-hoc harmonious merging of community and landscape, transforming them into a sacred unit which centers around Maqam Abu al-Hijja.

The immense geopolitical changes that followed the 1948 war led to the cessation of this annual procession. Along these lines the oral traditions, much like in the St. Besse example, transformed and paved the way for a military commander, a *mujahid*, to become a charismatic saint who performs miracles and sustains the locals in their times of need. In this questionable fashion, a general of a different ethnic origin, whose main (and probably only) connection to the villagers that used to worship him is the taxes he extorted from them, was transformed into a wali, that is, a charismatic saint who is considered a friend of God who is also capable of performing *karamat* (supernatural wonders) (Karamustafa 2018). In the case of Abu al-Hijja, he is famed for special healing powers that cure podiatric problems. In many of my conversations with pilgrims at the shrine, and certainly during interviews with village people, the term that often came up was *mukarsakh*. In the vernacular, Arabic this means someone who has walking problems, ailing in his legs, or a cripple. Once, while conducting ethnography and walking in the village, I was invited for coffee by a group of young people who were enjoying a late afternoon in their garden. Upon learning that I was exploring the Maqam, one of them attested that he himself saw a man who was driven to the site by his family as he could no longer walk. After spending the night at the Maqam, he returned home the following morning, walking unassisted on his own two feet (fieldnotes, April 12, 2007). Some of these traditions were recently collected and published by the village municipality (Arraf 2008). The following tradition, which I borrowed from this project, was narrated by Mahmud 'Abd al-Fattah, a resident of Kawkab who has since passed away: Mustafa al-Hasan was herding his goats in the fields by the Maqam when he saw two men carrying a sick person who could not stand on his own two feet. They wanted to place him inside the Maqam by the tombs, but the man beseeched them not to leave him alone. So, Mustafa volunteered to stay with him and convinced him to spend the night inside by the graves. He himself returned home with his herd and only came back the following morning, to see the man outside the Maqam, capable of walking. Mustafa invited the man to his house and there, as they were sipping coffee, the man described what had transpired overnight. "After you left," said the man,

> the shaykh (i.e., Abu al-Hijja) arrived, carrying a staff in his hand. He swore in the name of Allah and as he was holding my hands, he hit me with the staff and said: Stand on your feet by the will of Allah, and suddenly I was healed, and I managed to get up and stand on my feet. The shaykh sprayed water on the ground and prayed the evening prayer (ṣalāt al-Maghrib). After the prayer ended, he bid me farewell and vanished, and here I am in front of you, healthy as if it were all but a bad dream.
>
> (Arraf 2008: 37)

This tradition is one of many in which the healing saint motif is repeated, along with miracles that occur to those who spent a night between the two graves inside the Maqam. This is not unique in any way and most villages in pre-modern Palestine cultivated their own local patron saint (Canaan 1927). In the case of Abu al-Hijja, a certain duality is maintained as he is remembered and recognized as both a military official and a virtuous saint. This duality furnishes and sustains a complex politics which is also attested in the changing landscape and materiality of the maqam and the significance assigned to it by the community. This will be discussed at length in the subsequent paragraphs.

The Changing Landscape of the Maqam: A Socio-Spatial Analysis

The early beginnings of the Maqam cannot be substantiated through historical sources, but they are cast in stone. The earliest and most central part of the maqam is a humble rectangular compound consisting of two rooms, each adorned with a dome. A low door leads inside the first room which also has a prayer niche (*mihrab*) and an opening in the western wall that leads to the second room in which two tombs are to be found, one of which is considered to be the tomb of Abu al-Hijja. It is unclear when, but probably at a later date, a surrounding wall was added to the compound, thus creating an inner yard surrounding a water cistern. This type of compound is not a singular example and represents an architectural template which can be found throughout the region during the late Ayyubid to early Mamluk period (thirteenth and fourteenth centuries CE). As part of the re-Islamization of the region following the battle of Hattin and the religious competition with the Christian Crusader kingdom, numerous Islamic sacred places were constructed in the region (Frenkel 2001; Luz 2002). Many of these sites, especially those located in rural areas, share a general building pattern and architectural motifs (Luz 2014a). This allows us to establish the *terminus post quem* for the inauguration of the Maqam to the early Mamluk period. Indeed, in comparison to similar sites in the region, Maqam Abu al-Hijja manifests many of the characteristics of vernacular Mamluk architecture. The Maqam remained active during the Ottoman period (1517–1917). This can be inferred from two inscriptions on two graves that were built adjacent to the northern wall, both bearing the date 1182 AH/1769 CE. Indeed, from early on the village people buried their dead in the vicinity of the Maqam. Today, the village graveyard surrounds the Maqam and still serves as the main burial site of Kawkab.

During the 1960s, two storage rooms were built at the eastern part of the inner courtyard. This was probably connected to a renovation that took place in 1967, as can be inferred from the date and insignia of a certain Ahmad Nimr Qasim inscribed onto a rather crude cement supportive beam, constructed on the north side of the Maqam. A significant change in the Maqam and its surroundings occurred in the early 1990s. This happened under the leadership of Ahmad Hajj, who served at the time as the mayor of Kawkab (1989–93). Hajj launched the renovation of the Maqam as part of a larger project which included all the historical sites in the village. It was part of his vision to brand the village as a tourist attraction:

> I wanted to renovate all historical sites. True, I am not a religious person, but I think that some places need to be preserved by the people they belong to because they are part of their history. If you do not have a history, you do not have anything, and especially because I am not religious, I renovated the place because I wanted my history in the region not to be erased.
>
> (interview, December 28, 2005)

The renovation included a complete remodeling of the internal parts of the Maqam. In addition to renewal of the plaster and repainting of the walls, the external side of the two domes was painted in the traditional Islamic green. A significant change took place in the area surrounding the Maqam. A new parking lot was constructed close by, and trees were planted around its perimeters. A small picnic area was also added by the parking lot and a new gate was opened toward the bustling main regional road, to facilitate an easier approach to the Maqam. The physical changes brought forth by the renovation contributed directly to a surge of visits to the Maqam. Many of the visitors were not concerned with the sacred virtues of the place but rather took advantage of the new facilities to enjoy a picnic or a short break from a long drive. During the years of the Second Intifada (2000–5), tension mounted between the Jewish majority and Palestinian minority. Jewish municipalities were trying to ban, or at least minimize, the use of their public facilities by non-resident Palestinian visitors. The small park by the Maqam enabled an alternative venue where one could be less observed, scrutinized, or marginalized by the hegemonic Jewish group. It was during that time that the internal landscape of the Maqam changed, expressing an upsurge in the display of identity politics, be it Palestinian or Islamic. In addition to pictures showing the sacred centers in Mecca and Medina, which are (almost) customary in such places, one could also find a growing number of depictions of al-Haram al-Sharif, that is, the most revered Islamic landmark in the region which in recent years has also become a Palestinian national symbol.[4] The Maqam was thus adorned by representations of al-Aqsa Mosque and the Dome of the Rock, alongside placards carrying traditional Qur'anic verses. Additionally, it also hosted pictures which are iconic in Palestinian contemporary culture such as the olive tree or the picture of a weeping young boy clad in a Palestinian keffiyeh. This picture is an iconic self-representation of the current predicament of the Palestinians. The boy personifies Palestine and the struggle for the lost lands, as well as a sign of the catastrophe of 1948 (the Nakba). And should this unsubtle symbolization escape the visitor, the following caption is inscribed: "My beloved Palestine, how can I sleep when my eyes are clouded by the shadow of agony?" An even more outspoken expression of anger and defiance was inscribed on the wall in the winter of 2002. I was conducting a field trip with students and as I was discussing the political nature of the internal landscape of the Maqam with them, one of the students pointed out to me a short graffiti by the small entrance door. The handwritten Arabic inscription read: "please God, help Osama bin Ladin" (*Allah unsur bin Ladin*). During those post-9/11 days, at the height of the Second Intifada, a pilgrim expressed his support for this most controversial Islamic figure. On my following visit the inscription could no longer be found, an unknown hand was bothered enough to expunge it from the wall. In 2003, a new council was elected in Kawkab and one of their first resolutions was to block the new gate facing the main road. This was done consciously to try and minimize "unwelcome" activities that took place by the renewed Maqam (conversation with Mahmood Qasim, April 12, 2012). This affected a change in the numbers of visits but did not prevent young people from the village from meeting there at night to engage in less accepted social activities, such as smoking hookahs and drinking alcohol.

As the Second Intifada was ebbing away in 2005, the more contested political pictures (i.e., those of a Palestinian national nature) were removed from the walls. When I asked 'Ali Abu al-Hijja, the volunteer caretaker of the Maqam, if this was his own doing, he smiled and said nothing. But indeed, a change was easily discerned. Once again, the walls of the Maqam were used to inscribe the more traditional personal vows and requests from the saint. This is a rather typical example which is undated, but sums up nicely the gist of many other inscriptions found at the Maqam:

> Oh God, make me successful at work and assist me in the following things:
> A new and upscale job
> Oh God allow the righteous people to take care of me and send
> Me a man with clear intentions to build with him a pure relationship.

Recall that this chapter started out with a short ethnography of a fire that raged in the Maqam in February 2016. The results of the fire forced the council to launch a massive renovation project at the site. This was a rather telling moment, which reflected that tremendous changes that have occurred in the community of Kawkab since the last renovation in the 1990s. The estimated cost of the renovation project was around NIS 100,000 (Assad Daoud, personal communication, March 15, 2017). The council was in difficulty for a few months trying to secure the total sum. As it so happened, at the same time a gargantuan new mosque was built at the center of the village, not far from the council building. The estimated cost of the mosque was over 20 million shekels (Mahmood Qasim, personal communication, April 5, 2017). When I tried to understand how a small project with a relatively meager budget was running into difficulties while at the same time a much larger project was proceeding smoothly, I was informed that whereas the money for the renovation of the Maqam came directly from the council budget, the funding for the mosque was based mostly on donations. Indeed, during the twenty-odd years I have been exploring the Maqam I could not help noticing that the number of visitors constantly diminished. While during the early 2000s I always met pilgrims during my weekly visits, in recent years I find myself time and again spending hours on my own before anyone arrives, if at all. The difficulty in financing the renovation on the one hand and the dwindling of interest in the shrine on the other reflect a fundamental change that village society has undergone in recent years. This was summed up very succinctly to me by S., a woman in her late twenties who I met outside the purview of my ethnographic work, in a totally private capacity. When I learned she resides in Kawkab, I asked her if she ever visited the shrine. Not only had she never visited the place, but she also hardly knew anything about it as, according to her, she only moved to the village following her marriage in 2011. The following is the gist of her explanation: "I think we have changed, and my generation simply does not go to those places [i.e., local sacred places] anymore. And certainly, when I want to have a picnic or a vacation, I would not go to a park that is so close to a cemetery" (personal communication, June 15, 2022). This is surely not a unique case, and I have received similar responses from others of her age group in the village. This is the outcome of meaningful changes in education and impacts of modernization, as well as a steady rise in the standard of living.

The long process of restoration ended in late 2017. Once again, the Maqam has undergone a significant change. The inner parts were stripped of all former layers of plaster that were laid one above the other over the years. The inner wall that separated the two rooms was removed and transformed into one hall. The restorer insisted on the most advanced techniques and materials and painted the entire Maqam anew, using mostly bright pastel colors.[5] The domes were painted in a very light green which utterly changed the external look of the Maqam. The storage rooms in the yard were transformed into an open visitor hall (Arabic: *madafeh*). And yet, the council refrained from conducting any formal ceremony to inaugurate the renewed Maqam. It would seem that the new appearance of the Maqam only intensified the already existing process of transforming this sacred place into a heritage site. Put bluntly, the renovation was also a museumification of a sacred place. This was easily discerned during a Heritage Day organized for an elementary school in Kawkab. During that day, the children were taken, among other places in the village, to the Maqam and were engaged in various activities under the slogan "Kawkab through the ages" (Arabic: *Kawkab 'abr al-'usur*), which was also printed on special T-shirts they all wore. Following a short lecture about the site from the regional archeologist, which was by and large an historical analysis of the site, they all entered the Maqam. As I was watching them, I was astounded to see no one was removing their shoes, as per the custom in Muslim sacred places. I read this as another indication of a process of forsaking the religious importance of the place and regarding it solely as an historical landmark of Palestinian heritage. This could also be inferred from the lack of any ritual performed at the Maqam nor a communal prayer throughout the field day (fieldnotes, March 20, 2018). These changes are certainly not endemic to Kawkab and reflect fundamental changes in Palestinian Muslim societies on both sides of the Green Line. Along with the growing influence of the fundamentalist-Salafi position that categorically prohibits pilgrimage to sacred places save those approved by the Prophet Muhammad, this society is also experiencing growing impacts of modernization and secularization. These two seemingly opposing trends affect changes in the activities performed in sacred places and the ways they are perceived. A recent exhaustive survey of sacred places conducted in the Palestinian Authority reached similar conclusions regarding the heritagization and folklorization of these sites. The survey revealed a significant decrease of religious activities in those places and a transformation in the ways they are perceived, and specifically, how the Islamic component is played down or totally ignored (Lecoquierre 2019). Maqam Abu al-Hijja shares these trends. Since the restoration in 2016, not only has the council refrained from any formal ceremony or gathering therein, but a clear decrease in visits and public attention is detected.

The Politics of Maqam Abu al-Hijja: Dynamics of a Sacred Place

The ethnographic survey of the place started out during the years of the Second Intifada and shortly after September 11, 2001. The socio-political tension between majority and minority in Israeli society reached a new height. The politization and, indeed, nationalization of the sacred were well attested in the landscape and materiality of the Maqam. The Palestinization of the minority struggle for recognition and civil rights in Israel permeated and influenced the ways the place was perceived by its community. Alongside the more traditional and rather typical ornamentation of Islamic sacred places, more and more indications of current affairs could be observed, be it the picture of the boy who symbolizes Palestine or the pictures of the holy sites of Jerusalem. The Maqam was charged with manifold meanings to accommodate urgent needs of the community. This type of identity politics is readily apparent in Ahmad Hajj's explanation as to his motivation to renovate the Maqam in the 1990s. Hajj is an outspoken secular person who was a member of the communist party in

Israel. Thus, when asked about his infatuation with the site and the person commemorated therein, his answer shed a direct light on the politics of place.

> Q: What is so special about Abu al-Hijja? After all is said and done, he was but a military figure, a general in the army of Saladin. What do you have in common with this man from the twelfth century, who was a Kurd and exploited the peasants in the region?
> A: I feel close to Abu al-Hijja, not because he was a general or a Kurd, but because he was involved and helpful with the battle against the Crusades. Through fighting the Crusades, he ultimately helped the Palestinian cause and people.
> (interview, December 28, 2005)

This discourse reflects the nationalization of the place in response to larger socio-political processes at the national scale. A regional impact on the ways the place was understood may be found in the following rejoinder by J., a young man from Kawkab who I met in one of my ethnographies at the village. Jamil, who was twenty-four when we met, confessed that he is not a religious man and yet claimed he visits the Maqam quite often. When I was puzzled by his answer, he explained:

> I do not go there because I believe in the sanctity of Abu al-Hijja or that I pray there. For me this is my place, and it is important for me that it will look nice and particularly now because of the new Jewish places that were recently developed around us. I am not ashamed of what I have, far from it. Abu al-Hijja is a part of my history even though I am not a religious person.
> (interview, June 6, 2005)

J. is responding to major changes that have occurred in the region surrounding the village, in the shape of a new Jewish regional council established in 1980 consisting of thirty-five new villages. These are nothing short of affluent gated communities destined to accommodate Jews only, to which he and his friends would never have been accepted. This was the outcome of a state-led project called the "Judaization of the Galilee" (Luz 2007). Against this demographic-cum-administrative change in the landscape surrounding the village, the Maqam serves as a bastion of Islamic-Palestinian identity. The historical Abu al-Hijja and his mythical confrontation with the Crusades are thus fused to serve current needs of the community. Surely, as previously argued by Massey a place is always a complex web of relations, of domination and subordination, and reflects socio-political processes that far exceed its immediate spatiality (1993). Against the current plight, the past, or a certain version of it (Nora's *lieu de memoire*), is recruited and manufactured. As time passed and the tensions between the communities lessened during the late 2000s, so the national symbolization in the Maqam was replaced with more general religious messages. The internal landscape of the Maqam aptly reflected this direction, as the pictures changed and more personal requests regarding mundane life reappeared on the walls. Given that a place is a spatial metaphor through which individuals and communities represent themselves and give meaning to their culture, needs, ideologies, and more, this is hardly surprising. As the localization of the national Palestine struggle symbolized in the Maqam was ebbing away, a renewed understanding of the religious-historic significance of the place emerged (Rekhess 2002).

Dr. Hamza Hamza is a resident of Kawkab who, in addition to his role as an imam in the new mosque, serves as a qadi in the sharia court of the city of Tayyibe. His analysis of the Maqam adds a new dimension, which on the one hand wishes to downplay the national politics assigned to it, and on the other hand to create a clear separation between its historical significance and the rituals preformed therein. Put simply, he condemns pilgrimage and other attributes of folk religion, which to him are inconsistent with Islamic jurisprudence and therefore unacceptable:

> The place has much historical significance and conveys the routes of our people in this region. It expresses the presence of Islam in the land and the belonging of the village people to the place.... But from a juridic perspective [pilgrimage and taking vows therein, N. L.], it is a problem as graves are not considered holy in Islam and it is forbidden to visit them for a religious quest. In the last ten years people have stopped visiting the tomb to seek healing ... this place has historical implications because he was one of the leaders of the Islamic *umma*.... But under no circumstances does this need to motivate anyone to worship this historical figure but rather show to respect for a righteous person (Arabic: *salih*) of our history.... The place is an historical landmark but should not be read as a Palestinian one. It is a place which is a part of Islamic history.
>
> (interview, May 22, 2015)

Hamza, as a religious authority and as an Islamic scholar, dilutes the national-cum-political aspects of the place as they played out since the 1990s. He does not conceal the fact that the place was indeed part of such a process and part of his Palestinian heritage. Nonetheless, his approach is purely religious and follows the Salafi "purist" understanding. He is engaged in a delicate scalar analysis, moving between the individual, the community, and the national scales. In summing up this part it is plain to see how the community responds to external processes which, time and again, effectively alter the spatial, as well as the social, characteristics of the Maqam. With this in mind, I will turn to address the shrine of Mariam Bawardy and the village of I'bbelin.

The History and Mythology of Mariam Bawardy of I'bbelin

It is not every day that a would-be saint appears in one's lecture hall. But in 2009 Mariam Bawardy, a Melkite Carmelite nun known also as "the Little Arab Nun," or in her ordained name Sister Mary of Jesus Crucified (1846–78), appeared in my "Politics of Conservation" seminar. I was introducing the students to my "Politics of Sacred Places" project, to explain how politics is always spatial and subsequently why they should regard their new vocation as inherently political and surely not, as some would have it, based on solely professional principles. In the discussion that ensued, one of the students, Assad Daoud, challenged me to visit his ongoing one-man conservation of the birthplace of Mariam Bawardy. I was totally oblivious to her at the time, and little did I know that this saint and her shrine in I'bbelin would have such an impact on my work. This was also the time when, together with Nurit Stadler, we began to conceptualize our joint project on "Enchanted Places on the Margins."[6] So, I duly visited the place and indeed was taken not only with Daoud's visionary venture but also with its relevance to our said project. Mariam's "apparition" proved to be highly beneficial, and her emerging shrine became one of the pivotal sites we explored. From 2010 to 2018, Nurit Stadler and I jointly conducted numerous ethnographies and interviews, joined in the annual processions, followed the restoration project of Mariam's house and were as excited as the locals when, following an announcement of Pope Francis, Mariam was canonized on May 17, 2015. My own ethnography of the site continues to the present. In what follows I will narrate Mariam's history and mythology, based on locals' traditions transmitted during interviews, as well as to be found in various biographies published about her life. This will also entail a discussion of her road to canonization in the present.

According to local traditions, Mariam Bawardy was born in the village of I'bbelin in the Lower Galilee, on January 5, 1846, to a Christian family. It is not clear what the circumstances were that brought her mother, Mariam Shahin, and her father, Jirjis (George) Bawardy, from their Galilean villages of origin (Tarshiha and Hurfeish) to reside in I'bbelin (Brunot 1981). As their surname divulges, the Bawardys were involved in the manufacture of gunpowder (Arabic: *barud*), which was typically used for quarrying. Jirjis is often described as a poor man who was temporarily incarcerated by the Ottoman authorities on false charges of murder and for the illegal manufacture of explosives for quarrying building materials (Daoud 2008: 19–20). This was but part of the hardships her parents endured, which portrays them as Christian martyrs. Along those lines of suffering, traditions have it that their first twelve children, all boys, died in infancy. Inspired by a vision, the couple set out on a pilgrimage to Bethlehem to entreat the Virgin Mary for a daughter who they promised would be called Mariam and who would dedicate herself to Christ (interview with R., January 9, 2016). Their prayers were answered when Mariam was born, followed two years later by her only surviving brother, Boulos (Paul), in their humble home in I'bbelin.[7] However, when Mariam was two years old, both her parents died, and Mariam was taken in by her paternal uncle, who also resided in I'bbelin. Struggling to earn a livelihood, the uncle moved to the vicinity of Alexandria, Egypt, when Mariam was eight. Against this backdrop, her mythologization echoes that of the Holy Family (Butler and Burns 1995: 263). At the tender age of twelve, Mariam was betrothed to an in-law of her uncle. However, a subsequent religious experience inspired her to pledge a vow of celibacy (Daoud 2008: 55). As part of her mythologization as a martyr and a suffering female saint, it is narrated that just before eschewing the marriage, Mariam summoned a Muslim servant to deliver a letter to her brother. When the servant learned about her plight, he suggested that she convert to Islam, to which she emphatically refused. The enraged servant lashed out at her so gravely that her wounds necessitated a month of convalescence at a local monastery. Following this near-death experience and thanks to a generous patron, Mariam subsequently relocated to Marseille in 1863. While in France, she decided to enter a religious order. Rejected by the Franciscan monastery of her choice, she was ultimately accepted into the Congregation of the Sisters of St. Joseph of the Apparition in Pau. Soon after joining the cloister, Mariam was imparted with stigmata. The marks of Christ were impressed on her body at the age of twenty during a vision she had while praying in the chapel (interview with Z., October 28, 2012; interview with R., November 6, 2015). These were the stigmata of the heart which became a recurrent theme in her mythology, in both written and oral accounts of her life (Buzy 1921; Brunot 1981).

In 1870, Mariam was among the first Carmelite Apostolic Sisters to serve in Mangalore, India. After twenty-four months of service Mariam returned to Bethlehem where she laid the foundation of the first Carmelite monastery (Daoud 2008: 58). Just a few months later, she fell down the nunnery's stairs, her arm broke and became infected by gangrene. She passed away on August 26, 1878, at the age of thirty-three, yet another point of resemblance to Jesus' life. By the time of her death, she was already recognized as an extraordinary mystic who endured a very harsh life amid the trials of her undeterred faith. Her birthplace in I'bbelin began to attract pilgrims, although in very small numbers. The Patriarch of Jerusalem opened her case for beatification in 1919 (Buck 2004). The drawn-out canonization process culminated with a decree of heroic virtue on November 27, 1983. Two years later, John Paul II beatified her as "Sister Mary of Jesus Crucified" (Hasson 2015). Her case for sainthood was strengthened on December 6, 2014, with the documentation of a final miracle. Pursuant to a consistory decision two months later, Mariam was canonized by Pope Francis on May 17, 2015 (Associated Press 2015), together with another nineteenth-century nun from Palestine, Marie-Alphonsine Ghattas. The ceremony was attended by the president of the Palestinian Authority, Mahmud 'Abbas, and about 2,000 pilgrims from the region, some of whom waved Palestinian flags. Surely, this nationalization of the new saints puts us squarely within the politics involved with the shrine of Mariam Bawardy. This will complement this discussion, following an analysis of the changing materiality of the shrine which in many respects allows us a better understanding of the politics of place against its respective community and village.

The Changing Landscape of the Shrine: A Socio—Spatial Analysis

Although the small cult around Mariam Bawardy birthplace has its roots in the late nineteenth century, the place remained undeveloped until the late 2000s.[8] As local traditions would have it, a trickle of pilgrims and visitors used to arrive at a makeshift altar located in the vicinity of what was accepted as her birthplace, usually on Saturday evenings (interview with Z., May 11, 2018). Changes began to take place in 2009 when a local resident of I'bbelin, Assad Daoud, an architect and a budding conservationist, launched a renovation-cum-restoration project of Mariam Bawardy's birthplace, which, as it so happens, was part of his family's private property.

To understand the changes in landscape and the changing materiality of the shrine, it is pertinent to understand Daoud's pivotal role and motivations, as he is the major force behind the project. The ownership of the place plays a crucial role in everything concerning the complex's material culture and reconstruction. As it is part of the Daouds' private property, it remains less approachable to changes from external players. Though raised in the local Orthodox community, neither Assad is a practicing Christian nor does he attribute his involvement in this undertaking to a religious impulse. As he admits, he never attends the annual processions or other events dedicated to Mariam. Effectively, Daoud has taken upon himself the role of chief architect and restorer and de facto he is the main gatekeeper of all that concerns the material reconstruction of the place. This is how he narrates his vision for the restoration project:

> I started to think of restoring the compound when I was an undergraduate architectural student at the Technion [Israel Institute of Technology]. This was in the mid-nineties … At the outset, when these ideas began to germinate [in my head], I envisioned a chapel at her birthplace … My initial plan was to uncover the remains of the original house … It was not until 1998 that we applied for a building permit … but it was only for a chapel … In order to build a chapel, we were obliged to perform a salvage excavation, which was begun in late 2002. Upon completing the excavations in 2003, I decided not to implement the original idea of the chapel and opted instead to preserve our discoveries at the site…. [This stage began] in the summer of 2007…. In early 2009, I was approached by a small group of young residents of the village who offered their help. Together, we cleaned the site. We then got a permit from the Israel Antiquities Authority to expose the house under its supervision…. That same year we also received a permit to partially reconstruct the house…, Since then, we have continued to work very slowly toward our goal.
>
> (interview, October 20, 2012)

After finalizing his plans to "authentically" restore the compound "without ruining its spirit," Daoud completed a degree in conservation at The Western Galilee College[9] to obtain the fundamentals of professional conservation and reconstruction (interview with Daoud, April 22, 2012). In his estimation, "every piece of stone is important in places like this, and I must be certain about its specific period and the architecture of the time, in order to reconstruct the place according to the different periods, the designs, the materials, and the function of many objects that are scattered around the place" (interview, November 23, 2013). Along these lines, he proceeded at a very deliberate pace to reconstruct the shrine and the house of Mariam Bawardy. Once the work began, Daoud came to the following realization: "In the compound itself, there is a great deal of evidence of Mariam and her family's life that you cannot find anywhere else." Most of this information does "not appear in any photo or text; therefore, we have to think and imagine the place according to its period and according to the data that we have. Therefore, we cannot do whatever we want; we have a responsibility to the historical truth" (interview, November 23, 2013). This meticulous approach

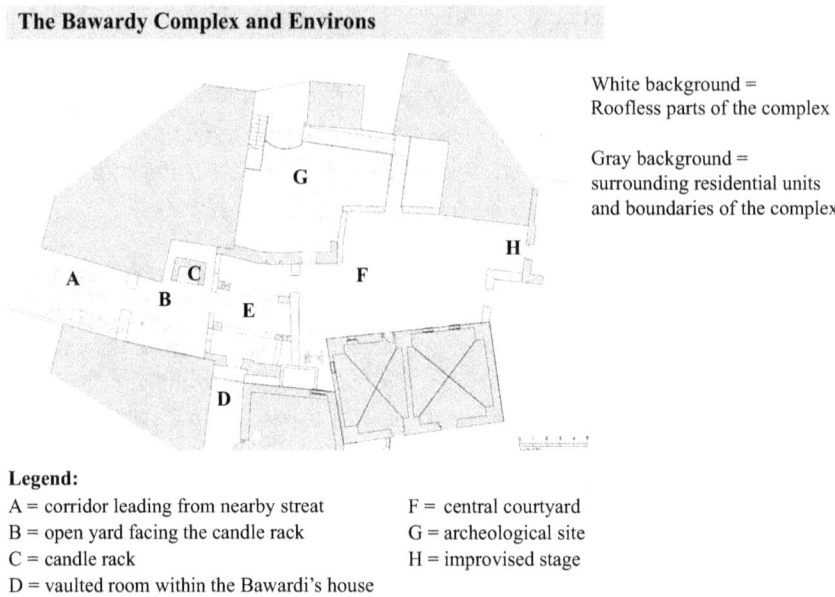

Legend:
A = corridor leading from nearby streat
B = open yard facing the candle rack
C = candle rack
D = vaulted room within the Bawardi's house
E = birthplace of mariam
F = central courtyard
G = archeological site
H = improvised stage

Figure 3.2 The Bawardy complex (courtesy of Assad Daoud).

was not the only reason for the slow progress. Whereas Jewish shrines in Israel usually receive considerable government funding, their Christian and Muslim counterparts are rarely even acknowledged by the state. In the absence of financial support from the government or state institutions, the Daoud family and other residents of I'bbelin are picking up the appreciable tab on their own. Ultimately, by 2015—prior to the canonization ceremony—most of the project's goals were achieved. The following drawing represents the complex at its present state.

The entrance to the shrine is from a small street branching out from the main thoroughfare. An open corridor from the main street leads to the central, most important part of the shrine, which is the actual room where Mariam was born according to local traditions (D). A new candelabrum and altar were added (C). East of the former house lies a central open yard, which is designed for public prayers and gatherings (F). On its southern parts are two doors (usually closed) of storerooms and a gate leading to the courtyard and house of the Daoud family. Bordering the northern side of the central yard is an excavation site, containing findings dating from Late Antiquity to the Ottoman Period (G). One of the most challenging aspects of the reconstruction involved the walls of the room in which Mariam was supposedly born. Initially relying on written material and visuals taken since 1926 to arrive at a plan for the reconstruction, Daoud also collaborated with restoration specialists from the Israel Antiquities Authority and other organizations. While Daoud is committed to his intellectual and professional integrity, other "players" are less hesitant to suggest changes which might not fit into any conservation charter, but may draw more attention to the site, raise the numbers of pilgrims, and thus turn the shrine into a recurrent theme on the local religious tourism map. To that end, some Christians residents of Iʽbbelin have expressed hope for a sacred place design that accords with mythological and spiritual interpretations of the site, while others have indicated the need to enhance Christian local identity. These demands include, among other things, putting pressure on Daoud to add a decorative roof over the shrine. As was the case with other ideas and innovations suggested to him, Daoud paid no heed. He remained faithful to his strict understanding of how the shrine should be reconstructed in the most professional and authentic manner (interview, March 15, 2017). Indeed, as he remains the final decision-maker, the shrine progresses according to his vision and matters are never finalized nor expedited in a fashion with which he cannot concur. The question of ownership is, therefore, crucial to the development of this shrine. Daoud's role in the reconstruction of the compound should be understood in terms of his own agency, scientific aspirations, and control of the site vis-à-vis town and church authorities.

Owing to intensive work between 2014 and 2015, Mariam Bawardy's birthplace has also experienced some architectural changes. Besides exposing the building, Daoud has realigned stones following meticulous reconstruction based on pictorial evidence from the 1920s. Photos and posters of Mariam were hung outside the chamber. Adjacent to the room, an area was reserved for candles. Even after the restoration, the Bawardy house remains highly suggestive from an architectural and material standpoint. This situation is due to the fact that all changes are made solely by the owner of the site and according to the strictest conservation standards. Following the canonization, a few changes took place at the complex. The vaulted room, which is part of the Bawardys' house, was adorned with logs and a few more ornaments and decorations were posted on its walls. At the very eastern end of the central courtyard, a makeshift wooden stage was built, which serves singers and bands participating in public gatherings and rituals at the site (H in the above layout of the complex). A 2x2 m. picture was hung on the northern wall of the central yard depicting the three local female saints: the Virgin Mary and the recent additions of Mariam Bawardy and Marie-Alphonsine Ghattas.

However, even against this meticulous restoration and after the seven years that have elapsed since the canonization, the shrine of Mariam Bawardy is still a rather peripheral pilgrimage destination, and in general is not considered a "must visit" site among Christian pilgrims, both local and international. Furthermore, although the canonization process aroused much attention and media coverage at the time, it did not effect any major and much anticipated changes in the village. These issues will be discussed in the next paragraphs, as part of my analysis of the politics of the place in multi-scalar settings.

The Politics of the Shrine of Mariam Bawardy: Dynamics of a Sacred Place

On the eve of canonization in 2015, the media—and certainly Palestinian media—were as excited about the upcoming event as the Christian community in I'bbelin. The following is an excerpt from a report by AP News Agency:

> The Holy Land's Christians are excitedly preparing for next week's canonization of two Arab nuns, bringing some joy to a tiny community that has had little to celebrate in recent years. Mariam Bawardy and Marie Alphonsine Ghattas, who lived in what was Ottoman-ruled Palestine in the 19th century, will be the first from the region to receive sainthood since the early days of Christianity. They will also be the first Arabic-speaking Catholic saints. The nuns were born in Jerusalem and a town in what is now Israel but come from an Arabic-speaking Christian community that has mainly identified itself as Palestinian for many decades. President Mahmud Abbas, a Muslim, will attend the canonization festivities at the Vatican on May 17, said Ziad al-Bandak, an adviser on Christian affairs to the Palestinian leader: "This canonization has a meaning for the whole Palestinian nation," al-Bandak said. "It's a very important thing for Palestinians, whether they're Muslim or Christian." In the birthplace of Christianity, Christians are a tiny minority, making up less than 2 percent of the population of Israel and the Palestinian territories.
>
> (Berretta 2015)

This short passage clearly reflects the ways in which a place is constructed and influenced by scales which far surpass its own locality. Surely, the most striking issue at play here is the Palestinianization-cum-nationalization of a local Arab-Christian nun. Another pertinent issue, which bears directly on the development of the shrine of Mariam Bawardy, is the predicaments of the Christian communities in the Middle East at large and in Israel/Palestine in particular. Against the ongoing Islamization process that has characterized the region since the seventh century CE, Christian communities experience a continuing demographic decline. This has enormous impact on different socio-political aspects of these communities, such as increased immigration, isolation, harassment by Muslim communities, and in general, social infringement (Murre-van den Berg 2021). To understand how these regional processes impact the community scale of the shrine, let us go back to the village of I'bbelin following the major geopolitical breach that followed the 1948 war. This is surely but one of the influences on the unfolding of the politics of the place, as will be explained below.

During the British Mandate (1917–48), I'bbelin was a humble agricultural village in which the Christian communities formed the majority of the village. Its estimated population in 1945 was 1,660 people, of which Christians of both congregations in the village amounted to 64 percent (1020) while the remaining 36 percent (600) were Muslims (Dabbagh 2016). I'bbelin surrendered to the Israeli army on July 14, 1948, as part of Operation Dekel (Palm Tree), which was launched to complete the takeover of the Western Galilee (Pappe 2006). As the war subsided, Israel imposed martial law on all its Palestinian citizens, which was maintained until 1966. One of the outcomes of this geopolitical change was an influx of Muslim refugees to the village. Thus, a significant demographic change was underway as the Muslims (as in most mixed villages in Israel/Palestine) over time became the majority group in the village. To date, it has a population of 13,300, of which 58 percent (7,714) are Muslims, while the remaining 42 percent (5,286) are Christians (CBS 2019). The Christians belong to two distinct communities, of which the Greek Orthodox is the larger (circa 4,500) and the Greek Catholic (circa 1,110) is the smaller community (interview with Father Demetrius, February 20, 2017). Thus, the group promoting Mariam's mythology, and the one that Mariam hails from, is the smallest in the village. To complicate matters further, the shrine is located within the private land of the Daoud family, a long-established and well-respected Greek Orthodox family that resides at the very center of the old historic kernel of the village. As the shrine is literally in the backyard of the family house, no changes or development plans can be implemented without the family's consent. Assad Daoud, who launched the long process of restoration, operates (to the chagrin of mostly the Catholic community) in accordance with his own secular perception and through his professional lens, which therefore renders the site less touristic and accommodating than others from the village would have wanted. As such, at the village scale the politics of the place are mostly influenced by the contradicting forces of the owners of the land, and the sentiments and aspiration of the Catholic Christian residents and the pilgrims. This is but one of the issues that construct a rather complex matrix of local forces that together inform the politics of the shrine and hence its spatiality and materiality. These intricate relations, and at times opposing forces, are revealed in the procession dedicated to Mariam Bawardy in I'bbelin.

Processions have long been an integral part of the study of religious life, as they are rituals which reinforce the presence, identity, faith, and piety of their participants in the public sphere (Kong 2005; Maddrell, Terry, and Gale 2015). They require organization and present a public face to others. Parading one's religious affiliation seems to have a significant effect on one's status and surely promotes the community involved. Processions are rituals which temporarily claim a place and take place, and as such, are always involved with questions of territoriality, belonging, dominance, and subordination. Indeed, processions are about making a stand and—intentionally or unintentionally—are a process of boundary-making and constructing an affiliation and statement about one's group. However, a public religious ritual is not only a process of identity marking or a display of the collective self: it entails collective labor as well as articulations with public authorities. It is also an evident quest for public visibility, which means both to "take place and make place" (Knott 2005). The procession of Mariam Bawardy started out in 1983, and since then has become an (almost) annual ritual in the village landscape. However, one of their characteristics is their ephemeral nature and constant flux, as they are negotiated among various forces within both Christian communities and surely vis-à-vis the dominant Muslim community. This was readily apparent already during the first procession that Nurit Stadler and I attended, in late October 2011. The procession started at the Church of Mar Elias, located on the southern hill of the village. Following a long indoors ceremony, which also included a homily by Father Elias Shakur, the Archbishop of the Melkite Greek Catholic Church (2004–14), the procession started meandering its 700-meter course along the streets of I'bbelin. While most of the participants were Christians of both communities, a small number of Muslims was present as well. There was no specific clergy leading the procession, nor anyone who seemed to be in charge, save a big van carrying a huge picture of the saint which set the general direction of the procession. Upon arrival at the shrine, the procession split. Some people stayed at the shrine, as their last destination, and some went toward the Catholic Church to pray and to enjoy the sweets on offer. The procession slowly ebbed away as participants retired to their homes at their own pace (fieldnotes, October 31, 2011).

In the years that followed (2012–16), we noticed various changes. One dramatic change was the procession that did not march in 2015. This was the outcome of various factors, mostly connected to internal rivalries within the Greek-Catholic community, which ultimately ended with the said result. Since then, the date of the procession shifted to May 15 in recognition of the canonization day. Another noticeable change is the course of the procession. While in the past the processions marched along the lines I indicated above, they center now on the streets surrounding the shrine. This is probably related to a reassessment and a fallout between the Greek-Catholic community and former Archbishop Shakur (interview with A., May 15, 2018). Thus, on May 15, 2022, the procession followed a short course from the old Christian cemetery to the shrine and ended in the Catholic Church of I'bbelin. The procession was organized by the new Greek-Catholic committee, which was also responsible for bringing a few sacred objects connected to Mariam's life from her Bethlehem monastery (Khoury 2022).

This is yet another indication that on the local village front, the Greek-Catholic congregation is entangled in internal debates and rivalries that bear directly on the activities regarding Mariam and her shrine. This is particularly true regarding its unchanged peripheral status and the lack of touristic and pilgrim interest in, and interaction with, the place. However, this is not solely a matter of internal village politics, but is also the outcome of larger spheres of influence. During our lengthy ethnographic journey, we tried time and again to fathom the lack of interest and enthusiasm, not just among locals in the Galilee, but also among Christian pilgrims from around the world regarding the shrine. This became an even more intriguing issue following the canonization and the media hype around it. It would seem that Mariam's affiliation with the small Carmelite order, which is insignificant in the Holy Land relative to the well-established Custodia di Terra Santa (i.e., the Franciscan order), presents a problem for the ongoing efforts to promote the site. Currently, the Custodia—which is the biggest organizer of Christian pilgrimage to the Holy Land—is not changing its pilgrimage map to enable its pilgrims to visit the site. In a religiously saturated region like the Galilee, in which the program for international pilgrims is already hectic, highly condensed, and comprehensive, without adding another stop, the new site is missed; or, as some of the interlocutors suggested, deliberately overlooked.

I want to conclude this discussion of the dynamic politics of the sacred place by transcending the community scale and looking at the national one, that is, the Palestinianization of the site which started out this discussion. Recall that the canonization ceremony in the Vatican was attended by the Palestinian president Mr. Mahmud Abbas. His presence there seems to suggest that Mariam Bawardy was heralded not only as a pious and an observant Christian Arab saint, but also as a Palestinian national hero. The small shrine in the Galilee is no longer just a birthplace of a sainted nun, but also of an iconic Palestinian figure. The nationalization of the sacred is a recurrent theme in the region, and will form the main theme of Chapter 6, which engages mostly with the national and global scale of the Haram al-Sharif. In the case of the shrine of Mariam Bawardy, there seems to be a discrepancy between the utilization of the site during the festive occasion of canonization, and the general indifference toward it since then. On the very day of the announcement in the Vatican, an Israeli-Arab Member of the Knesset, Basel Ghatas, who is also of Greek-Orthodox origins, was interviewed by a local Palestinian channel. As he was facing the camera while wearing a shawl with the Palestinian flag on it and other known national insignia, Ghattas unequivocally connected Mariam Bawardy with the Palestinian struggle. According to him, the sanctification of Mariam Bawardy (along with that of Marie-Alfonsine Ghattas) is surely part of the Christian struggle in the region for recognition and their importance in the construction of Eastern Christianity's culture and heritage. But there are greater political matters at stake. The announcement, he added, coincides not only with the commemoration day of the Palestinian Catastrophe (aka the Nakba, which is commemorated on May 15), but also with the recent statement of Pope Francis in which he recognized and endorsed the Palestinian State. Indeed, he emphasized: "This is an historical event of the highest importance" (Nabulsi 2015). That said, in the years that have passed, nothing dramatic has changed at the site nor has it emerged as a significant Palestinian-cum-Christian site.

To date, and against the multiple spatial changes that have taken place at the shrine in recent years, the site is still a rather humble pilgrimage destination. Pilgrims do not frequent the place, and even the attention received from the Christian communities is focused mostly on specific occasions throughout the year. What is rather intriguing is the general indifference of the Muslim community of I'bbelin. H. is a young man of twenty-six, who runs a family business of spices and seeds where we frequently meet. Recently, while I was already in the process of writing this chapter, we met at his shop and the conversation revolved around my visits to I'bbelin and to his surprise at my acquaintance with its past and present (fieldnotes, July 10, 2022). I explained that it is part of my research as I study the shrine of Mariam Bawardy. To my astonishment, he was unaware of it, perhaps even ignorant of its existence.

He is not alone in that, and other Muslims I talk to in the village, and certainly outside it, are not familiar with the shrine. This suggests that the sporadic efforts to nationalize this Christian site as a Palestinian heritage site have thus far been ineffective. Unlike charismatic sites such as Lourdes in France or Fatima in Portugal (Eade 1992; Reader 2007), which gained fame almost instantly and today draw large audience and millions of pilgrims, the shrine of the "little Arab nun" from a small village in the Galilee remains in its humble stage.

* * *

This chapter set out to explore the politics of rural sacred places and engaged with the extensive meanings they entail for their respective communities and explored place-community interactions. This exhaustive study of Maqam Abu al-Hijja and the shrine of Mariam Bawardy allowed us to penetrate both the micro and macro politics within and without their communities' scale. The analysis of the place at the village/community scale fleshed out various spheres of influence and complex politics which foreground the places and enabled us to cross their threshold, as suggested in Hertz's pioneering study of an Alpine saint.

In both places I have addressed the mythology and history of the saint in question against socio-political processes both within and without the village. Analysis of the changing landscapes of the places revealed how they are produced, constructed, and perceived within a complex matrix of forces and actants. Surely, these are all part of the politics of the places and exploring them against their communities enabled us to see how they are constantly changing and influenced within a multi-scalar setting. Maqam Abu al-Hijja experienced dramatic changes over the last three decades, which were informed by both internal village processes, such as an improved economic situation or the emergence of highly entrepreneurial leaders, as well as by external forces, such as demographic and administrative changes in its region or the escalation of the Israeli-Palestinian conflict. Conducting a relatively long ethnography of the place enabled us to see the dwindling of its religious/mythical importance and the emergence of a new understanding of the site as a heritage and historical landmark. The changing spatiality of the shrine of Mariam Bawardy was the outcome of mostly one impresario, who dictated the nature of the renovation and its final outcome. Following the processions to the shrine of Mariam Bawardy as a community activity demonstrated the complex relations within the Greek-Catholic community and, even more so, of the interactions among all groups in I'bbelin. The canonization of Mariam Bawardy transformed, albeit for a relatively short time, the shrine into a national-Palestinian landmark.

And finally, the hopes of the local communities that the canonization would put the shrine on the pilgrimage route failed against politics which concern rivalries among different Christian organizations in the Holy Land. In the next chapters I engage in the urban scale. In Chapter 4, the discussion brings to the fore three sacred places that stood at the center of urban conflicts and contestation over ownership and the right to the past. Chapter 5 focuses on Acre and first introduces the readers to the concept of *ReligioCity*, to be followed by an analysis of the politics of sacred places in the city.

4

Sacred Sites and the Right to the City

Lefebvre, Materiality, and Urban Sacred Places

In this chapter, I discuss the urban scale and explore struggles and conflicts over sacred places while engaging with Lefebvre's notion of the right to the city. This is achieved by harnessing his post-Marxist approach to the realm of symbolic goods and exploring the sacred as a resource in the urban sphere. His approach helps us to examine the ways in which different actors are conversing and contesting over their right of ownership and control of their past, their heritage, and of course their preferred urban culture. Along these lines, I will explore struggles of subordinate communities in Israeli cities as ways to "claim the city" through the sacred. These struggles have shaped and are still shaping the urban landscape, instigating dialogues and conflicts among different groups within the urban sphere. As such, I focus on urban conflicts over the Ottoman Friday Mosque in Beersheba, and the Hassan Bey Mosque in Tel-Aviv-Jaffa. To set these case studies in context, in what follows I will address the growing impacts of religion(s) in contemporary cities and the Lefebvrian concept of the "right to the city" and its theoretical implications.

At the beginning of the third millennium, our cities are gradually becoming more susceptible to the increasing influence and presence of religious components in urban conflicts. This is particularly true for cities in ethno-national regimes where urban struggles often erupt (Estonia, Bosnia, Israel, and more)—but also in seemingly peaceful cities worldwide, as the controversy over the Fazl Mosque clearly demonstrates (Naylor and Ryan 2002; Tong and Kong 2000; AlSayyad and Massoumi 2010; Beaumont and Baker 2011; Garbin 2012; Gökariksel and Secor 2015; Luz 2015). The (re)appearance of religion as a component in urban conflicts, most particularly in cities that showcase a highly heterogeneous and multi-ethnic population, need not surprise us. In recent years and under various names, religion and religiosity are moving center stage to become powerful players in the public arena (Latour 1993; Casanova 1994; Berger 1999). Some scholars might say reentering, while others, including this author, would assert that they never left. Religious-based struggles are becoming part of everyday life in cities worldwide. Once again it would seem that "God walks among us," in the main thoroughfares of cities. Religion, as previously suggested by John Agnew, seems to be "the political language of the time" (Agnew 2006: 183). Which probably explains why scholarly works in recent years have shown a renewed interest in uncovering connections between religion and politics (Asad 1999; Kong 2010; Pullan et al. 2013). This interest stems from the realization that previous scholarly positions regarding the role of religion in our (post)modern daily life merit further reflection, and ultimately failed to anticipate the contemporary surge of religiosity and religious conflicts in cities worldwide (Larkin 2010; Bakshi 2011; Komarova and O'Dowd 2013). That said, cities have always been the place of our meeting with the "stranger"; and places of encounters with others suggest the possibility of conflicts (Simmel 1903; Barthes 1981). Intrinsically, they are spaces where different social, cultural, and certainly political perceptions are negotiated and contested among different communities, who share the urban landscape and compete over tangible and intangible resources. Religions, and certainly sacred places as our main interest in the current context, clearly provide ample reasons for conflictual encounters among urban groups as they are replete with meaning and landmarks of the utmost importance to their respective communities. As will be demonstrated in this chapter, sacred places of subaltern groups are particularly vulnerable to confiscation, neglect, appropriation, and general mishandling in ethnocratic regimes. Therefore, it is hardly surprising that they have emerged as bones of contention in various Israeli cities.

I want to frame these struggles through a Lefebvrian lens as a demand to be part of the city, indeed, as a claim to the "right to the city." For Lefebvre, the right to the city is a demand for social justice, and surely for social change. It is a battle cry, calling for the abolishment of unjust inequality (Marcuse 2009). The right to the city stresses the need to restructure the power relations that form the root cause of continuously produced inequality within the urban space (Purcell 2003). This implies a restructure of urban resources and, at times, a rather simple step of returning these meaningful places to their former owners and surely reintroducing them to the urban landscape in their initial role. This can prove to be a rather difficult task, as the hegemonic group often finds it too much to endure, as these sites represent an alternative—and therefore a threat—to their own habitus. A case in point is the Fazl Mosque, which was built in a London suburb in the 1920s. Initially, the place was accepted by the majority group and regarded as an exotic, enriching, and modern addition to the urban landscape. During the 1990s, when its community applied for permission to renovate it, the responses were strikingly different. By that time Muslims were already a noticeable minority in the UK and the mosque's high visibility as a prominent center for its non-Christian community was met with growing resentment by the majority group and municipal agencies ultimately rejected the proposed project (Naylor and Ryan 1982). Similarly, mosques in the Netherland and in Western Europe, in general, are mostly located in marginal spaces, as are their respective communities.[1] However, resistance to them arises when they become too visible in the urban landscape. The construction of the Essallam Mosque in South Rotterdam has been a thorn in the side of various non-Muslim groups who reside in its vicinity. A non-Muslim resident who moved away from the neighborhood following its construction explained: "I step out of my house … it's like I'm in another country … that mosque is just too big" (Tamimi-Arab 2013). On November 29, 2009, Switzerland conducted a national referendum which resulted in banning the construction of minarets on mosques. In the village of Pigniu in the canton of Graubünden in the eastern part of Switzerland, nine people took part in the referendum. They all voted for a ban on building new minarets in Switzerland. A few days later, when a journalist came to inquire about this, the local village secretary and school bus driver explained: "It's not about Muslims. We don't know any Muslims; none of them live here." He went on to express distrust of the Swiss political elites and media, and finally explained why people voted against minarets by saying, firstly, "The world always wants to dictate to us how we should conduct our political affairs, but we do not accept that"; then, "Minarets are symbols of power. We do not need foreign power symbols here" (Mayer 2011). This semiotic reading of the landscape, and specifically the minaret, will reemerge as we explore conflicts over sacred places in Israeli cities. Regardless of any other issues involved, the reluctance to accommodate minarets and the emotions they evoke are part and parcel of what I will further elaborate on as part of my discussion of materiality and the spatial turn in the study of religion. To do so, I scrutinize some of my interviewees' engagement with the religious landscape and its impacts on them. This will facilitate a deeper understanding of the materiality involved in the two case studies that stand at the center of this chapter.

Nadim Rouhana is a professor of International Negotiation and Conflict Studies at Tufts University and the founding director of Mada al-Carmel–Arab Center for Applied Social Research in Haifa, Israel. This research center's mission is to expand critical thinking and broaden knowledge about Palestinian Israeli citizens. Rouhana hails from a Christian family from the predominantly Druze local council of Isfiya, atop Mt. Carmel. I wanted to interview him as I was interested to learn how he perceives the role and importance of Palestinian sacred places for Palestinian Israelis. His answer revolves around the importance of these sites, particularly the Islamic ones, as mnemonic landmarks which attest to Palestinians' continuing presence and existence as an anti-hegemonic message to the State and Jewish majority. Inadvertently, he taps into the importance of materiality in the urban landscape:

> The sacred places of Islam are more important for me than those of Christianity. When I walk in a city like Acre or Jaffa and I see a mosque, I feel immediately connected to the mosque and to the place, much more than if I would walk on HaNevi'im street in Haifa where one may find a Catholic church that was built after 1948. And why? Because the mosque in Jaffa and in Acre and the mosque in the ruined village are signs of continuity that this was Palestine. ... I will pay top dollar for a mosque to be built here on the [Mt. N. L.] Carmel, more than if a church would be built here .... Because a mosque challenges the Jewish-political identity of the State of Israel ... which is why I connect more to the ruined mosque in the village of Hittin than to a church.
>
> (interview, August 13, 2002)

Rouhana's analysis befits and follows his firm political stance that promotes Israel as a "state of all its citizens," as opposed to the current ethnocratic logic that purveys the idea of Israel as a Jewish and a democratic state (Rouhana 2001). What I find particularly intriguing and worth pursuing in his analysis is the suggested impact of the tangible on our intangible experience of the sacred. In the current context, Rouhana accentuates the political role of a mosque as a landmark of Palestinian identity, defiance, and resistance to the hegemonic powers. His analysis lands us squarely in the realm of materiality and the ways it has been theorized, following the material turn, and mostly the ways it mediates meaning. I totally concur with Hazard that despite numerous discussions, it is still rather difficult to arrive at an accepted definition of what materiality is and what it does (2013). However, we are not short of "material" to work with. With this in mind, I want to explore materiality further, as firstly, it bears directly on how I examine the politics of sacred places; secondly, it furnishes the concept of *ReligioCity*, which is presented to the reader in the following chapter; and thirdly, it is highly relevant to the conflict over the Hassan Bek Mosque.

Let me begin by stating what might sound rather trivial; materiality is about more than objects and it mediates a myriad of socio-political-cultural perceptions and processes. As such, materiality refers to the intermingling of sign and referent. Material objects along those lines both enable and enact perceptions and evoke responses (Morgan 2010). These responses are inseparable from the subjects that come into contact with them, and they reflect habitus, cultural and political affiliation, and surely experience. Materiality is about embodiment and sensation, social relations, devotion, taxonomies of cultural classification, epistemology, and the social nature of speech utterances and texts as artifacts (Morgan 2016). Materiality emerged in recent years as a highly important concept in the study of religion, as it became evident that the distinction that exists in older models of material culture between subjects and objects is highly problematic. Put bluntly, can the inscription on the gate of the mosque be distinguished or understood apart from the person who inscribed it, local and national politics, prevailing power structures? Following what is commonly referred to as the "spatial turn" in the study of religion, materiality has emerged as a concept that suggests a breakthrough from previous conceptions of material culture that focus on humans to include the much broader domain of non-human material conditions (Hazard 2013). Otherwise, it would be impossible to understand the materiality of a minaret in Switzerland from contemporary issues that preoccupy Swiss society, such as globalization, immigration, immigrant absorption, and surely its history as a predominantly Christian society. Materiality becomes a compelling register through which religious manifestations can be examined, as can matters of belief that account for, and interact with, various structures of social life (Morgan 2010). There is mounting acknowledgment not only of the tangible aspects of religion, but also of the way material objects are never neutral and devoid of social context or personal subjectivities (Navaro-Yashin 2012; Knott et al. 2016). Certainly, as a cultural geographer I see an intimate connection and many similarities with the ways landscape has been theorized in recent decades (Creswell 2014). This is easily discernible in Orsi's definition of material culture as "that segment of humankind's biosocial environment that has been purposely shaped by people according to culturally dictated plans" (1985: 5). It seems to me that Orsi's definition needs an expansion, or at least a clarification, that culture is inherently political (Mitchell 1995). This is precisely what engagement with materiality allows us to transcend, enriching the study of the politics of sacred places. As previously suggested by Keane, religions may not always demand beliefs, but they will always involve material forms. It is in these forms, that is materiality, that people experience, respond to, and influence the built environment. Since these forms enjoy relative autonomy, put plainly they are open to different interpretations and have differential influences. Keane rightly suggests that these objects are susceptible to acquiring features which are unrelated to the initial intentions of those who constructed them (2008). This understanding of materiality thus enables us to follow these changes, which, as I argue throughout this book, are at the heart of the politics of sacred places and emerge from their spatial nature.

Indeed, the Israeli case is surely more complicated than the current travesties with immigrants' religious compounds in Europe. The places I explore are negotiated and have emerged as conflictual within a settler-colonial context and involve native groups who are struggling for their heritage, history, collective memory, on their former land. It presents us also with complexities evolving from the implementation, indeed de-scaling, of the ethnonational logic unto the urban sphere. This is particularly relevant while engaging with mixed cities where, under the yoke of the ethnocratic logic, the city is shaped by an urban ethnocracy; that is, the dominant group appropriates the city's infrastructures to maintain and bolster its domination and privileged position (Yiftachel and Yacobi 2003). In his analysis of a mixed Israeli town (Lydda), Yacobi theorizes the Israeli construct of urban citizenship along ethnic lines, and the formation of ethnic enclaves that follow an ethnocratic urban logic (2003). This urban logic also informs the State's and municipalities' responses to struggles over the minority's sacred places. It is against this urban logic, and the might of the ethnocratic regime that seeks to eliminate the former Palestinian presence, that Palestinian sacred places are contested in the urban landscape. These struggles by local Palestinian communities within Israel are often perceived and framed as part of *sumud*, a concept that might be translated as "steadfastness" or "steadfast perseverance." This has certainly become a pattern of Palestinian life since 1948, which refers to endurance in the face of, and resistance to, Israeli policies (Zatari 2018). In the Israeli/Palestinian context, it implies a cultural value and ideological theme which relates to forms of resistance to the erasure of Islamic and Palestinian memories, heritage, and surely built environments (Peled 2019). In the protracted struggle over the ownership and right of access to the historic Ottoman mosque in Beersheba, known also as the Grand Mosque, this is precisely the background against which this conflict has erupted.

The Grand Mosque of Ottoman Bi'r al-Sabʻ in Contemporary Beersheba

From Bi'r al-Sabʻ to Beersheba

On March 30, 2000, Nuri al-Ukbi, a longtime activist for Bedouins' rights in the Israeli Negev (the semi-arid region in the south of the country) spraypainted "The Grand Mosque of Beersheba" on the closed gate of the Ottoman mosque of Beersheba (Nir 2001). This was inscribed in both Arabic and Hebrew.[2] While doing so, he also damaged a municipal billboard declaring the place a museum. He was duly arrested by the police for a violation of the public order, and was hauled into court a year later to be tried for this offence. The timing of this act of defiance and civil protest was not picked at random and was part of the unique day of commemoration called *yawm al-ard*, literally meaning "Land Day," which is celebrated annually by Israeli Palestinian communities on March 30 (Nakhleh 2011). It follows the day of the general strike held on March 30, 1976, among Palestinian communities in Israel to protest government plans to appropriate Israeli-Palestinian citizens' land in the Galilee. Since then, this day has come to symbolize the Palestinian struggle against Israeli plans, policies, and discriminatory practices against Palestinian communities and their determination to remain steadfast on their land (i.e., *sumud*). Al-Uqbi's protest is but one episode in a long-term struggle of Muslim, mostly Bedouin, citizens in the town of Beersheba and the surrounding communities to reopen the closed mosque and renew its former capacity as a Muslim house of prayers. The mosque of Beersheba is an intriguing case in point, as over its century-long history, it has gained profound meanings and deep veneration by its respective urban and regional communities in response to geopolitical transformations in the region. To understand these changes and the alternate significance this mosque has assumed since its construction, let us go back to the establishment of the new township of Beersheba by the Ottoman Empire in the 1900s.

During the late nineteenth century, the Ottoman Empire underwent major transformations, among them a renewed concern with its Arab provinces, particularly the southern parts of Syria namely the contemporary Israeli region of the Negev. There were several motivations for this new policy, among them the need to control and consolidate the nomadic tribes (Bedouins) residing in a border region that faced the growing influence of the British Empire in Egypt and beyond (Lewis 1961; Avci 2009). One of the outcomes that facilitated better control on the generally unmanageable tribes of the Negev (Arabic: al-Naqab) was the establishment of a new sub-district (*kaza*), to be followed by the construction of a new administrative center by the name of Biʾr al-Sabʿ (Beersheba) (Luz 2005b). The city was planned along a grid pattern, and most official and public buildings were constructed at its very center, among them the government house (*saraya*), the governor's house, a police station, a post office and telegraph station, and indeed, a luxurious and conspicuous central mosque (Berman 1965). Like many other colonial powers, the Ottomans exploited the most concise and efficient plan to convey a clear message regarding the identity and nature of their hegemonic power (Luz 2008b).

The establishment of Biʾr al-Sabʿ, along with the rearrangement of the regional administration, diminished the Bedouin threat by the beginning of the twentieth century. The establishment of the new town was a profound change and a deep intrusion into the nomads' way of life (Gelber 1986). At the beginning, this certainly did not bode well for the local tribes and the Ottomans had to maneuver very delicately between oppression and coercion to quell sporadic Bedouin rebellions or the possibility of such reactions (Nasasra 2015). The location, architecture, and ornamentation of the Ottoman Grand Mosque convey these dual—at times conflicting—meanings. The mosque was built at the behest of local Bedouins, a term that usually designates nomads, who had already moved to the new town and was built on *waqf* (endowment) land donated by the tribespeople after collecting donations from Bedouin shaykhs (Nasasra 2017). This notwithstanding, the compound as it was located in the budding city, and surely the symbols it bore, was another symbolic landmark of the sultanic presence in the town. The building bears the sultan's monogram (*tuğra*) on its heavily ornamented entrance and features some of the latest fashions to be found in Istanbul at the time (Luz 2005b). The minaret is a highly conspicuous edifice of fine craftsmanship, which ultimately became the sign of the new town and the omnipresence of the Ottoman Empire (often referred to as the Sublime Porte) in the region. The mosque gained recognition and was regarded as an architectural gem by the local population, admired for its beauty and august presence in the town (al-ʿAref 1999).

During the British Mandate, the mosque was often the preferred location for highly political speeches and declarations on the part of local Bedouin and Palestinian leaders of the region. (In the current context, by "Bedouins" I mean the nomadic Arab-Muslim tribes of the region and "Palestinians" refers to urban and settled communities.) These gatherings in the mosque were mainly connected to the growing tensions between the Bedouins and the mandatory

Figure 4.1 Mosque of Beersheba 2022 (courtesy of Dr. Mansour Nasasra).

regime particularly during the major Arab Revolt (1936–9) (Nasasra 2017). It was considered the most important mosque of the region (Shimoni 1947). And like the entire region, the mosque was about to experience dramatical changes following the establishment of the State of Israel.

From Mosque to Museum: The Unsuccessful Struggle of the Local Muslim-Palestinian Community

On the eve of the 1948 War Bi'r al-Sabʿ was predominantly an Arab town with a population of circa 6,000 people. On May 15, 1948 (during the 1948 War), the State of Israel was founded and quickly established the Israel Defense Forces (hereafter IDF). In October 1948 the city was conquered by the IDF and most of its Palestinian inhabitants either fled prior to the conquest or were forced out of the city following it; thus the city was emptied of most of its former population (Morris 1991). Shortly after the war, the mosque was used as a court and a detention center.[3] In 1953 it was handed to the municipality which converted it into the Museum of the Negev. The museum closed down in 1991, following a "hazardous building" warrant from the municipal engineer. It remained closed for eleven years, until a petition was submitted to the Israeli Supreme Court (HCJ) by several civil rights organizations, along with Muslim citizens of Beersheba (Adallah 2002). The gist of their demands was that the municipality renovate the mosque and reopen it for prayers. This was not the first nor the last time the mosque became a battleground between Muslim communities and the Beersheba municipality and state agencies. Since the 1970s the mosque had time and again become an arena of confrontation between the municipality and the city's slowly growing Muslim community, civil rights organizations, and Muslim religious and national figures. As early as 1974, Nuri al-Ukbi, as the chair of the Committee for Bedouin Rights, approached the municipality, as well as several governmental agencies, demanding the reopening of the mosque. Even though he received initial approval from the Ministry of Religion, his request was denied by the municipality on the grounds that "there are no Muslim residents in Beersheba." This demographic reasoning would appear in later episodes of the same conflict. This claim was dubious when it was first made in the 1970s, and certainly became even more misleading as time passed and the number of Muslim residents in Beersheba grew steadily.[4] This was the outcome of a number of combined processes. The growing need for skilled and highly educated professionals, be it in the regional hospital located in Beersheba or teachers for the local Bedouin communities, as well as faculty of Ben-Gurion University also located in the city, has swelled the ranks of professional Palestinian-Israelis in town overtime. Among them are also the main activists who signed the said petition. The petition was also rejected on the grounds that it was submitted by politically motivated non-residents of the city, to incite and exacerbate an already complex problem (Reiter 2017). Another argument that features in both municipality and state responses to this request relies on security reasons. Since 1948 an army base has been located opposite the mosque and hence the authorities expressed concern that opening the mosque would be hazardous. Put bluntly, they were worried about the possibility of Muslims assembling at the mosque five times a day near an army camp. The petitioners were not deterred, and during the 1980s several attempts were made to reopen the mosque (Reiter and Lehrs 2013). In June 1997, another petition was submitted to the Minister of Religion, expressing grave concern regarding the physical survival of the mosque and therefore demanding it be turned over to the urban Muslim community of Beersheba. This was also complemented with receiving permission from the police for a public prayer session by the mosque. Upon hearing about this initiative, Eli Boker, a member of the municipal council during the 1990s and a steadfast opponent of all initiatives to restore the mosque into Muslim hands made sure that municipal workers spread manure on the main lawn facing the mosque on the eve of the prayer. This did not deter the Muslim devotees, who came prepared with layers of canvas and conducted the prayer as Jewish demonstrators faced them, shouting "Beersheba is for Jews" (Shchada ibn Bari, oral communication, August 2, 2022).[5] When all options were exhausted, the activists along with several civil rights organizations submitted a brief (2002) to the Supreme Court. It was only in 2011 that the court arrived at a final ruling, decreeing that the compound should remain a museum, as it had been since 1953. However, the decision also stated that "the purpose of the structure would be a museum that would be devoted uniquely to Islamic culture and the Peoples of the East" (HJC 2011). In an interview conducted with Eli Boker following the decision of the Supreme Court, he explained why the mosque must remain in its present capacity:

> Beersheba will never be considered a mixed city.... Its identity must remain Jewish.... In 1948 our commandos conquered the mosque first; it is the symbol of the conquest of Beersheba.
> (interview, July 1, 2011; cited in Reiter 2017: 213)

This analysis certainly raises questions which are fundamental to the ongoing internal discussion regarding the Jewish versus democratic nature of the state of Israel. Against the claims of Israeli-Palestinians for reparation and restitution of land and heritage sites, there is mounting Jewish opposition to such arguments. Shortly after the Supreme Court published its ruling, the protests were renewed upon learning that the municipality was about to hold a wine festival which was slated to take place in the courtyard of the mosque (Kais 2022). The steering committee of the Arabs of the Negev hurriedly put up a protest tent by the mosque, as they were outraged by the probable consumption of alcohol at the mosque. This time the protest went global and Muslim leaders from across the Middle East responded and condemned Israel for "lack of respect for Islam." The Beersheba Municipality said in response: "The festival will not take place inside the museum, but in the courtyard between it and the Negev Museum. During the past few years, the event took place with exemplary quiet and without any disturbance or complaints. It's unclear why the complaints are being made now" (Yagne and Khoury 2001). This was not the last time the municipality's conduct at the mosque would steer local Muslim residents to protest what they considered to be a violation of a Muslim sacred place, indeed a metaphorical act against their very existence, both past and present, in the city (al-Tihi 2022).

On Friday, July 2, 2022, a demonstration was held at the mosque by Muslim activists, protesting public events initiated by the municipality during which alcoholic beverages were on offer. When interviewed about this by a local radio station, Shimon Tubul, the vice-mayor, responded in the following manner:

> I do not think we need to legitimize them [the demonstrators—N.L.], they are a bunch of bored people. Since 1953 the place is not a mosque. There is a group of people with vested interests who try to achieve political legitimation and gains. No mosque will be built in Beersheba and this compound will remain a museum. Beersheba is a Jewish city, traditional and a city of people who care deeply about Judaism, about the Bible and if you want to "do politics," go to Rahat and Hura [Bedouin towns established by the state near Beersheba—N.L.].
>
> Q: So how many Muslims are in town?
> A: Very few. We are talking about dozens and not hundreds, and certainly not thousands.
>
> (Tubul 2022)

I ask S. if indeed there are so few Muslims in the city. S. was born and raised in one of the satellite Bedouin villages that emerged in the hinterland of Beersheba since 1948. Due to his position as faculty at Ben-Gurion University in Beersheba, he moved to the city. According to him, there are many Muslim-Bedouins who come to town for work, shopping, or for municipal facilities which the state usually denies the Bedouin settlements, regardless of their size. In his estimation, Beersheba serves tens of thousands of nonresident Muslim citizens a day, who would certainly appreciate a mosque that could cater their needs while in town. He is puzzled by the 2011 decision to transform a mosque into a museum, which according to him "less people than the fingers on one hand enter." Furthermore, he laments the lack of sensitivity on the part of the municipality and the museum director for organizing events during which alcohol is consumed. As a Muslim who resides in town, he estimates there are some 20,000 Muslim residents whose very existence the municipality traditionally denies, and therefore provides not even one mosque in town for them. This policy makes these citizens transparent or even non-existent. For S., the most disheartening thing is the fact that his city is denied to him and nothing in it represents him: "I also want to belong and to be part of the city's landscape and for my culture also to be part of the urban sphere" (oral communication, July 31, 2022). Specifically, as a practicing Muslim the current situation forces him to pray at home, except for the Friday noon prayer, for which he drives to his hometown mosque. His analysis echoes Sandercock's almost utopic vision of a just city where all groups are represented. In the case of the Muslim residents of Beersheba and their mosque, the right to the city is yet a distant, currently unattainable goal. Against the ongoing and relentless efforts (and blatant denial or myopia) of officials at both urban and national scales, Beersheba is gradually becoming a mixed city. In the current Israeli context, this is a very charged and laden concept. Initially the term referred to pre-1948 Palestinian urban centers that following the war were transformed from predominantly Arab majority cities into Jewish towns with a small Palestinian minority (Monterescu and Rabinowitz 2007). Beersheba was not considered among them, and yet, like other cities in Israel it is becoming de facto a mixed city, much to the chagrin of its municipality. As long as the denial is successful, these municipalities, as portrayed in S.'s narration of his life in Beersheba, can remain free to refuse to provide municipal services to this allegedly nonexistent minority. In the prolonged struggle over the mosque, on the one hand the descaling of the ethnonational conflict to the urban level was readily apparent, while at the same time also upscaling the conflict by allowing players from the national level to engage in this urban conflict. The case of the Hassan Bek Mosque in Tel Aviv-Jaffa represents a more successful struggle of a minority group to cling to its sacred place, as will be narrated in the following paragraphs.

The Hassan Bek Mosque Conflict and the Semiotic of a Minaret in a Mixed Israeli City

Semiotic Readings of Hassan Bek Mosque

'Abd al-Qadir Satil is an Israeli-Palestinian who was born and still resides in Jaffa. He is one of the more prominent activists struggling for equal rights for the Arab community of Jaffa. When interviewed in 2001–3 about the mosque affair, he was serving as the chairperson of al-Rabita—the League for the Arabs of Jaffa. As part of his efforts to commemorate Jaffa's Palestinian past, he conducts tours in Jaffa, mostly for Jewish-Israelis. For him, the mosque and certainly its minaret is a landmark of the utmost importance and an aide-memoire device for his "history" of the city:

> During the tours I show them Palestinian Jaffa and I present them with facts on the ground. I introduce them to the neighborhood of Manshiyya, its past and what survived until today, and all that is left is the mosque of Hassan Bek, which is more a symbol than a mosque. Hassan Bek is a compass for the people of Jaffa: here was my neighborhood, from here I would go to the house of this and

that. It is our only possession in this neighborhood which was our neighborhood and was subjected to a transfer of the entire community ... Hassan Bek is an anchor and a symbol for the Arabs of Jaffa. Everyone knows how to find the place that was one's house according to the minaret of Hassan Bek.

(interview, October 21, 2001)

His analysis portrays the minaret as a landmark of yearning and a symbol of a lost Palestinian past. The visibility of the minaret acts as a form of agency. Visibility as a form of agency, Göle suggests, comprises materiality of culture, aesthetic forms, dress codes, or architectural genres (2011). In a similar fashion to the dynamics that led to the minarets' ban in Switzerland, this form of agency does not sit well with the Jewish majority. It is hardly surprising, therefore, that Satil's narrative of the minaret is not shared by the Jewish majority. As late as 2005, the official site of Tel-Aviv municipality contained the following paragraph in the section devoted to the history of the city:

The city of Yafo [the Hebrew version of the toponym Jaffa—N.L.] was a center of activities and riots against the residents of Tel Aviv since its establishment. The Arabs turned the Yafo neighborhood of Manshiyya to a frontline outpost against Tel Aviv, and from the height of the Hassan Bek Mosque Arab snipers fired on Tel Aviv and were responsible for many causalities ... Yafo surrendered on May 13, 1948.... The mayor of Tel Aviv at the time decided that it would be appropriate that the Hebrew city that emerged from Yafo should reunite with it and thus the merging of Tel Aviv and Yafo was declared. On October 4, 1949, exactly 40 years after the foundation of Tel Aviv, the first Hebrew city embraced defeated Yafo, after serving as one of its urban suburbs for many years.

(www.tel-aviv.gov.il)

This short passage appeared the municipal website during the years (2001–8) I was conducting my ethnographies involving the Hassan Bek Mosque conflict. Firstly, it conveys a different semiotic reading of the materiality of mosque and minaret than that narrated by Satil. Secondly, it is no longer to be found, as in the time that elapsed since then, the municipality has put up a new website and it stands to reason that someone realized that there might be more accommodating ways to narrate the city's history for its Palestinian citizens. This was also one of the outcomes of what Monterescu defines as the fourth moment in the contentious relations between Jaffa and Tel Aviv following the civil unrest of October 2000, which suggests "the emergence of new conditions of possibility for coming to terms with Jaffa's past and present from a post-Orientalist position. Thus, the exotic strangeness that characterized the Orientalist imagination of Jaffa since the founding of Tel-Aviv gave way to new political claims for equal citizenship, bi-national collaboration, and Palestinian presence" (Monterescu 2009: 650). This will be explained in the next paragraphs as I engage in an analysis of the mosque against developments in the urban sphere. However, crude as this short historical narrative might be, it is indeed an abridged version of the ethnonational conflict as it unfolded between the two urban entities that ultimately merged into one following the 1948 war. It also supplies us with the initial background for understanding the two opposing semiotic readings of the materiality of the minaret of Hassan Bek.

The Premeditated Erasure of Manshiyya

During the late nineteenth century Jaffa became the political, intellectual, and definitely the most important economic center of Palestinian society, which endowed it with the title "the Bride of Palestine" (Arabic: *'Arus Filastin*; LeVine 2005; Monterescu 2015). The city experienced an economic and demographic prosperity which also brought about significant changes in its urban development, among them the building of a new suburb named Manshiyya at the northernmost edge of the city. In 1914, a new and highly entrepreneurial Ottoman regional governor, by the name of Hassan Bek al-Jabi, was appointed. Even though these were the troubled years of the First World War and despite the general decline of the Ottoman Empire, he initiated many building projects in the city, among them a mosque bearing his name in the ethnically mixed blue-colored suburb of Manshiyya (Dabagh 1972). One may only surmise as to Hassan Bek's motivations for that building spree in such uncertain times, but it stands to reason that the conspicuous mosque with its decorated minaret was also intended to set a cultural-religious-symbolic boundary against the rapidly growing modern Jewish suburb of Tel Aviv, which was inaugurated in 1909 due north of Jaffa. This new suburb (and city in the making) was, since it was first conceptualized and surely following its inception, conceived as antithetic to Palestinian Jaffa (Rotbard 2005). It expanded very quickly through a series of land purchases that were clearly intended to block Manshiyya's northward expansion. This probably prompted Hassan Bek to build farther north into Manshiyya and construct the imposing mosque as an authoritative symbol competing with fast-growing Jewish Tel Aviv (LeVine 2005). During the Mandate Period (1920–48), these two urban entities continued this cat-and-mouse expansion and rivalry and quickly became each other's nemesis. The Jaffa/Tel-Aviv area became a focal point of the escalating national conflict between Palestinian Arabs and Jews. The "contact zone" between them, the mixed border neighborhood of Manshiyya, featured time and again as the place where these encounters were spatialized. Indeed, this would not be the last time Manshiyya served as a microcosm, a condensed multilayered symbol of the escalating Jewish-Arab conflict. Against the growing mutual hostility, most of the Jewish residents of Manshiyya left and moved north to Tel Aviv by 1943 (LeVine 2005). Following UN Resolution 181 in November 1947, which divided Palestine into two states, symbolic-cultural urban borders became concrete, and practically war zones, between Jaffa and Tel Aviv. From December 1947 to April 1948, Manshiyya effectively became a military outpost of Jaffa's armed militants, with the minaret of the Hassan Bek Mosque featuring as the favorite spot from which snipers shot at random on civilians in Tel Aviv (Hamuda 1985; interview with Shlomo Lahat, former mayor of Tel Aviv-Yafo, November 5, 2001). In late April 1948, Manshiyya was conquered by a Jewish paramilitary organization (IZL), which also completed the entire conquest of Jaffa on May 13, 1948 (Morris 1987).

The tables had now turned, and the small, newly established suburb was now in control of the historic Palestinian city, of which only a fraction of its former 70,000 inhabitants remained (Golan 2001). The residual Jaffan community of some 3,500 people was concentrated in the southern neighborhoods of the city. Manshiyya was emptied of its former population and the gates of the Hassan Bek Mosque were closed (Fabian 1999). Jaffa, a city that boasts one of the world's longest urban histories, ceased to exist as an autonomous entity and on August 18, 1950, was officially annexed to the municipality of Tel Aviv, to be known hereafter as Tel Aviv-Yafo (Golan 1995). In the wake of the war, the young State of Israel constructed highly sophisticated legal mechanisms to ensure its control and the transfer of ownership of about 5 million dunums of former Palestinian lands and a myriad of public compounds, including religious institutions (*awqaf*), houses, and more, in both rural and urban environments as the spoils of war (Kedar 2000; Naamnih 2018).

These vast tracts of land, formerly belonging to Palestinians who were defined by the new state as absentees, were handled by the Custodian of Absentee Property, operating according to the Absentee Property Law (1950) (Israel Book of Laws 37/b, March 1950). Section 19a of the said law allowed the Custodian to sell the land only to another government agency, called the Development Authority (Kedar 2000). In practice, this section ensured that absentee-owned land and property would be sold only for purposes approved by the state and suiting its agenda. In 1965, following an amendment (29/b) to the Absentee Law, a new legal entity called the Muslim Charitable Trust was formed in seven municipalities where substantial Muslim land and properties still existed. Allegedly, these trusts were established to ensure better care of Muslim properties by their respective communities. However, these trusts were only allowed to manage property released to them by the Custodian. Additionally, the people nominated to the trusts were handpicked by the state, not the community, to ensure their cooperation (interview with Ilan Sharqon, May 11, 2003).[6] Initially, the state-appointed committees were heavily scrutinized by the state and could only release their entrusted properties to a Jewish third party (interview with Victor Herzberg, July 22, 2003).[7] This is the background against which the Hassan Bek conflict emerged.

The Struggle over the Mosque: Early Beginnings

The conflict started in 1973, when the Muslim Charitable Trust of Jaffa approved a covert (at first) transaction, which leased the mosque compound to a Jewish entrepreneur by the name of Gershon Peres. The transaction was made public when one of the trust members approached both the press and the courts asking for the annulment of the contract, on the grounds that it was illegal. This was the first time the Jaffa community was made aware that the trust had leased the mosque for forty-nine years, to be transformed into a tourist and shopping center (Tel Aviv-Yafo Archives, 146–724). This was another step in implementing the Tel Aviv municipality's urban planning policy and master plan, according to which the area of Manshiyya and its mosque would serve as part of the newly planned Central Business District and an urban recreational park by the seaside (Hashimshony 1968). Prior to that, and under the guise of constructing Manshiyya as a contact zone between Tel-Aviv and Jaffa during the 1960s and early 1970s, most of the neighborhood's houses were razed to the ground (Alexandrowicz 2013). The old, historic Palestinian Jaffa was erased from the urban landscape and succumbed to modernistic planning, and especially to the habitus of officials in municipal and national planning agencies (Hatuka and Kallus 2006; interview with Shmuel Penn, September 9, 2002).[8] This was surely part of the municipality's overall strategy, accurately defined by LeVine as "erasure and re-inscription" (2005). The Hassan Bek Mosque was saved from the same fate as it was earmarked for conservation as an historical building. However, the complete annihilation of the neighborhood to which it belonged left it as a prominent and highly conspicuous landmark. This visibility and contentious materiality were to feature in the nearly three decades' struggle to reinstate it as an active mosque and return it to the Jaffa Muslim community, as will be narrated below.

Since 1948 and the annexation to Tel Aviv, the gates of the mosque had remained closed. Over the years the structure began to deteriorate, its roof caved in, and it was mainly used for activities typical of blighted urban areas: a den for drug trafficking, prostitution, and the occasional garbage dump (interview with Nassim Shaqar, March 15, 2001).[9] Following the creation of the Jaffa Charitable Trust in 1967 and in line with the city planning programs, the time was deemed ripe for the implementation of the next phase in the "erasure and re-inscription" policy and the elimination, or at least mitigation, of the mosque's visibility and impact. Peres, the entrepreneur, recalls how he was approached by a few people, among them the mayor of Tel-Aviv at the time, and was asked to "lend a hand" and assist them in getting rid of the mosque:

> Rabinowitz [mayor of Tel Aviv] saw that the south [namely, Jaffa] was decaying and all of a sudden there is this mosque of Hassan Bek that was deserted ... while at the same time people began to put in gigantic investment in hotels and this [the mosque] was like a thorn in the flesh of the system.... So they paid money [to the Jaffa Charitable Trust] but they did not deliver ... they told me do it as a service for the state ... so I met with the Trust people and told them: Listen, guys, there is no money here but for once in your lives put a smile on your faces, and we will all work together ... but I told them: keep your mouth shut or else it will be noisy and dirty.
>
> (interview with Gershon Peres, June 15, 2002)

And noisy and dirty it became. It should be recalled one of the trust members went public in 1973 and revealed to the Jaffa community the shady details of the deal, which included also bribe money delivered covertly to trust members to relinquish Hassan Bek. Notwithstanding, the transaction was signed and sealed on November 11, 1974, and Peres committed to renovate the mosque and preserve it as part of a new shopping compound (interview with Victor Hertzberg, July 22, 2003).

However, the election of a new mayor in 1974, followed by the election of a rightwing government in 1977 and growing resistance from the Jaffa community, caused the project to grind to a halt, even though it was approved by the municipal planning committee in 1981 (Luz 2005a). Resistance started in the 1970s with 'Abd Badawi Kabub, a Muslim citizen of Jaffa who, upon hearing

Figure 4.2 The proposed plan for the Hassan Bek tourist compound.

about the transaction, formed the al-Maqasid Islamic Association of Jaffa, with the sole purpose of stopping the Hassan Bek transaction (interview with 'Abd Badawi Kabub, September 29, 2003). But while Kabub and his colleagues were conducting the struggle in what he himself called a "polite and civilized manner," a new NGO named al-Rabita—the League of Jaffa's Arabs adopted a much more confrontational approach.

Winning Back the Mosque: The Rabita and the Renovation Process

The Rabita was formed in 1979 by the first generation of Jaffa Arabs who were born into the State of Israel and were much better equipped to demand their rights against official agencies. The Rabita entailed both Muslims and Christians, secular and religious, working together to empower the Arab community, and strengthen its Palestinian Arab identity (interview with 'Abd Satil, October 21, 2001). When the Hassan Bek transaction was approved by the municipal planning committee, Kabub organized a protest prayer at the mosque, which was indeed the first prayer held there since 1948. Inasmuch as Kabub was trying to walk the middle ground and coordinate his struggle with Lahat, the new mayor, the members of the Rabita seized this opportunity to express their discontent with the meek and subservient conduct of Jaffa's old guard. It was indeed time for a generational change in the leadership:

> To us, in the Rabita, it was clear that since this [the mosque] is the last relic that memorializes the Arab existence in Manshiyya.... And as you well know, that if one sees such a relic, one understands that Tel Aviv was not a wasteland as we were taught in fourth grade books, but one learns that here was a neighborhood and it had a mosque and it had a cemetery and it had a life, and this life was ruined. And from all that, only Hassan Bek remained, which is why the struggle was symbolic, and this is why we felt that whoever wanted to topple the mosque ... and who ever neglected the place, wanted to destroy it. And why was it neglected? It was neglected and its community was forbidden to pray therein so it would collapse and then the last memory of the Palestinian community of Tel Aviv would also fade.... So, when I got a call one day and this journalist on the other side of the line informs me about the approval of the development plan by the Municipal Planning and Building Committee to transform the mosque into a commercial center, boom boom boom! We immediately prepared ourselves [to struggle] against this development.
> (interview with Nassim Shaqar, March 15, 2001)

Elsewhere I have described at length the ins and outs of this complex public and legal conflict that stretched over a decade and ended with the government's repudiation of the transaction in late 1981 (Luz 2005a). I would argue that it was not in the legal or political sphere that the struggle against the development plan was won, but in the realm of the semiotics of its minaret and the shockwaves in the Jaffa Arab community, prompted by the changes in its materiality.

On April 2, 1983, the minaret of Hassan Bek collapsed. According to the municipal officials and police experts, this was an unintentional misfortune inflicted by the poor state of the compound (interview with Shmuel Penn, September 9, 2002). That said, the community's unwavering conclusion to date is that the collapse of the minaret was deliberate sabotage (interview with Samih Tuhi, December 20, 2001; interview with Yusuf Reyhan, August 18, 2003).[10] The Rabita, as a non-religious association which includes both Muslims and Christians, worked under the assumption that the mosque is first and foremost a Palestinian national symbol, and as such should be reconstructed and reinitiated into the urban landscape (interview with Nachla Shaqar, May 11, 2003). Kabub, who by that time was nominated as the chair of the Jaffa Muslim Trust, pursued a different philosophy that confined the mosque to its purely religious function. This is but one reminder that the Arab community was neither cohesive nor united, and there were indeed various forces over the years who pushed in different directions and had conflicting views on what the best course of action for the community and for the mosque might be. The Rabita's approach proved to be the most effective in the struggle, as they were not intimidated by nor shied from confronting state and municipal agencies. As part of their efforts to encourage public support, they published a booklet about the mosque history calling themselves, for the purpose of the publication, the Committee for the Defense of Hassan Bek. The following is their narrative regarding the collapse of the minaret and the ample meanings it conveys. It involves a very critical spatio-political analysis and critique of the erasue of Manshiyya and—what was already underway—the transformation of the area into a commercial and tourist zone:

> What is the meaning of an Islamic mosque among the crowded hotels that were founded on the ruined houses of Manshiyya? What is the meaning of the survival of its mosque, which is a symbol of Islam, in the middle of hotels designed to cater for Westerners who support Israel? Joshua Rabinowitz, the former mayor, saw it is a sign of disgrace that needed to be eliminated ... the minaret is the only symbol of the entire mosque and therefore once it fell, one would assume it would be easier to get rid of the mosque ... the conclusion of both the police and Tel Aviv's engineers is that the fall of the minaret was caused by heavy rains, but this conclusion does not convince the people of Jaffa, who were greatly shocked by its collapse. This criminal act led to their firm resolution to protect the mosque.
>
> (Hamuda 1985: 40–1)

As the mosque was legally an absentee property (i.e., not under the management of the Jaffa Charitable Trust), the Rabita received informal approval from the mayor to rebuild the minaret. However, against their verbal commitment not to deviate from the previous plan of the mosque, the Rabita extended the original height of the minaret by 130 centimeters (interview with Shlomo Lahat, November 5, 2001; interview with Shamai Assif, September 4, 2002).[11] In late 1985 the mosque was handed back to the Jaffa Charitable Trust. This was the end result of fifteen years of struggle, during which different forces among the community were working toward that aim (interview with Ahmad Asfur, November 27, 2003). The renovation of the mosque required the cooperation of different factions within Jaffa's Arab community. It also entailed going global and receiving donations from both the Hashemite Kingdom of Jordan and Saudi Arabia (interview with Nachla Shaqar, May 11, 2003). Following a festive inauguration ceremony on May 21, 1994, during 'Id al-Adha (the Muslim Feast of the Sacrifice), the mosque resumed its original functions and since then it is regularly used for prayers (interview with Yusuf Reyhan, August 18, 2003).

In a picture of the mosque with the David Intercontinental Hotel in the background that I took in 2003, it is easy to read the semiotics of an Islamic-Palestinian historical landmark in the midst of a rejuvenated modernistic area of Jewish Tel-Aviv. I should however alert the reader that the picture misrepresents the "real" differences in heights between the approximately 12 m. minaret and the circa 80 m. hotel. And yet, it precisely narrates the diametrical readings of the mosque among the majority and minority groups in the city, and in particular, the politics involved in its very existence.

Another aspect, hitherto neglected and surely underplayed in my take on the "right to the city," is the relationship, power-structure, and scalar-politics involved in political-economic restructuring and urban governance, namely, global capital effects on the urban sphere. It should be recalled that the booklet published by the Rabita during the heated years of the struggle alluded to the mosque as a "symbol of Islam in the middle of hotels designed to cater for Westerners who support Israel." The erection of a grand, modern hotel on the ruins of historic Manshiyya is surely a pertinent case in point of the intricate scalar politics at national and supranational scales, and of the ways capital is shaping current cities. This rescaling demonstrates how urban citizens' basic right to their city is disenfranchised as the responsibility and authority of the urban scale devolve and succumb to national and supra-national powers (Purcell 2002). These changes in urban governance and the growing impact of global capital have certainly curtailed urban inhabitants' abilities to affect and be part of the decision-making process that shape their city (Peck 1998). In the case of the Hassan Bek Mosque, what seemed to deflect and thwart the power of capital—at various scalar settings—to take over the mosque is the power of the sacred and the intricate politics it entails.

The struggle of the subaltern Jaffan community ended successfully and unlike the mosque of Beersheba, the Hassan Bek Mosque "came home." However, the community' relative unity was quickly shattered. By 1996, following the split in the Israeli Islamic Movement the mosque changed hands and since then is governed by the "Council of Jaffa," which is an offshoot of the Islamic Movement—Northern Branch headed by Shaykh Raid Salah.[12] Most of the

Figure 4.3 Mosque of Hassan Bek against the David Intercontinental Hotel.

activists who were interviewed (as they had a pivotal role in the struggle) lament this situation and admit that they no longer visit there. Basam Abu-Zayd is a former member of the trust and a former imam of a mosque in Jaffa. He is still very active in the community, and sadly and candidly narrates this situation:

> Hassan Bek is now in the hands of Raid Salah's guys, I will tell you we are going against each other … this is not good for Jaffa, and I tried to talk to the people but to no avail.
>
> (interview, September 4, 2003)

The mosque was again in the eye of a storm during the Second Intifada, alternatively known as the al-Aqsa Intifada. On June 1, 2001, a Palestinian suicide bomber detonated himself in a crowded night club, and consequently twenty-one people, mostly teenagers, were killed, and 120 were wounded. The following morning, a few hundred people gathered around the Hassan Bek Mosque, which is across the street from the site of the attack, and besieged the place while throwing stones at it. The word on the street was that the suicide bomber spent the night before the attack within the mosque's precinct. Eliran, a 23-year-old Jewish man, from a nearby town, was particularly resourceful in the stone throwing department. He explained his behavior thus:

> Last night I turned on the television around midnight and learned that there was another attack. People cannot take it anymore. Everyday 5–10 more people are killed. I am afraid to wake up tomorrow to learn that my uncle, or someone else in my family, was killed. In one split second they take your life, and I am too young to die.

As the reporter persisted and tried to understand why the mosque was targeted specifically, he replied: "Go figure, maybe he (i.e., the suicide bomber) spent the night here and probably even got their blessings" (Waqid and Pais 2001). The uncanny ease of connecting this deadly bombing with the mosque speaks volumes for the importance of materiality, and certainly for the alternate reading of the mosque's materiality among different groups both at the urban scale and among Israeli society at large. Hassan Bek Mosque, from its very beginning, has been in between these two conflicted communities. The struggle over it on the urban scale is also part and parcel of the national conflict, descaled into the city. Its materiality is a mnemonic device for both Jewish and Palestinian communities in town. While for the minority it stands as a sign of resistance, endurance, and belonging, it constantly constructs a complex and undesired geography of the other in the predominantly Jewish city. Geography, to use LeVine's metaphor in a slightly dodgy way, was apparently not completely overthrown. There were surely many reasons for the successful end of the Jaffa community struggle over the mosque. I highlighted a few of them and focused on the semiotics and impact of materiality on the unfolding of the conflict. However, the growing prowess of leading figures within the community, as well as changing dynamics within the municipality and indeed at the state level, was also contributing factors to the (successful) outcome for the Jaffa community.

As in the case of the mosque of Beersheba the struggle was also about belonging to one's city and clinging to one's heritage. Ahmad Asfur, who was very active, along with 'Abd Badawi Kabub, during the early stages of the Hassan Bey conflict, sums up concisely the reasons that enthused him and drove him to pursue this goal:

> This mosque is mine. Supposedly, Gershon Peres would have managed to destroy the mosque and construct those shops. My grandson would arrive there with his father and would not know anything … but now that it remains, your grandson would ask you what this minaret is, and he will know there were other people here. As soon as the mosque is no more, no one would ask, and should it

remain, your grandson would ask [about it]. There is a history here, and it is my history, and these are my roots, and religion has nothing to do with it.

(interview, November 27, 2003)

Asfur is surely not the only one who emphasizes the political aspects of the mosque and the politics that involved in the struggle. Against the ethnocratic nature of the municipal and national spheres, religion and ethnic-religious affiliation are bound to become important identity markers, regardless of one's individual stance and approach to belief. For Asfur, the mosque is an identity marker and a landmark of his community. The triumph of the community for him is that they managed to safekeep the mosque and thwart its erasure, frustrating both municipal and national agencies' plan to undermine its Palestinian roots. Furthermore, the real goal was achieved and that was to prevent the mosque from disappearing from the urban landscape, which is a spatialization of Asfur's personal and national history. Asfur's analysis stresses memory and materiality as crucial components of belonging to the city. Unknowingly, he echoes Sandercock's critique of the modern planner as a "thief of memory." She argues that one of the failings of modern planning is the unequal representation (and surely misrepresentation) of minority groups' landmarks by removing them from the urban landscape (Sandercock 1998).

For many of the people from the Arab community of Jaffa, the mosque was synonymous with their existence in the city. Therefore, a wide variety of people from both religious communities and those who define themselves as secular could join hands in the protracted struggle. This also explains why, when it finally returned to the community, its political-national component gave way to internal religious-political rivalries. This is surely part and parcel of the inescapable political nature of sacred places. The materiality of the mosque was also a key factor in its unfolding history, ever since it was constructed in the late Ottoman period up to the present. It started out as landmark intended to frustrate Jewish expansion in the newly established suburb of Tel Aviv, becoming a military outpost during the conflictual decades leading to the 1948 war. Following the war, it turned into a "thorn in the flesh" of the development of "modern," "Jewish" Tel Aviv. It was nearly taken from the community, were it not for the struggle I discussed above.

* * *

For Henri Lefebvre, who advanced the idea, the "right to the city" implied more than the right of access or use of the entire city. It also inferred the right to influence the form and development of the city and to assign alternative meanings to the urban landscape. Following these thoughts, Leone Sandercock muses on the essence of a new type of planning needed for a just city:

> I want a city ... where city planning is a war of liberation fought against dumb, featureless public space as well as the multiple sources of oppression and domination and exploitation and violence; where citizens wrest from space new possibilities and immerse themselves in their cultures while respecting those of their neighbors, and collectively forging new hybrid cultures and space.
>
> (Sandercock 1998: 218–19)

Time and again, in the analysis of both urban conflicts these were exactly the sentiments expressed by members of the subaltern group aspiring for greater impact and influence on their city. In Israeli mixed cities, minorities' sacred places are found over and over at the very center of urban conflicts, as they become grounds where subaltern groups compete to share the city. This has to do, as I demonstrated in both cases, firstly, with the intrinsic contested nature of sacred places, and secondly, with the fact that they are replete with meaning which is there to be owned and controlled. Thirdly, as I emphasized here, it has to do with their materialities, their complex and often contradicting semiotics and visibility. Visibility, as argued by Göle, is a form of agency in the public domain. It comprises, among other things, materialities of culture and architectural styles (2011). But most of all, it is a discursive agency which is articulated through materialities and evokes semiotic readings. Following these semiotic interpretations, I was able to take up the challenge of the hidden (hi)stories of the politics of sacred places in the urban landscape. In tapping into the realms of materiality, I also wanted to offer a more expansive understanding of how cultural-political analysis of the sacred, and heavy engagement with matters of control and ownership, may benefit from introducing the ways in which people experience the landscape, and more specifically, matters of belief and religious objects. This understanding will inform the next chapter, as I introduce the concept of *ReligioCity* as a way to account for material expressions and influences of religion at the urban scale, through readings of urban infrastructures and matters of belief. Therefore, my analysis remains in the urban scale and looks at the numerous ways the religion(s) and religious actants are shaping and reading their city. Taking Acre, a multi-religious, multi-ethnic city as a case study, the chapter also expands the theory of urban ethnocracy by engaging with its religious dimensions and how it is played out through religious infrastructures. This will be complemented with a case study of decolonization through the sacred, that will be narrated by the struggle over the Lababidi Mosque.

5

ReligioCity and Decolonizing Acre through the Sacred

Urban Religion and the Urban Sphere

The study of urban religion is now a burgeoning field across several disciplines, ranging from sociology to anthropology, geography, urban planning, and more (Garbin and Strhan 2017). The cornucopia of studies engaging with the growing role of religion in the urban scale notwithstanding, religion, religious groups and organizations, and their ample impacts on cities are still greatly understudied and undertheorized in current critical urban theories (CUT). This can be discerned in the scholarly fascination with the idea of the "right to the city," which is mostly constructed as a way to respond to neoliberal urbanism (Purcell 2002). My engagement with this concept in Chapter 4 demonstrates clearly that it need be broadened to other aspects of the urban condition. Unpacking the right to the city through the religious factor seems even more sensible given the unparalleled urban growth entwined with the (re)emergence of religion in the public sphere (Casanova 1994; Berger 1999; Burchardt, Becci, and Casanova 2013). In 2018, an estimated 55.3 percent of the world's population lived in urban settlements. By 2030, urban areas are projected to house 60 percent of people globally and one in every three people will live in cities with at least half a million inhabitants (UN 2018). This fast-growing urbanization, combined with the de-secularization of cities, surely explains the growing interest in urban religions (Kong 1993b, 2005; Eade and Garbin 2006; Eade 2011; Dwyer, Gilbert, and Bindi 2013; Dwyer 2016). My long-time engagement with the urban sphere and urbanism on the one hand, and religion (mostly as a social-political category and through the exploration of the sacred) on the other hand, has convinced me that religion needs to be further engaged in urban theory in order to cover the range of explicit and hidden, tangible and intangible, ways in which it impacts the urban. This introspection is complemented by my growing interest in matters of belief or, as discussed above, materiality. This understanding was explained rather elegantly by Burchardt and Becci:

> Religious discourses, practices, and communities, like sacred spaces, are part of the urban experience, but they also contribute to changing the urban environment. Processes of collective and individual identity formation, of constructing and maintaining power relations, occur in cities on the local, national, and transnational levels, on each of which they are traversed by religious elements.
> (Becci, Casanova and Burckhardt 2013: 18)

Against this backdrop, I developed the concept of *ReligioCity* as a way to account for and understand the interrelated and intricate relations among cities and religions. Therefore, this chapter further studies the urban scale and offers *ReligioCity* as an umbrella term to understand both the tangible and intangible aspects of urban religion, religion in the city, and the reciprocal relations between religion(s) and city. That said, *ReligioCity* in Acre (as in other Israeli cities) is inescapably linked to the naissance and the development of Jewish Israeli society as a settler-colonial society. Settler-colonialism is theorized as an inclusive, land-centered project that coordinates a comprehensive range of agencies, from the metropolitan center to the frontier encampment, with a disposition of eliminating indigenous societies. Its operations are not dependent on the presence or absence of formal state institutions or functionaries (Wolfe 2006). While colonialism reproduces itself and the freedom and equality of the colonized is forever postponed, settler colonialism, by contrast, (supposedly) extinguishes itself. Settler colonialism justifies its operation on the basis of the expectation of its future demise. Colonialism and settler colonialism are not merely different; they are in some ways antithetical (Veracini 2010). However, as settler colonialism proves impervious to change, the main task of the colonized remains to challenge and alter its continuous domination and effects on political stratagems. Decolonization may take place when the exogenous colonizer departs but in settler societies, this is unlikely to happen. Therefore, equality between former colonizer and former colonized replaces a relationship of domination. Indeed, decolonization in the full sense of the word is that which enables the colonized to rupture the colonial cycle. Successful settler-colonies, suggests Veracini, end up establishing independent nations, effectively repressing, co-opting, and extinguishing indigenous alterities (Veracini 2010). Applied to the urban landscape of Acre, this facilitates a framing of decolonization (also) as the struggles of indigenous people to claim their past places, as will be narrated hereafter.

The chapter starts with a theoretical introduction to *ReligioCity*, and then takes Acre, a multi-religious and multi-ethnic mixed city in the north of Israel, as a case in point to study the intricate connections between religion and the urban sphere through religious infrastructures. This will be preceded by a contextualizing of the city by adding the concept of urban ethnocracy (following Yiftachel and Yacobi 2003) into the 'mix" of a multi-ethnic, multi-religious, "mixed" Israeli city. Following that, I engage with a plethora of voices of religious actants and their personal readings, needs, and visions of Acre that emerged from a decade of ethnographic survey in the context of religion and urban infrastructures in the city. The chapter concludes with an analysis of the struggle over the Lababidi Mosque under what I frame as the decolonization of the city. This engagement with colonization/decolonization theories permits a deeper insight into the role of urban religion(s) as a site of converging and conflicting visions and voices, practices, and orientations, which arise from the complex desires, needs, and fears of many different people in the context of urban ethnocracy.

ReligioCity Introduced: Toward a Theory of Urban Religion and Materiality

During the inauguration ceremony of a new upmarket neighborhood in Acre, designated for Jewish religious citizens, the city's chief rabbi declared: "We have yearned for many years, and we have dreamt of this moment … more strong families are arriving in Acre … and Acre will remain for ever and ever a Jewish town" (Yashar 2017). Given that Acre is a city composed of circa 70 percent Jews and 30 percent Arabs (both Muslims and Christians), one may wonder what is implied by his wish that Acre would "remain a Jewish town." Is it about making sure Acre remains a city in which Jews form a demographic majority? Perhaps other, more pertinent issues are concerned, which involve providing for more religious needs of Jews living in an urban environment? Taking a more radical interpretation, perhaps it is about a city for Jews only? I will leave the rabbi's yearnings to their own devices by suggesting that this is a case in point of the way religious affiliation combines with urban ethnocracy to heavily influence the mixed-Israeli city. Further still, it also highlights the influence of religious agents on urban infrastructures and, in this case, the planning and constructing of a new, gentrified and ethnically segregated neighborhood (Luz 2022b).

In his urban project, Lewis Wirth aspired to define the essence of the city and what is inferred by being urban (1938). He wanted to distill the fundamental nature of urban life, as opposed to other forms of human settlement, by asking whether cities give rise to distinct subjectivities. Surely, there is a flipside to this query and that is: do these urban "subjects" give rise to a distinct urbanism and urban spatialities? In recent years, these questions have become highly pertinent with regard to the growing impact of religion and belief systems on the urban sphere and their complex relations with each other (Orsi 1999; Tweed 2006; Qian and Kong 2017). These two categories of inquiry should be conceived as mutually constitutive, jointly shaping and being shaped in response to each other (Woods 2019). The re-emergence of religions and belief systems in the urban, and certainly the public, sphere (Casanova 1994) has already met with an abundance of explorations among geographers of religion (Kong 2010). A few theoretical notions have been proffered to grapple with these changes in urban environments. Al-Sayyad and Massoumi suggested the concept of the Fundamentalist City as an explanatory mechanism for the growing religious nature of cities (2010). Following Habermas's theory of post-secular modernity(ies) (2006; 2008), perceptions of cities as post-secular were soon to follow (Molendijk, Beaumont, and Jedan 2010; Beaumont and Baker 2011; Cloak and Beaumont 2013). Although in vogue, this understanding has already been criticized as not conducive to understanding cities. (Beckford 2012; Becci, Burchardt, and Casanova 2013). Wilford reminded us that our task is not to assess the extent to which religion in modernity has declined or increased, but rather to follow the ways "religious thought and practice changed in relation to modernization" (Wilford 2010: 333). Following Vatrovec's construction of cities as super-diverse (2007), Becci, Burchardt, and Giorda suggest religious super-diversity as a way to account for the plethora of religious innovations in cities (2017). Although not engaged solely with cities, della Dora developed the idea of moving from post-secular narratives to infrasecular geographies (2016). She thus aims to account for the fluidity of the sacred in everyday life and for what she defines as the "religious subconscious" that characterizes contemporary Western societies. However, one may ask, following Robinson, if this is conducive enough to promote a globalized theory of urban religion (2006). Qian and Kong suggested "religious urbanism" as a category of inquiry that prioritizes investigations into the ways in which urban space is negotiated by religious groups (Qian and Kong 2017: 1; Woods 2019). That said, recent debates among urban theorists, and particularly readings from the South or South-East (Parnell and Oldfield 2014; Roy 2014; Yiftachel 2016; but see also Peck 2015), caution us against unitary theories that offer one-size-fits-all conceptualizations of the urban. Against these crucial developments, I offer *ReligioCity* as a place-based dynamic concept to grapple with the role of religion(s) in cities rather than a unitary logic to account for faith within global-cities theorizing. As such, *ReligioCity* does not indicate a type or class of cities, nor does it address a certain "cityness," but rather it is a concept that opens myriads of opportunities to engage in urban-religion encounters and explore these intricate relations. *ReligioCity* needs be seen as a frame of reference, indeed a concept that allows us to account for urban-religion(s) dynamics and the importance and multifold influences of these intricate relations in cities.

The notion of *ReligioCity* fuses two broadly defined bodies of scholarship: the de-secularization of cities and the spatial turn in religious studies. Starting with Weber, urban sociologists and geographers have observed the modern city predominantly through a secularist lens (Lanz 2013). Thus, in tandem with the dominance of secularization theory, cities were considered bastions of the secular in which the influence of religion would ultimately diminish (Berger 1967). This assumption has continually eroded in recent decades, given numerous studies that demonstrated how the urban environment becomes the very material for innovative religious imagination and experiences and, of course, the mounting presence of religions in the urban public sphere (Eade and Garbin 2006; Dwyer, Gilbert, and Bindi 2013; Dwyer 2016). Individuals and groups are indeed placing their faith in the possibility of sustaining, projecting, or even reinventing a sense of self through urban religious place-making (Garbin 2012). This is but one aspect of *ReligioCity*, which now will be complemented by the theoretical impact of the material turn in religious studies.

Following the pioneering works of the likes of de Certeau (1984) and Latour (1996), both the humanities and the social sciences have taken a material turn (Hazard 2013). This means to suggest that material things and phenomena—objects, practices, places, built environment, landscape, bodies, sensations, affects, and so forth—are becoming pivotal in scholarly endeavors across a variety of disciplines. More pertinent to geography of religion, and following Lefbvre's theory on the production of space, Knott incorporated new spatial dimensions in the study of religion. Her seminal work presents us with a spatial methodology that allows for a critical study of religion in various scales and locations (2005; 2008; 2010). This was complemented with a material turn in the study of religion (Morgan 2010). Reincorporating phenomenological aspects of belief and the materiality of religions and belief systems is highly suggestive for the study of religious presence and influence in cities (Ash and Simpson 2016). While welcoming this development, I wish to add to the exploration of the urban context, the study of infrastructures through which material aspects become viable and can be further analyzed to account for both materiality and culture. In the current context, infrastructures are defined as socio-technical apparatuses and material artifacts that structure, enable, and govern circulation—of energy, information, goods, and capital, as well as people, practices, and images in the urban realm (Burchardt and Höhne 2015: 3). The study of infrastructures as outcomes of cultural and political processes opens the possibility of a research that dialogues between urban infrastructures (as part of the material aspects of the urban) and urban diversity (which also accounts for religions in the urban), as a way to explore politics and meaning in the urban built environment. In that sense, *ReligioCity* consists of the interconnectivity of urban infrastructures and the ways religion(s) are involved, influencing, and changing in contemporary cities by being part of their everyday politics. This allows incorporation of the ways religion and urban space are co-constitutively transformed by current socio-political processes, but also of the ways the city's landscape encompasses new expressions of religious materiality in the urban and is changing in their light. This enables an exploration of the city as an arena of competing forces that aim to shape, be, and place (and practice) belief in the city by competing for symbolic and tangible resources and thus influencing and changing the urban. *ReligioCity* takes into consideration religion and its spatialities, and new understandings that stem from recent explorations of the material aspects of the imagined and perceived (the phantasmatic, to borrow from Navaro-Yashin 2012), as to that which is the material of belief and organized religions. It marries Bourdieu's theory of religion (1980; 1985; 1991) as a field of symbolic goods to Knott's seminal exploration of "locating of religion" (2005; 2008; 2010), to reveal how, through the mediation of cognitive mechanisms operating at multiple entangled levels, the spatial manifestations of religion influence urban infrastructures and diversity and serve as a field where ideas, resources, identity politics, and belonging are being discussed, competed with, and altered. This theoretical construction was explored empirically through the study of urban infrastructures in Acre. Among other things, I looked at urban planning, religious services and structures, urban processions, education system, and impacts of religious organizations (faith-based organizations) on the urban landscape. In the next section, I will introduce Acre and discuss mostly recent urban developments against the notion of urban ethnocracy to further contextualize the city.

Contextualizing Acre: "Mixing" Religion into Urban Ethnocracy

Acre is a coastal town located on the shores of the Mediterranean in northern Israel. The city boasts a long and convoluted history, starting as early as the fourth millennium BCE which surely makes it one of the oldest living towns (Gibson and Negev 2001). Its natural harbor won it a unique importance which culminated during the latter part of the twelfth and thirteenth centuries CE, when the city became the formidable capital of the Crusaders' kingdom (Galili et al. 2010). Following the Mamluk conquest in 1291, Acre was deliberately destroyed, as a preemptive measure to prevent future crusades from arriving at its shores. Most of the city remained in ruins and sparsely populated until much later in the Ottoman period (Amitai 2017). After the Ottoman conquest in 1516, Acre became a regional capital and reached its height in the latter part of the eighteenth century (Ben-Bassat and Ben-Arzi 2016). Following the Napoleonic siege in 1799 and during the course of the nineteenth century, the city experienced several internal major armed conflicts which destroyed several compounds in town and caused havoc to its economy and demography (Philipp 2001). The emergence of Haifa as a major port during the second half of the nineteenth century was a leading factor in ensuring Acre's humble status as the capital of a small Ottoman administrative district (*sancak*). In 1840, following a short period of Egyptian rule, Acre returned to Ottoman rule which lasted until 1917. It experienced a slow process of urban recovery, mostly due to initiatives and urban projects instigated by the Ottoman administration. Part of the Ottoman efforts to revive the city was through implementing modern urban planning. The plan was suggested as early as 1909, but it was primarily executed during the British Mandate (1920–48) (Waterman 1971).

This early twentieth-century plan is still very much apparent in the central parts of the city, located between the seashores and the railway lines built by the British due east and two kilometers beyond the Old City. This central part, due north of the historic city walls, is known as the Mandatory Quarter. During the British Mandate the city experienced significant demographic growth. While in the 1922 census there were 6,420 residents in town, on the eve of the 1948 war (1946 census) the population stood at 13,560, of which 10,930 were Muslim, 2,490 were Christian, 90 were from other denominations, and 50 were Jews (Abbasi 2010). Pre-Israel Acre was an overwhelmingly Arab-Palestinian town.

The establishment of the Jewish state of Israel in 1948 instigated the most significant changes to contemporary Acre (Dabbagh 1972; Torstrick 2000). In the aftermath of the 1948 war, most of its population was either expelled or fled, leaving the circa 3,000 inhabitants who remained in complete disarray and stripped of any local leadership, who had fled the scene (Abbasi 2010). The small community that stayed was forcibly moved into the intramural historic part of Acre, known until today in the local parlance as *al-'Atiqa*, that is, "the old [city]." Originally, according to the UN's 1947 partition plan, Acre was destined to be part of the future Palestinian state. However, during the latter part of the war, Acre, which served as the major stronghold of the Arab fighting force of the region, was captured by Israeli forces on May 17, 1948 (Karsh 2010). This new urban reality was part and parcel of the Nakba (Ar.: catastrophe), the destruction of the Palestinian society and homeland in 1948, and the displacement of most Palestinian Arabs. This is also when Acre (as other mixed cities in Israel) was greatly transformed under ethnocratic logic and urban religion and affiliation became paramount. *ReligioCity* is suggested to theorize and accommodate this growing importance of religions in cities. This situation is manifested on many levels and has many implications which still weigh heavily on the Palestinian minority of Israel and surely beyond.

In the following excerpt from an interview with Fakhri al-Bishtawi, the founder of a local NGO named *'Akka* Baladi ("Acre My Town"), one may directly understand the repercussions of these dramatic personal, geopolitical, societal, and demographic changes brought forth by the war:

> Originally, I am from Haifa, I was born there. We were expelled from Haifa and escaped under fire and gunshots. I was twelve-thirteen years old at the time. We ran at night, we left everything behind, ousted from Haifa [breaks down and weeps, N. L.], we left our family, our friends, and everything. Our childhood was ruined, we had no childhood and suddenly we found ourselves here [in the old city of Acre], a new reality.
>
> (interview, April 14, 2013)

And a whole new reality it was! The city quickly succumbed to the ethnocratic logic of the newly emerging state, promoting the Zionist vision of Judaizing Israel/Palestine (Yiftachel 2006). The abandoned houses of Palestinian refugees were placed in the hands of the Custodian of Absentee Property and quickly became the residential solution for the influx of new Jewish immigrants and army veterans arriving in town. In the wake of a state-led public housing project (Amidar) for the immigrant Jewish population during the 1950s, the formerly

Arab town became a city dominated by a Jewish majority. Once this project was completed, the Jewish population of the city stood at 6,200, comprising approximately 65 percent of the total population (Heidecker 2022). So, from early on and under the ethnocratic logic of the state, the city developed along the lines of ethnic segregation and separation between Jewish and Arab populations when possible. This is but one outcome of urban ethnocracy, which will be discussed below and by adding the religious component to the Acre "mix." Like other cities, Acre has undergone a rapid involuntary process of "mixing."

It must be recalled that *ethnocracy* is a distinct regime type, established to enhance the expansion and control of a dominant ethno-nation in multiethnic territories. In such regimes, ethnicity, and not citizenship, forms the main criteria for distributing power and resources. As a result, such regimes usually display high levels of uneven ethnic segregation, and a process of polarizing ethnic politics. In ethnocratic contexts, the city becomes a site where the crucial connection of (ethno)nationalism and urbanism dictates the city's development and prevailing urban logic. That said, in the Israeli case formerly Arab-Palestinian towns (like Jaffa or Acre), that following the establishment of the state of Israel were transformed into predominantly Jewish cities in which the Arab-Palestinian community became a minority, are generally defined as mixed cities. "Mix" is a rather neutral definition which relates solely to the urban demographic composition and potentially obfuscates the power structure and inequalities that inform these cities. As such, mixed cities in Israel are effectively "ethnocratic cities," by which it is suggested that they are subject to a persistent Israeli policy of deliberate Judaization, to Arab resistance, and often become sites of constant ethnic conflict and instability (Yiftachel and Yacobi 2003). The ethnocratic city, Yiftachel and Yacobi argue, is characterized by the domination of one ethnonational group, being a place where urban citizenship is unequal, and resources and services are allocated on the basis of ethnicity and not urban citizenship. The new religious Jewish neighborhood recently constructed in Acre is but one case in point. Since urban politics are ethnicized, over time ethnic identities are essentialized and become pivotal to one's urban identity. Against the veneer (thin as it may be at times) of urban democracy, resources such as housing, municipal facilities, cemeteries, houses of prayer and other religious needs, and access to public spaces are marked by deep patterns of ethnic segregation.

To illustrate this urban condition, I will provide an overview of and allude to religious processions in Acre. These were observed in my *ReligioCity* project from 2013 to 2019, when following the outbreak of Covid-19 all public events were halted. While Jewish processions during specific Jewish holidays were orchestrated by the municipality and facilitated with municipal resources, non-Jewish processions were, by and large, sponsored by the organizing body. Additionally, Jewish processions took place along central city boulevards, which required the police to halt traffic and demarcate central zones of the town for the said activities, while most non-Jewish processions were confined to the predominantly Arab intramural city (Luz 2022a). This ethnocratic urban logic is reflected also in planning, development strategies, and surely allocation of public land. This will be further elaborated as I engage with voices of *ReligioCity* and urban infrastructures but suffice it to point here to a sizeable lot (ten dunums) given by the mayor for the construction of a new yeshiva (Jewish religious educational institution) in the eastern parts of the city, not far from the Jewish neighborhood (interview with Yossi Stern, October 18, 2018). In 2008, Acre was ablaze as riots and urban street fights between Jews and Arabs erupted for three days following what was perceived as a young Muslim man's transgression of the holiness of the Jewish Day of Atonement. Under his capacity as the rabbi and leader of a central yeshiva in town, Rabbi Stern expressed his opinion on the latest unfolding: "Co-existence is a slogan after all. Acre is a city like Ra'anana, Kfar Saba and Haifa [cities that are not defined as mixed, N. L.], which must preserve its Jewish identity. We are here to safeguard the Jewish identity and strengthen the spirit and to pass the national test with dignity" (Izenberg 2008). His narrative, indeed, his discourse, unreservedly combines the national with the religious to inform an ethnically Jewish-Israeli urban identity. In Acre, as in other mixed cities in Israel, there is a growing presence of Jewish settlers, motivated by a combination of national ideologies, economic incentives, and symbolic rewards (Shmaryahu-Yeshurun and Ben-Porat 2020). Stern represents these new arrivals in town, who at times express an unconcealed ideological creed of "saving Acre," which means Judaizing Acre. This is not always consistent with the veteran Jewish communities. H. is a religious Jewish native of Acre. As a religious person who regards Acre's ethno-religious mix as a blessing, she resents what she sees as the condescending attitude of these new ideological neighbors:

> We are the old residents of Acre and they have just arrived ... I do not like the idea that someone has come to rescue me as I am supposed to be weak. I am far better than you, we [veteran Jews, N. L.] are the nobility! All the people of Acre that were born here, worked here and are in good positions in life ... and I find it highly problematic to come to an existing community and proclaim, I came

to fix you as I find you faulty. No one needs to be fixed. If you want, you can become partners in a shared path, in a process that is already underway here.
(interview with H., August 3, 2020)

In cities like Acre that are deemed "mixed," against the ethnocratic logic of the state which is usually involved with urban colonialism and constant infringement on the colonized populations' rights and material exploitation, religion has emerged as one of the main bones of contention and as a breeding-ground for radicalization and urban conflicts (Yiftachel and Roded 2010). I argue that in such conditions, the religious factor is essential in order to unpack urban reality and needs further integration with the conceptualization of urban ethnocracy. I will address this fully while attending to the multivocality of religious voices in Acre, against municipal allocation of resources and religious infrastructures.

Thus, following the 1948 war, geopolitical changes, urban demography, power structures, and urban patterns in Acre were radically altered. New arrivals, consisting mainly of Jewish citizens, were channeled by the state's authorities to reside in the city (Kipnis and Schnell 1978; Heidecker 2022). During the 1950s and 1960s, new neighborhoods were planned, offering housing solutions for the Jewish population in the newly developed modern parts of the city due north and east of the historical city. These were immigrants primarily from the MENA region, who following their religious heritage established numerous synagogues. Part of their absorption in the new country, while trying to hold to their existing cultural-religious beliefs, was manifested in establishing synagogues as centers for their respective communities. As such in the modern part of Acre, alternatively known as the Mandatory Quarter, over ninety synagogues were registered in a survey conducted in 2017–18 (*ReligioCity* survey).[1] However, due to the continuing withdrawal of Jewish residents from these parts of the city, most of the synagogues are struggling and regular prayers and rituals are not always possible due to lack of sufficient congregations.[2] And yet, when the Muslim community, now (most likely) the overwhelming majority in this part of town, wanted to re-open a mosque shut down following the war, Jewish residents of Acre were outraged (Luz and Stadler 2015). Indeed, no accurate statistics exist, yet my ongoing ethnographies and interviews with residents in the central parts of the city and election patterns[3] reveal that the central parts of the city (those adjacent to the Old City and due north) were gradually populated by Arab residents. The following maps clearly indicate this changing demography (Ram and Aharon Gutmann 2017).[4] They are also useful

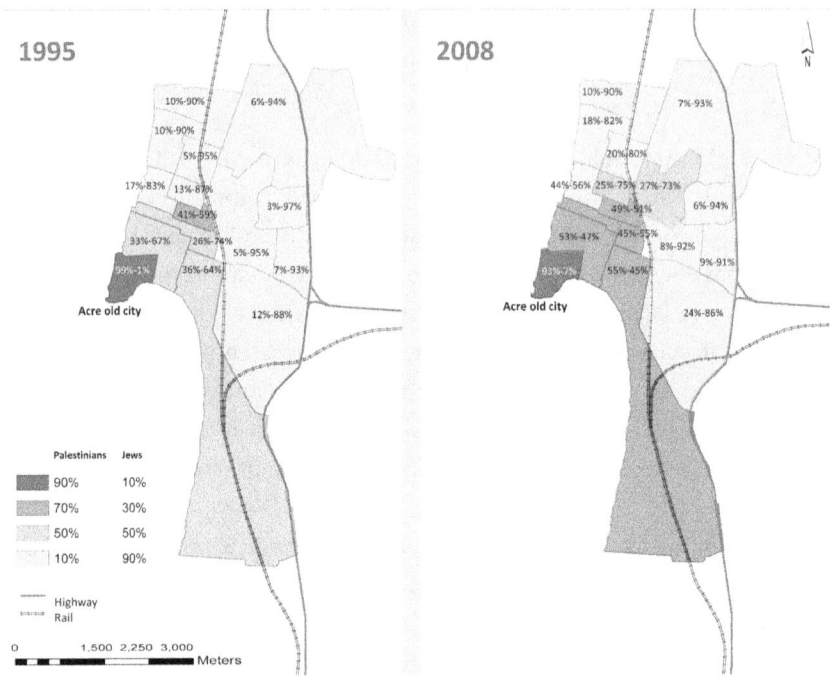

Figure 5.1 Demographic maps of Acre, 1995 and 2008.

to understand the importance of the railway line as an internal urban boundary, which also functions as a porous ethnic-religious one.

Religion, and more so ethnic-religious affiliation, time and again is allowed to effect changes in Acre (as in other cities in Israel) and construct predominantly Jewish residential areas. This is achieved in Acre by constantly shifting the ethno-territorial boundaries within the city (Moore 2016). Put plainly, Jewish residents constantly seek residential solutions as far as possible from Palestinian residents. In recent years, this generally implies moving to the northern and eastern parts of the city. These boundaries are not lines demarcated onto the city plan, but rather daily micro changes. So, as one moves from the Old City, which is predominantly Arab, north to the Mandatory Quarter and east of the railway lines, the number of Jewish residents rises concomitantly with the decrease of Arab ones. In the neighborhoods east of the railway lines (known locally as the "Eastern Projects"), the number of Arab residents is meager to hardly existing. This situation was exacerbated following the 2008 riots, as Jewish residents targeted Muslim families still living in this part of town and eventually forced them to move (interview with N., March 15, 2013).[5]

In recent years, under the leadership of the mayor, Shimon Lankri (in office since 2003), a new building spree has taken place in Acre. Though housing cannot by state law be marketed solely to Jewish citizens, this is indeed the general outcome in the much gentrified newly established neighborhoods, located mostly east of the railway lines. This recent endeavor coincides with a general planning policy, aptly defined as state-led ethno-gentrification (Shmaryahu-Yeshurun and Ben-Porat 2020). Consequently, state agencies and the municipality are promoting religious affiliation as inescapably political, but also as identity markers within the city. Again, this indicates the need to acknowledge the importance of religion and religious affiliation in urban ethnocracy. This is also the background to the May 2021 riots in town, which erupted across all Israel "mixed towns" in response to the confrontations between police forces and Palestinians taking place at the Haram al-Sharif/Temple Mount compound in Jerusalem, which was followed by Hamas launching missiles on Jerusalem during an annual Jewish Flags Parade in the Old City of Jerusalem. During the four days of riots, young Arabs from Acre took to the streets, raised Palestinian flags, and engaged in vandalism of mostly Jewish business places within the Old City. This spectacle of rage came as a shock to Israeli officials at both municipal and national level and as a natural outcome of years of neglect and marginalization of the Palestinian minority in Israel to members of the community (Tzaban and Luz 2021). Ashraf Amer is a resident of Acre, and a social worker and activist who succinctly explains the situation while interviewed following the riots:

> We are second-class, when the Jews can see us at all. The Nakba is a continuous thing, it's not over. You see it in Sheikh Jarrah [a Jerusalem neighborhood where Palestinian residents face eviction, N. L.] to make way for Jewish settlers, and you see it here in the economic problems, job issues, neglect, lack of access to loans that drives Palestinian citizens out.
>
> (Cohen 2021)

By "out" Amer refers to the process of gentrification that is underway in the Old City of Acre, which forces Arab residents (usually from low socio-economic echelons) either to sell their properties or evacuate state public housing (interview with N., June 11, 2019).[6]

Today, Acre is a multi-ethnic multi-religious city where urban ethnocracy dictates the city's conduct and lends its residents their urban status mostly based on their religio-ethnic affiliation. Of its circa 54,000 inhabitants, 69 percent are Jews and the remaining 31 percent are Arabs (CBS 2019). However, the Arabs are further divided into religious denominations, thus 28 percent of the city's residents are Muslims, 2.8 percent are Christians, and 0.2 percent are Druze. Additionally, the city is also home to major Baha'i sacred sites that attract many pilgrims year-round. As a way to account for and further explain the merits of *ReligioCity* to unpack the city, I will engage in the next section with voices of Acre citizens, as they reflect on their city, their urban identity, and their citizenship vis-à-vis urban infrastructures.

ReligioCity in Acre: Voices, Materialities, Religious Infrastructures

To unpack its main questions and themes, the *ReligioCity* project drew on two main methodological approaches. The first was a range of qualitative methods, and in particular participant observations, mainly of religious ceremonies and daily rituals in religious sites; in-depth open-ended interviews with local players, devotees, and municipal officials; and textual analysis of local newspapers, social networks, religious decrees, and religious authorities' public statements. The second approach was spatial-geographical in nature and consisted of surveying, mapping, and documenting the material aspects of *ReligioCity* and the spatial aspects of the urban-built environment. The project focused mainly (but not exclusively) on the following urban aspects: a. urban planning; b. religious and sacred places; c. faith-based organization and civil society; and d. educational institutions. Naturally, because of the abundance of data harvested in the city for over a decade, I am only able to highlight a few examples as a way to bring the multivocality of Acre's *ReligioCity*.

The Israeli Ministry for Religious Services caters solely to the Jewish population. Religious services for the non-Jewish population are provided by the Branch of Religious Communities, which is part of the Ministry of the Interior. A recent report of the Israeli Ombudsman reveals that the burial of non-Jewish citizens of Israel remains unresolved since 1948. It is unclear who is in charge of providing burial services to these communities, and many of the existing cemeteries are poorly maintained and cannot accommodate to the current needs of visitors and surely of bereaved families (Ombudsman 2020). While Jewish citizens' burial is supervised by official and authorized bodies of the state, among non-Jewish citizens the burden of burial is still borne mostly by the immediate family and the religious community. In late 2019, the Al-Jazzar Charitable Trust (commonly known as the Waqf), which is the main body that officiates religious services for the Muslim citizens of Acre, initiated a much-needed maintenance project in the central Muslim cemetery in the city. The purpose of the project was to extend the reservoir of empty lots, as it had become nearly impossible to bury the deceased in the overcrowded cemetery (fieldnotes, January 2, 2020). However, as soon as the works started the municipality hastened to issue an order of cessation of work, as according to municipal officials, the Waqf had not obtained the proper authorization. In response to this claim, Ahmad Auda, a Muslim member of Acre city council, issued the following statement:

> The works were stopped by the municipality under the pretext that this is a public space and permission was not properly obtained. However, the Waqf decided to launch this project against the current distress and to keep things in an orderly fashion and prevent individuals from starting to dig graves by themselves. The project includes also a much-needed fortification to prevent future collapse of debris on existing graves … The municipality's claims are fraudulent. What are we supposed to do? Where will we bury our dead? Are we not also the "public"?
> (Baranes 2020)

While the Muslims are struggling to find space for the dead, things are rather different regarding the urban burial infrastructure designated for the Jewish citizens of Acre.

Rubi Luzon is the Director of the Religious Council of Acre. The council provides religious services for Jewish citizens, among them marriage registration, Kosher certificates, and indeed, burial services. The council is funded by the state and need not answer directly to the mayor although, as Luzon explains, "it is better to work in harmony to provide proper service to the people" (interview, June 28, 2018). He elaborates on the current digitalization project he launched, which also includes the cemeteries under his responsibility:

> I can provide marriage registration online at the moment, but we are working on expanding our abilities. … We live in 2018 …. Say a family is performing a memorial service, they can enter the name of the deceased and immediately get everything you need and print it from our site … As for burial and cemeteries, I need to move to the next phase and modernize matters, but before I do that, I need to coordinate meetings with the mayor and the general manager, because if I want to change the burial system from individual lots to more sophisticated methods due to lack of space, I will need their support.
> (interview, June 28, 2018)

Against the digital revolution Luzon envisioned, the plight of the Muslim community seems all the more crucial, and above all, highlights yet another aspect of how religion is played out and informs urban ethnocracy. Let us take this one step further, as I discuss the municipality's differential approach to religious compounds in town.

On February 21, 2017, the Anglican Archbishop of Jerusalem, Suheil Dawani, conducted a special service of rededication at St Savior's Church in Acre. In his sermon he stressed his gratitude and happiness at the re-opening of the church:

> This evening we, the Anglican Diocese of Jerusalem, with our sister churches, and the people in Acre, although we are from different backgrounds and affiliations, unite together to celebrate this important and historic event of rededication of this spiritual place after so many years of waiting. God has empowered us to revive God's house of prayer, and to re-open it as a space of welcome to all people without exception.
>
> (ANCS 2017)

The church was inaugurated in 1947 to serve the Protestant community which developed in Acre during the Mandate period. However, following the war the church was closed and most of its parishioners no longer lived in Acre. The closed church's condition deteriorated over the years, and in 1987 it was subjected to arson and deliberate harassment, and racist slogans ("Arabs Out") were sprayed on its external walls (interview with Hatem Fares, April 12, 2018). The initiative to re-open the church and resume activities therein started with Hatem Fares, a member of Acre city council, who is also a Maronite Christian. Since 2010, he tirelessly tried to convince the Anglican Archbishop to renovate the church until finally he received a positive response in 2015. During the archbishop's visit to the church on June 12, 2015, Fares obtained his permission and financial support to launch the renovation project, which was supposed to transform the church also into a cultural center for all citizens of Acre (interview with Hatem Fares, April 12, 2018). Since its inauguration, regular services are conducted at the church on Sundays under the leadership of the pastor Imad Diabes who arrives weekly from Haifa (interview with Imad Diabes, February 18, 2018). The congregation is rather small and consists of ten to twenty devotees, most of whom are women who are by and large not Anglicans (interview with Z., May 15, 2018). I was eager to learn about their motivations to attend Sunday mass there and not in their original churches. The reason was revealed during interviews with parishioners and relates directly to the mundane aspects of being religious in cities. The following is an excerpt from an interview with L., a retired public servant, a Greek-Orthodox woman who resides in the Mandatory Quarter and regularly attends the mass at the Anglican Church:

Q: So why is it that you say you do not go anymore to your church?
A: I am not interested anymore. Once this church [the Anglican Church] was open, it is hard to park the car in the Old City and I do love the Anglican prayer, it seems deeper like you are more faithful ... and there are many things I do not like in other churches ... so we formed this group of women, including Maronite women, and we meet once a week ... Look, they are my friends.

(interview with L., June 13, 2018)

L.'s answer highlights the importance of facilities, that is, infrastructures for the conduct of religious life and rituals. The easy access to the Anglican Church, which is not far from her house, and the short distance on flat ground are becoming important at her advanced age. The ambience at the church and the conviviality and comradery she finds there also push her to prefer a church to which she does not belong over "her" own original church. As an aside, this phenomenon was also seen in Acre's more veteran synagogues in the Mandatory Quarter.[7] That said, toward the end of the nearly three hours' interview, L. asked for my assistance in obtaining a permit from the municipality to construct lavatories on the church lot. My positionality (belonging to the majority group? my professional status?) was perceived by her as conducive to receiving a favorable response from the mayor, should I approach him on this issue. This has become a recurring theme during interviews with other women of the makeshift congregation. I was even rebuked, during one of my ethnographies at the church, by L. and a few of the other women attending the mass for not advancing a solution to this problem. This is a rather telling episode, as it reflects not only the power-structure in the field, but also the way this ethnic-religious minority perceives its status within the city. This is a vivid manifestation of urban ethnocratic logic, which renders the municipality generally not responsive to the religious needs of its non-Jewish citizens. Not only it did not donate any money during the renovation, the upkeep of the church is also outside its jurisdiction. Incidents like this never happened during over a decade of interviews and ethnographies among Jewish communities in the town. The case of the Northern Wind Yeshiva depicts a totally different power-structure and relations among urban subjects and municipal agencies.

The most prominent Jewish religious compound in the eastern parts of Acre is the Ruach Tzfonit (i.e., Northern Wind) Yeshivat Hesder of Akko. This type of yeshiva is a Zionist religious college/yeshiva for students who integrate their army service with religious studies. It was established in 2003 with the expressed goal of "strengthening the Jewish and Zionist character of the city" (http://yakko.co.il/eng/). The yeshiva started out in a very humble building at the Wolfson neighborhood, which is one of the first public housing projects, built in 1968 on the outskirts of the Mandatory Quarter in Acre. In the early 2000s, the neighborhood had already gained an overwhelming Arab majority, so the idea was to construct "a Jewish bastion" therein. However, following the plan of the head of the yeshiva, in 2007, ground was broken for a spacious new compound in the eastern-Jewish side of the city. The new compound was inaugurated in a glamorous, well-attended public event held on June 30, 2011 (Akkonet 2011). It must be remembered that such attendance by municipals and state official was not registered during the inauguration ceremony of St. Savior's Church. In a circular to his students, Rabbi Yossi Stern, the entrepreneurial head of the yeshiva, expressed his reading of the city in theological terms:

> The city of Akko, as the ancient capital of the Galilee and one of the holiest cities in Israel, represents thousands of years of Jewish history. For generations, Akko served as the port of entry to the Holy Land. The Talmud relates that the Sages would kiss the stones of Akko when arriving at this vital seaport. Renowned as a center of religious study, Akko attracted many great scholars ... Akko is remembered as the site of the 1947 prison breakout by Etzel [a Jewish paramilitary organization, N. L.]. Later, the city became home to many Holocaust survivors seeking refuge at Israel's shores.
>
> (Stern 2007)

Stern promotes and enhances the Jewish historical narrative of the city that enables him to reconstruct a Jewish chain of memory (Hervieu-Léger 2000). This establishes the yeshiva as an important link in an already well-founded Jewish heritage (and claims) in the city. Then he addresses the core of his activities and major concern in the city:

> Currently, the Jewish existence of the city hangs in the balance. Nearly 20,000 Jewish residents have left the city in recent years, only to be replaced by thousands of Arab families from the surrounding Galilee. The city may very well lose its Jewish majority ... What happens today in Akko could very well happen throughout Israel tomorrow. The Yeshiva of Akko was established in 2003 to help stem the shift in population, to strengthen and maintain the Zionist character of this ancient city, and to infuse hope for the future of Akko. Since its founding, the Yeshiva has succeeded in bringing a spirit of Jewish revival and identity to the city.
>
> (Stern 2007)

Stern envisions a city that is Jewish both in the sense of a demographical majority and in its religious urban conduct and culture. In an interview conducted at the yeshiva compound, he reflects on the behind-the-scenes process which enabled the establishment of this rather impressive and successful institution:

> Q: I must confess, I admire you for your energies and fund-raising abilities. How did you accomplish this?
> A: I am a man of faith, so it is not a big deal … Sometimes it is a supporter from the United States who gave us three million dollars, another time it is a fund that we have managed to get its trust. And of course, it is also the state that was a partner …
> Q: Was the state a partner?
> A: In a certain way, the Ministry of the Negev and the Galilee was a partner.
> Q: And the municipality?
> A: In the early years, the municipality was very nice … it allocated this lot for us. It happened on the very first day after Shimon [the current mayor, who was first elected in 2003, N. L.], he decided it was important enough and was very generous.
> Q: And then did you meet with the city engineer?
> A: Yes, everything, the entire drill. Opening this, suggesting that, preparing blueprints, dreaming. But it was already after six years of work which started in our first location in Wolfson. …
> Q: I specifically ask about the municipality, as the interface between people like you and the urban agencies is what I am particularly interested in.
> A: So, as I say, during the early years after Shimon arrived, we felt that we are working together … later it was less so.
> Q: But were any budgets being channeled by the municipality?
> A: Not really. Once he gave us half a million NIS but due to an auditing mistake it turned out we had to return a million NIS in tax.
>
> (interview with Yossi Stern, October 18, 2018)

Stern may of course lament the deterioration of the yeshiva's relationship with the mayor, and through him—the entire municipality over time. However, against the plight of the St. Savior devotees who struggled for three years to receive a permit to build a lavatory, his worries seem rather negligible. As a member of the "right" ethnicity in town, his goals are much more in sync with the prevailing urban logic. As such he has received over time both land and money, which allowed him to establish a prosperous and highly successful religious-education campus in town. The yeshiva serves as a material outcome of a theological settler-colonial approach. However, as indicated by H.'s remark above, and surely by the demographic and material existence of Muslim and Christian communities, there are other competing and coalescing voices in town: the veteran (mostly) Mizrachi Jews, who continue to hold on to the city and cling to their old synagogues, and certainly the Muslim and Christian communities, for whom safekeeping the materiality of a church or a mosque is also a quest for Palestinian identity.

These tight connections (covert and explicit) and shared goals between members of the ethno-religious Jewish majority in Acre and municipal and state agencies were also instrumental in the emergence of a new religious Jewish neighborhood in town. On August 30, 2017, a small crowd gathered to celebrate the inauguration of a new Jewish neighborhood in Acre (www.facebook.com/watch/?v=1389040691217597). Its official name is Eliyahu Oasis (Hebrew: Neve Eliyahu), commemorating Rabbi Mordechai Eliyahu, a former chief rabbi of Israel whose son, Rabbi Shmuel Eliyahu, was a strong supporter of the neighborhood. He was also the main ideologist behind the establishment of Ometz (Heb: "courage"). Ometz is a faith-based organization that has operated in Acre since 1996. Among its main goals one may find the following:

> City and community advancement; community involvement; creating value-enriched central activities for Akko's residents; establishment of an active young community and encouraging young families to join the city.
>
> (http://www.omezakko.co.il)

This is in effect a religious-nationalist group operating through a colonial logic of territorializing the city by weaponizing middle-class Jewish religious families, mostly young and educated, who began arriving in Acre in 1996 and onward as a way to strengthen its Jewish character and prevent further Arab population from living the city (interview with Yishai Rubin, April 5, 2019). Part of their modus operandi is to purchase apartments and move into poorer neighborhoods to volunteer with disadvantaged populations, Judaize space, and disseminate Zionist and religious ideology among the general population (Shmaryahu-Yeshurun 2022).

Ometz's people were very instrumental to the establishment of this new neighborhood and some of them purchased houses therein. Arguably, the person who first envisioned the neighborhood was Rabbi Nachshon Cohen. In 2005, he registered an NGO whose main objective was to construct a religious neighborhood in Acre. Cohen himself had arrived in the city in 1998 to serve as the rabbi of Ometz, at the behest of Rabbi Shmuel Eliyahu and Rabbi Yosef

Yashar, the longtime chief rabbi of Acre, as they were both concerned with the "dire state of the city" (interview with Nachshon Cohen, March 14, 2019). This last idiom is often used by Jewish citizens of Acre when they refer to the 1980s and 1990s, during which thousands of the city's Jewish citizens left it, mostly to the nearby town of Nahariyya. This statement closely follows the ethnocratic urban logic that regards the possibility of a changing demography and a relative increase of the non-Jewish population as nothing short of a "danger to the very existence of the city." This is how Cohen explains the rationale behind his initiative to build an upscale neighborhood:

> I knew that, if I was to construct a religious neighborhood, which would be a prestigious one, it will naturally draw a strong population. Even if people do not live within the neighborhood, they will purchase houses on its perimeters, and I knew, with divine providence, that people would be attracted to live nearby this neighborhood.
>
> (interview, March 14, 2019)

Cohen was farsighted indeed, as contemporary Acre and current building patterns in the proximity of the neighborhood clearly demonstrate. But it would take a few years for this visionary blueprint to materialize in the urban landscape. Along with local forces within Ometz, in particular Yishai Rubin who served as its CEO during the 2000s, Cohen worked to find an empty plot within the town that would accommodate a considerable number of houses. Furthermore, he came to the realization that, against Acre's problematic urban image and the failure of previous plans to bring new Jewish population into town, his only hope of luring strong, middle-class families there would be to offer them luxurious housing solutions set within a "bourgeois landscape" (interview, March 14, 2019). This, however, stands against the *raison d'être* of the main government agency in charge of planning and land allocations, the Israel Land Administration, that usually promotes high-rise buildings to ensure bigger revenues from the would-be residents. Armed with the support of the mayor and various governmental departments, including at ministerial level, by 2010 Cohen and Rubin, along with other private citizens in Acre who shared their vision, managed to affect a change in the urban statutory master plan. A plot that was initially planned to accommodate 590 residential units in high-rise buildings was altered significantly to become a typical suburbia-style neighborhood of detached homes. Rubin, who was very active at this stage, explains the hurdles they faced and the story behind the formal tender for the neighborhood:

> Q: We received a lot of help from both the Minister of Interior Affairs as well as from the Minister of Housing, which surely had to do with their political interests as they aimed for the religious-national voters … We managed to secure the trust of various factors within the city … the mayor was very involved and, whenever I approached him for something, he would promptly issue a letter … we decided that in order to achieve the goal of changing Acre's demography, no less than 60% of the future residents would be external to the city, 30% would be locals and no more than 10% members of our FBO.
>
> Q: When the tender was finally out, was it clear that it was planned as a religious neighborhood?
>
> A: No! It is against the law to write religious and additionally, when it was out, we faced many problems. One of which was that one is not allowed to register for a tender as an NGO, so, once it was out, we had to come up as soon as possible with 153 names. Everyone around me was applying for the new neighborhood. In retrospect I should have applied too [Rubin laughs] as they all made a killing … but I was so focused on the project that it never occurred to me at the time.
>
> (interview with Yishai Rubin, April 5, 2019)

Cohen further reveals some of the hitherto hidden forces that facilitate the construction of a Jewish-religious neighborhood. As Rubin has rightly stated, it is officially illegal to select people according to that criterion, that is, based on their religious affiliation.

> Q: Tell us the covert story of the neighborhood—how did it play out?
>
> A: Look here, it did not happen one sunny day in a flash but [as] the outcome of numerous initiatives. Let us begin with Sharon [former Israeli prime minister Ariel Sharon, N. L.]. He took Acre as a project … the location of the religious neighborhood was initially planned for high-rise buildings … and he came and said: Change the plans and flatten the neighborhood to one story houses. … this boded well with our plans for the neighborhood because we kept talking about a religious neighborhood consisting of attached housing. … and indeed, the Administration [Israel Land Administration, N. L.] changed the plans and then I seized the opportunity and registered a new NGO for the religious neighborhood. … the idea was to lure people through inexpensive quality housing … the Ministry of Housing was sympathetic to the plan even before the tender was officially announced.
>
> (interview with Nachshon Cohen, March 14, 2019)

Let us go back to the inauguration ceremony. Among those invited were the mayor, the city's chief rabbi, its general manager and members of the city council, and dignitaries who were instrumental to and supportive of the project from within and outside the city. During the ceremony, the speakers were united in presenting this new gentrified neighborhood as part of a divine plan and the fulfillment of the biblical prophecy of the Israelites' return to the holy land. Rabbi Shmuel Eliyahu pointed to the nearest house wall and exclaimed: "Indeed, this is not the Wailing Wall, but it is nonetheless sacred, it is sweet, it is the Land of Israel and the joining together of the sons of Israel and the construction of the people of Israel." He concluded his short speech by kissing the wall and by blessing the audience. Lankri, the mayor, expressed his joy that another neighborhood was constructed in Acre which attracted people from nearby towns as well, and reminded the audience that nothing may be accomplished in the city without the consent of the municipality.

This short ceremony, a distilled moment of the local power structure, makes it abundantly clear that one cannot separate the idea of a religious Jewish neighborhood in its local urban context from the governing ethnocratic logic. In the case at hand, one would be hard pressed to try and discern between religion, urban ethnocracy, and the multi-scalar dynamic in which religion connects and moves between city, state, and nation. For A., a local resident, such a separation simply does not exist:

> I grew up in Acre not far away from here. But things deteriorated in the city during the 1990s and like others, I left for Nahariyya—mainly because it was the sensible thing to do tax-wise … The only thing that would have brought me back here is the possibility of a house with a garden, but not in a mixed neighborhood as might be found in some other places in Acre.
>
> (interview with A., October 6, 2019)

The religious neighborhood was initiated by a group of highly motivated private individuals who were following their aspirations and religious ideology to enhance the Jewish character of the city. They set in motion a process that ultimately materialized in the shape of a gentrified religious neighborhood. However, the project would never have seen the light of day were it not supported by various municipal and national agencies operating under the same ethnocratic logic and motivated to promote a specific scheme of social engineering and a particular demography in Acre. These different motivations could be easily depicted in the inauguration ceremony of the religious neighborhood, during which diverse players and stakeholders could unite under one ideological umbrella. Surely, the incentives of the neighborhood's initiators—and ultimately, its residents—were not necessarily identical. These forces successfully executed the project by allowing a solution befitting the capabilities and aspirations of middle-class residents, namely a gentrified neighborhood that fused, in a neatly tied package, the luxury of detached homes and religious-cum-national ideology. Compared to the process of reinscribing the St. Savior Church unto the urban landscape and the rather desperate moves on the part of its congregation to include a lavatory facility, urban ethnocracy's logic is readily apparent. What is also obvious is the crucial role played by religion and its influence on urban infrastructures. In the last section of this chapter, I will focus on the struggle of Acre's Muslim community while working to reinstate the Lababidi Mosque that operated in the Mandatory Quarter until 1948. In analyzing this conflict over a sacred place, I add a crucial dimension to my reading of the politics of the sacred in Israel/Palestine: decolonization through the sacred in settler-colonial society.

De-Colonizing Acre: Exploring the Lababidi Mosque

During the interview with Rubi Luzon, the director of Acre's religious council (see above), the conversation digressed to a short discussion of the nature of the relationship between the Arab community and the municipality:

> Q: Their relationship with the municipality is great … some of the Jews claim it is too great … but ok, I will not dwell on that.
> Q: What is inferred by "too great"?
> A: What is too great? Say on Ben Ami Boulevard [the main shopping street in the Mandatory Quarter, N. L.] there was a mosque, actually it is doubtful if it was a mosque or not. It is an historic building from many years ago … and they have decided it is theirs and that it is a mosque, and they want to renovate it. So, they approached the municipality who recommended to the Ministry of Tourism to come here and renovate it. But then after the Ministry of Tourism renovated it as a tourist attraction, all of a sudden now they want to open it as a mosque, in the heart of the city so people are angry … this instigates resistance ….
> (interview with Rubi Luzon, June 28, 2018)

The building in question is the Lababidi Mosque, built in 1930 by Ahmad Lababidi, a member of a prominent Muslim family of Acre in the growing bourgeois suburb known today as the Mandatory Quarter. It is not on Ben

Ami Boulevard and was open for prayer already in 2012. The fact that Luzon, a native of Acre and a long-time public figure in town, is incorrect on its history, location, and current status, speaks volumes about the nature of interreligious and interethnic relations in the city. Luzon is not alone in Acre's Jewish majority in expressing such opinions regarding sacred places of the Muslim minority. The mosque in question, which is indeed in the center of town, instigated more emotions and harsh responses, as it was perceived as a direct assault on Jewish hegemony in the town. In what follows, I will narrate the struggle over the mosque within the framework of the indigenous community's effort to decolonize its city. Let us begin with a short introduction to the mosque, to be followed by a conceptualization of urban decolonization in colonial settler-societies.

The Lababidi Mosque was the first mosque to be constructed outside the walls of the historic city. The mosque was meant to accommodate the needs of Acre's small population of wealthy Muslims who lived outside the walls (interview with N., April 18, 2012). A modestly proportioned rectangular building was built on an empty lot owned by the Lababidi family, which also turned it into a religious endowment (Reiter 2009). It served its immediate community until 1948, when in the aftermath of the war it was closed and stood derelict and dilapidating for decades (interview with Muhammad Zahra, April 27, 2018). In the summer of 2005, the Branch of Religious Communities initiated a project that provided for a limited renovation of the Lababidi Mosque. The restoration, that more than anything else was an emergency response to a demolition order on the compound issued by Acre's municipal engineer, was confined to the mosque's external perimeter (Yaacov Salama, oral communication, December 6, 2013).[8] In order to avoid any misunderstanding or misinterpretation of the renovation's goal, a letter was sent to the director of the Al-Jazzar Charitable Trust (which is the legal body in charge of the endowment) informing him that the renovation should not be regarded as a pretext for any changes in the function (or lack of it, as the case may be) or future of the mosque (Salaama 2004). The emergency renovation of this small compound caused a strong and phobic backlash among the Jewish citizens of Acre. As they expressed it, their main fear was of an orchestrated campaign launched by the Arab citizens to "take over the city center." The miniscule restoration project of the mosque was suspected—as part of a covert scam, it would be also appropriate to say—to take over the city. Following a post on the local internet forum, Akkonet, about the mosque-renovation project, talkbacks appeared expressing grave concern and basically suggesting that this is just the beginning of a complete and disastrous urban change. An anonymous user named "aka2005" summed it up as follows:

> This place on Ben Ami Street was never a mosque! It was a Muslim school and not a mosque!!!!!!!! A mosque is a compound with a dome and a minaret, and the roof of this place was always flat. Why do you [i.e., the forum manager, N.L.] put words in the mouth of the Arabs? And besides, they already dug two holes and cast heavily fortified concrete pillars in order to support the heavy dome to be built here … soon enough, if we will not do something to stop it, this will become an official and sacred place of prayers—to the glory of the Jewish state—the state of Israel.
>
> (http://www.akkonet.co.il/forums/viewtopic.php?t=294)

This response reflects the essence of the debate and the almost unanimous view expressed by the participants, that the renovation is a very hazardous step toward an imminent Muslim-Arab "conquest" of the city center and the loss of the entire city through this struggle over a sacred place. Given the fact that the Muslim community was not consulted before or during the renovation, the responses among the Jewish majority group are rather telling; they mainly narrate fear and mistrust. Incidentally, the debate and the emotions it evoked soon subsided, as no visible changes occurred that manifested what was feared and apprehended, not in the mosque and certainly not in the surrounding neighborhood. There were simply no changes in the built environment that could sustain this analysis and support concrete steps to counter this rudimentary renovation. However, these reactions, which attest to a specific state of mind, lead us into encounters between colonial settler society vis-à-vis indigenous groups in the context of urban ethnocracy. This enables a framing of the Lababidi Mosque conflict as decolonization by indigenous people to claim their past places and their very existence in the city.

In 2009, a new director and board members were appointed to the Al-Jazzar Charitable Trust.[9] The new board in Acre represented a fundamental change, which also reflects the empowerment processes Muslim communities have undergone over the years since the establishment of the state in 1948 (Rabinowitz and Abu-Baker 2005). This change is personified in the newly nominated director of the Trust, Salim Najami. He is a self-proclaimed secular man, who although coming from a Muslim family does not practice Islam in his daily routine: "I am not a religious man … I came from a place of not knowing what a mosque is, or how many times one has to pray during the day …" (interview with Salim Najami, December 26, 2012). Najami challenges and affects changes in the city through his claiming of his own indigenous heritage. He makes the urban landscape his very own through urban-political claims that are framed as religious claims, and not through his own religious identity. To be clear, Najami harnesses his indigeneity and religio-ethnic affiliation to hamper the superimposed logic of the settler-state.

Early in 2011, Najami, as the director of the Trust, initiated a complete renovation of the mosque with the unconcealed intention to re-open it and allow it to operate again after a dormancy of 65 years:

> There was a need for a place where Muslims could pray in the new city, indeed there was a need. It is not that I wanted to provoke someone. The mosque was already there in 1948 and I do understand the circumstances [the manifold repercussions of the establishment of Israel as a Jewish state, N.L.], but what I do not understand is the situation in which the majority of the Muslim community lives outside the Old City, but we are not allowed to build anything. We are a third of the city's population. Two-thirds of the community live outside the walls. Yet they do not have as much as one mosque. Why must an old man who lives in the new city walk and pray in the Old City? I acted with no backup from any religious authorities, and I did not ask for one. I wanted to act quietly and without any publicity or provocation.
>
> (interview with Salim Najami, December 26, 2012)

The reactions toward indigenous claims over the urban sacred ranged from expressions of fear that the city will become dominated by its Arab population (as one of the participants in Akkonet forum discussions exclaimed, "this is a Trojan horse") to accusations of negligence on the part of the mayor for not doing enough to stop this "shameful act." As one of the regular Jewish participants of the Akkonet forum posted: "As a citizen that supports co-existence in the city, I respect the freedom of worship of all religions in the city. However, I do not accept a Muslim house of prayer in the middle of the Mandatory Quarter" (http://www.akkonet.co.il/forums/viewtopic.php?t=294).

This response illustrates the tension between the (allegedly) liberal attitude toward religious worship and the fear of a Muslim majority and surely of Muslim presence in central parts of the city. Most responses express grave concern for the disruption of the fragile "status quo" between the communities. The following is an excerpt from yet another comment on Akkonet:

> In principle, I have no problem with the construction of a mosque in Acre. My problem is with its location … it is no secret that there are "certain" bodies that push Arab residents to purchase flats and assets within Jewish neighborhoods

to take them over. ... Look at what happened in Wolfson ... as soon as Arab families began to buy houses over there, Jewish families began to leave. Next thing, all the streets in Mandatory Acre that were Jewish are slowly but surely turning into Arab streets. Where will it end?
 (http://www.akkonet.co.il/forums/viewtopic.php?f=11&t=1603&p=109469)

The "fragile status quo" is an oft-repeated slogan, used mostly by members of the Jewish hegemonic group and state officials. This discourse is often used to justify and explain the continuing exclusion of minorities from the urban sphere. Najami was aware of these voices and tried to avoid public debates or polemic discussion. However, he remained undeterred, even after being approached openly and covertly several times by officials from within various corridors of power:

> I told them I do not need the mayor or the Ministry of the Interior, I alone took this decision because of all these people that sit at home yearning for this place and remember their father praying there ... and then he [an official from Ministry of Interior] asked for another meeting and another meeting until he realized that we would not turn back, and then he said: maybe the State of Israel can help—but nothing direct. It was always very subtle and cleverly done. So I told him, all I want is the mosque and nothing scares me. I care about the status quo, sensitivities, and the "fragile texture of relations" more than you do.
> (interview with Salim Najami, December 26, 2012)

Since the mosque was a Muslim endowment (*waqf*) and outside the jurisdiction of the municipality, the mayor—even if he wanted to intervene—has no legal standing to influence the project. While the debate raged, public figures from both communities voiced their opinions about either the importance or the futility of the renovation respectively. Undaunted by the brouhaha, Najami carried on with the renovation until the project was completed. On March 11, 2012, the mosque was inaugurated, and a prayer service conducted therein for the first time since 1948 (interview with Muhamad Zahra, April 27, 2018). To avoid further public debate or protests, only two hundred local Muslim dignitaries were discreetly invited to this festive occasion. Najami also committed himself to refraining from the customary Muslim call to prayer (*adhan*) to prevent further confrontations with the Jewish community (interview with Salim Najami, March 18, 2016). This has to do with his own personal politics and relates also to the unique materiality of this mosque, which was initially built without a minaret. Najami's decision meant that no external voices are heard from the mosque affecting the urban soundscape in its vicinity. Najami inadvertently tapped here into a contested bill proposal at the Israeli parliament, which suggested banning the Muslim call to prayers through loudspeakers. Since then, the proposal has been tabled, and yet it follows an ongoing controversy between Jewish majority and Muslim minority that is particularly relevant to their encounters within mixed cities, wherein communities are to be found in close proximity. Although similar laws were confirmed in predominantly Muslim countries such as Turkey and Egypt, within the Israeli context of settler-colonialism society versus indigenous Muslim minority it becomes a highly conflictual subject.

The mosque is kept closed and locked at all times, except during prayers. Since its inauguration in 2012, no urban conflicts surrounding it were registered. In my visits and observations at the mosque, I often encounter devotees from within and outside Acre. Some of them are retired and elderly citizens of Acre who, as suggested by Najami, yearn for their heritage, but—beyond the politics of the sacred which I dwell on—simply enjoy the modern facility, easy access, and convenient parking that a modern city can offer. The Lababidi Mosque and the struggle that revolved around its renovation and its re-opening is indeed a decolonizing process on the part of the colonized against the colonizing logic that constantly threaten to eliminate it from the city. Against this expected development, the Lababidi Mosque has undergone a process which not only preserved it as a landmark within the ethnocratic-colonizing city but also returned it to its deprived community and re-inscribed it as an active religious site unto the city's landscape. This, as I argue throughout this chapter, manifests the successful deployment of religion as a sociopolitical category and its growing role in shaping the city. This allows indigenous groups to claim the city and, at the same time, to decolonize the prevailing urban ethnocratic logic.

* * *

In this chapter I expanded on the politics of the sacred within the urban scale through an expansive discussion of a variety of religious-related issues in Acre, a multi-ethnic and multi-religious city. To explore the tangible and intangible aspects of urban religion and religion in the city and the reciprocal relations between them, I presented *ReligioCity*. This concept emerged from my on-going engagement with cities and religions, mostly through the realm of the sacred. It follows recent theoretical developments defined herewith as the de-secularization of cities and the material turn. *ReligioCity* was empirically explored by means of Acre, a mixed city in the north of Israel. This also allowed me to engage with urban ethnocracy and compliment this theoretical notion with the growing impacts of religion. The ethnocratic logic proved to be crucial for understanding Acre, and indeed the politics of sacred places in Israel/Palestine. To further explain *ReligioCity*, a myriad of voices of religious "citadins" was explored, mostly in relation to urban religious infrastructures. This facilitated a deeper engagement with the ample ways religion and city are interacting, but also with the ways the religious subjects experience, envision, and produce their city and are affected by it. This unequivocally showed that one simply cannot understand the prevailing urban logic in Acre (as a case in point of the mixed-ethnocratic city) separately from urban ethnocracy. This situation also informs the ethno-religious urban identity. The chapter was concluded with the politics of the Lababidi Mosque. I framed the discussion and conflict along the lines of the decolonization of an indigenous minority within a colonial-settler society. This theoretical lens allowed an analysis of the role of urban religion(s) as a site of converging and conflicting visions and voices, practices, and orientations, which arise out of the complex desires, needs, and fears of many different people in the context of urban ethnocracy. Following this exhaustive discussion of the politics of the sacred within the urban scale (both Chapters 4 and 5), in the last chapter of this book I move to the national and supranational scale (and global, as the case maybe). The theoretical discussion is grounded around the most iconic sacred place in Israel/Palestine: Jerusalem and its holy basin.

6

Glocalizing the Sacred: The Haram al-Sharif/Temple Mount as the Hypocenter of Israel/Palestine

Entering Jerusalem: The Ultimate and Most Conflictual Sacred

In this final chapter, I engage with scaling the sacred and scalar politics which involves the move from the national to the supra-national and global. I focus on Jerusalem which I conceptualize as a hypocenter, that is, the point within the earth where an earthquake begins. An earthquake's hypocenter is the position where the strain energy stored in the rock is first released, marking the point where the fault begins to rupture. This metaphor befits this enchanting and unique city, which time and again over its long history has served as the focal point for dramatic episodes that affected changes that reverberated across the world (Luz 2021a). It is also evocative and corresponds to the age-old notion of the Temple Mount being constructed on the foundation stone from which the world was created and where the Last Judgment will take place; a tradition that emerged in Jewish theology and was accepted both in Christianity (with a slight diversion to the Hill of Golgotha) and Islam (Gonen 2003). A case in point of the enormous impact and indeed importance of the city is the lengthy confrontations between Christendom and Islamdom over ownership, control, and dominance in and of Jerusalem.

Islam arrived in Jerusalem in 630 CE, following three centuries of a process of Christianization of the urban landscape (Busse 1968). On July 15, 1099, the forces of the First Crusade captured Jerusalem, then under the rule of the Ismaili-Shi'i Fatimid Caliphate. The Holy City had been the goal of the expedition-cum-pilgrimage from the outset and specifically the Holy Sepulcher, its most sacred Christian place (Riley-Smith 2003). Such was the lure of this holy destination that it carried thousands of people from across Europe on a three-year march into the unknown Outremer, "beyond the sea," until they arrived at the gates of the city. Jerusalem was soon chosen as the capital of a new and unique political entity: the Latin Kingdom of Jerusalem (Ellenblum 2003). The shockwaves bringing the news of the (re)conquest of the holy city from its Muslim rulers quickly arrived at the shores of western Christendom. Consequently, during the twelfth century Jerusalem became the most important destination for Christian pilgrims (Hamilton 1994). Under Frankish rule Jerusalem underwent a significant urban renovation, involving mostly sacred places, churches, monasteries, and pilgrimage centers. Indeed, the Holy Sepulcher was at the forefront of these endeavors, but this comprehensive Christianization process also included the Muslim places atop the Temple Mount. However, for lack of the financial means to demolish and rebuild these magnificent Islamic compounds, and perhaps also due to serious concern that the destruction of these sacred places might bring upon them the wrath of their Muslim adversaries, the Franks took an alternative direction. The solution found to resolve this contradiction was to identify the Muslim edifices as the first and second Jewish temples and accordingly, to name them *Templum Solomonis* (Solomon's Temple) and *Templum Domini* (the Lord's Temple) (Boas 2001). Accordingly, the Dome of the Rock was transformed into a church and was adorned by a conspicuous gold cross, while al-Aqsa Mosque became the King's palace and later, the headquarters of the Order of the Knights of the Temple (Bahat 1991).

Following the fall of Jerusalem to Christian forces, its revered religious status as the first *qibla* (direction of Islamic prayers, before Mecca was finally chosen) and the city third in holiness (after Mecca and Medina) was used to transform it to the destination of a jihad with the ultimate goal of rallying Muslim forces against the Crusader kingdom (El-Azhari 2016). This sacred task was accomplished by Salah al-Din (commonly known in English as Saladin) in 1187, following his decisive victory over the Crusader army at the Battle of Hittin. When Salah al-Din was negotiating Jerusalem's surrender with Balian d'Ibbelin, the Frankish commander of Jerusalem at the time, the latter threatened to dismantle the Dome of the Rock and al-Aqsa Mosque if his claims should not be met (Cobb 2014). This had the desired effect and Salah al-Din accepted his terms of surrender and granted the safe passage of most of the city's inhabitants. Once the city was in his hands, Salah al-Din was quick to launch a re-Islamization project that involved massive construction and renovation of religious endowments (*awqaf*) as an effective tool to transform Jerusalem into a city with a distinctly Muslim landscape (Frenkel 1999; Luz 2002). The Haram al-Sharif received special attention and not only were former Christian symbols such as the gold cross upon the Dome of the Rock quickly removed, but new shrines and cenotaphs were constructed, scattered around the compound (Mujir al-Din 1973).

This sacred center's capacity to evoke responses, steer emotions, and be involved in multi-dimensional and multi-scalar politics has not waned over time, and perhaps was even exacerbated against the emergence of nationalism in the region. It verges on the impossible to present an exhaustive list of case studies of such conflicts, disorders, and political storms in which the Temple Mount/Haram al-Sharif stood at the center, and I will narrate but one recent example that demonstrates the ways in which it is found to be upscaling the national into the supra-national and global.

Following the June 1967 war (known also as the Six-Day War), Israel assumed direct control over East Jerusalem, including the Old City and its holy compound (Lustick 1997). This geopolitical change instigated a very volatile religious-political situation, in which a non-Islamic entity was in charge of an Islamic sacred place of the utmost importance. The problematics of the situation was explained to the Israeli authorities a few days after the 1967 war by a group of Palestinian Muslim jurists calling themselves the Supreme Muslim Authority. This *ad hoc* organization issued a formal legal opinion (Arabic: *fatwa*) which stated the following:

> Because Muslim religious law clearly stipulates that Muslims must take the initiative and run their religious affairs by themselves in the situation that exists today and because Muslim religious law prohibits non-Muslims from running the religious affairs of Muslims ... therefore the signatories have appointed themselves as the "Supreme Muslim Authority Responsible for all Muslim Matters in the West Bank including Jerusalem" until the end of occupation.
> (cited in Reiter 2017: 25)

To accommodate this highly sensitive situation, Israel tacitly agreed to allow the daily conduct and responsibilities over the Haram al-Sharif to remain as they were under the previous Jordanian rule (Reiter 2008; 2017). This is the background against which the Haram al-Sharif has been managed since 1967, and which also informs the "metal detectors episode" that occurred in the summer of 2017. On July 16, 2017, Israel installed an additional security measure in the shape of metal detectors at the gates leading to the Haram al-Sharif. This was done in response to the actions of three Israeli-Palestinian citizens, who had brought concealed weapons onto the sacred compound, and fired at a police post near one of the gates, killing two Israeli officers before being shot dead (Berger 2017).

This soon became another chapter of the national dispute between Israel and the Palestinian Authority and Muslim Palestinians, and quickly escalated. This mobilization was very much led by Ra'id Salah, the leader of the Northern Branch of the Israeli Islamic Movement, who was very instrumental in galvanizing the response. Soon enough, ripples were reaching out to and from international players. Local Palestinian Muslim devotees refused to submit themselves to being searched by the detectors, and as an act of defiance, conducted their prayers outside the compound. The Palestinian president Mahmoud Abbas immediately severed contacts with Israel until the metal detectors were removed, claiming that the Palestinians have sole sovereignty over the compound (Booth and Eglash 2017). Jerusalem's most sacred place proved once again to be vulnerable to external forces of a multi-scalar nature, in tandem with the growing social and political unrest in the city. Condemnations of Israel's unilateral action quickly began arriving from across the Muslim world. A group of Turkish citizens protested outside one of the central synagogues in Istanbul to denounce Israel's security measures at this sensitive holy place in annexed East Jerusalem (Express Tribune 2017). Turkey's president, Recep Tayyip Erdogan, announced it was unacceptable for Muslims going to pray at al-Aqsa to be treated "like terrorists." Speaking at the Turkish parliament, he called on Muslims to visit the al-Aqsa Mosque: "From here I make a call to all Muslims. Those who are able must visit the al-Aqsa Mosque in Jerusalem as recommended by the Prophet. Those who cannot, go should send help to our brothers there" (Efe-epa 2017). The Arab League, an umbrella group of Arab countries, and the Organization of Islamic Cooperation each issued separate statements calling on Israel to lift the security measures. When Israel decided to remove these detectors from the gates of the Haram al-Sharif, the Trump administration praised Israel for its efforts to reduce tension in the region (Cortellessa 2017).

The power of this sacred place to engage with supranational and global scalar politics clearly demonstrates that scalar configurations are not predetermined platforms upon which socio-political life simply takes place. They are constantly being remade through sociopolitical struggles. As such, in this chapter I explore the politics of sacred places as they are upscaled from the national to the supranational and the global. This chapter, therefore, portrays an intricate and highly nuanced picture of the ways the Haram al-Sharif is assuming a unique and unparalleled position in the ethno-national conflict between Israel and Palestine. I frame this as the glocalization of the sacred. Following a theoretical discussion of glocalization as part of the scalar configurations discussed throughout the book, I contextualize Jerusalem and its most holy and contested compound under the yoke of nationalism and as part of the Israeli-Palestinian conflict. The empirical focus of this chapter revolves around the Israeli Islamic Movement as a significant agent of change through its ongoing efforts to glocalize the conflict over the ownership of the Haram al-Sharif. This is a way to resist Israeli control of the site, to better its position vis-à-vis other Muslim stakeholders and internal Israeli politics and as part of the personal project of its charismatic leader, shaykh Ra'id Salah.

Glocalization as Overthrowing the State: Local to Global Flows of Sanctity

The notion of "glocalization" emerged during the 1990s in the wake of the scholarly interest in globalization (Robertson 1995). This neologism is a linguistic hybrid of globalization and localization, which was hypothesized originally by a Japanese economist to theorize Japanese global market strategies. Glocalization is generally understood as the simultaneous occurrence of both universalizing and particularizing tendencies in contemporary social, political, and economic systems. It has come to suggest the interaction between the local and the global to produce unique hybrids in different socio-political and geographical settings (Roudometof 2016). As the global and the local are assumed to mutually constitute each other, hence "glocal" relates to a process where the global and the local entangle together to construct a new reality (Robertson 1995). This loaded concept is often understood as a two-level system (global and local), which through dialectical processes such as hybridization result in greater interconnectedness (Korff 2003). As a theoretical framing device, glocalization has become increasingly prevalent across various disciplines even though, to date, it is still used in a rather unclear manner and has received numerous interpretations.

Among geographers, Erik Swyngedouw was probably the first to engage in scalar understandings of glocalization by stressing its spatial nature. Unlike Robertson, who appears to treat the global scale as an independent variable, Swyngedouw argues against an *a priori* privileging of spatial scales. For him, scales are historically constructed and mediated through social relationships, forming possible terrains for action and inaction (Swyngedouw 1997). Swyngedouw's rationale for emphasizing the importance of place rests with his critiques of how the local and the global are exhibited: place is socially frozen whereas globalization is precisely the opposite. Neil Brenner's approach to glocalization complements Swyngedouw's characterization of the national scale under glocalizing conditions.

He follows Swyngedouw's criticism of state-centrism because the naturalization of the nation-state blocks a potentially more nuanced analysis of social formations' relationship to globalization's time-space compression (Brenner 1999a). However, he calls for a decentering analysis of the state to get away from state-centrist approaches and move toward more territorially nuanced enquiries that recognize complexity (Brenner 1999b). In this way, the orthodoxy of nested territoriality is challenged, because a decentered state analysis rejects the *a priori* favoring of one scale over another. Instead, changing scalar architectures produces new forms of nested territorialities that serve to shape other spatial scales' opportunities and constraints. This brings us to the question of power and power-geometries while trying to fathom glocalization.

Power indeed does not rest in the single scale of a spatial container. Beck stresses power in his analysis of globalization and defines it as a locale's ability consistently and persistently to originate waves across the world stage. This he describes as a locale "globalizing" itself from within (Beck 2000). In overcoming the state and using glocalization as a scalar strategy, I want to suggest that minorities may venture to "overthrow" the state by reaching beyond the national scale. This involves a slightly different approach to glocalization, which neither looks at how the global is affecting the local nor at how the local is accommodating the global, but rather how the local is approaching the global to overcome constraints and power structures of lesser scalar levels. Let us explore this understanding. To do so, I return to October 2000 in Israel/Palestine.

Following the failure of the second Camp David Summit on July 25, 2000, the region was quickly succumbing to another round of armed conflict between Israelis and Palestinians. On September 28, 2000, Ariel Sharon, then a member of the Israeli Parliament and later Israeli prime minister, visited the Haram al-Sharif under high-profile media coverage. This was the final spark in the already highly explosive atmosphere which led to the combustion of the Second Intifada. Civilian acts of resistance and defiance of Israeli state authority spread among Palestinian communities within and outside the Green Line. When interviewed about the riots (also known as the "October 2000 Events") and the reactions among Israeli Palestinians, 'Abd al-Malik Dahamshe, MK and head of the Islamic party in the Israeli parliament at the time, supplied the following rejoinder:

> It is a war that every Muslim should be part of. There is no Green Line when al-Aqsa is concerned and this [the reactions] will continue throughout Israel ... I cannot see this murderer transgress the most holy place in this land and idly observe from the sideline. Am I not a human being? Am I devoid of emotions, am I not a Muslim? He entered the most holy mosque of the Muslims in order to

defile it as a murderer, as a powerful man, a Zionist. Do you honestly believe that we will not face up to it? This act is addressed against our very existence, but we do exist. Our sole culpability is that we are humans and that we have a life and that we have a mosque and a land.

(Gal 2000)

Dahamshe engages here with an intriguing spatial language and weaves a complex multi-scalar configuration. He was known for his provocative oratory style in the Israeli Parliament and often abrupt conduct with the press, which is why I was rather surprised, when we met in his parliamentary office in his hometown of Kufr Kana, to be received not only with very amicable and accommodating hospitality but to find a softspoken, open, and reflexive person. During the interview he narrated his side of this statement, which appeared in an Israeli newspaper in the very first days of the Second Intifada:

> I was on my way to meet with people in 'Amman and this reporter caught me as I was just passing the bridge [one of the international entries between Israel and Jordan—N. L.]. This was indeed a very emotional response, as the events touched upon the very core of my being. This is something Israelis do not like to acknowledge ... I will tell you: the problem ends there and does not begin there. It starts between us, between Jews and Arabs—if the Jews would ever agree to see us as equals, brothers for life, for geography, for existence, for a shared destiny, real partners ... once there will be peace and cooperation, all those things [violence, confrontations—N. L] will be taken down from our daily lives, this place will return to its former capacity as a religious place and a mosque.
>
> (interview with 'Abd al-Malik Dahamshe, September 29, 2002)

However, this is but one approach to be found among members of the Israeli Islamic Movement. Many of those I met with, and certainly among the more influential leaders, oppose all negotiations and even dialoguing with Israel, and Israeli Jews for that matter. But at this stage I want to address Dahamshe's spatial language and his engagement with scalar politics regarding the holy compound in Jerusalem. He begins with the global scale by asserting that the defense of al-Aqsa against the transgression of profanation is the task of all Muslims. He then moves to a supranational scale and addresses the role of Palestinians on both sides of the Green Line. Subsequently, he touches on the national scale by focusing on the Israeli Palestinians' role within Israel. I frame these endeavors as glocalization, which I see as the contested restructuring of the institutional level from the national scale, both upwards to supranational or global scales and downwards to the scale of the body or the local, the urban or the regional configuration. Therefore, glocalization is also concerned with process of deterritorialization and reterritorialization. This is achieved through the reconfiguration and the contestation over spatial scale. Since all social life is inevitably situated and locally placed, the global is local at every moment (Latour 1993). The global always takes place at the local, as the local is constantly being shaped and altered by the global. That well may be, but regardless of the importance and magnitude of world globalization, we need to pay special attention to the localities in which these changes are taking place (Swyngedouw 2003). Glocalization, as I conceptualize it, refers to the changes and struggles over scalar configurations and entails the possibility of jumping scale and moving the local into the global sphere. This understanding is informed by the notion that scale is a constitutive dimension of sociopolitical processes. It demarcates the site of social or political contest. It is also about setting a context to the struggle. Scale is an active progenitor of specific social processes; it sets the boundaries for struggles over identity, and control over places. In the face of a scale superimposed by a hegemonic power, subaltern groups may opt to thwart this power by actively jumping scales.

Against the backdrop of Israeli control over the Haram, Dahamshe moves between scales as a way to subvert and resist a given geographical production of scale in that specific place. Jumping scales allows subordinate or controlled groups to dissolve spatial boundaries that are largely imposed by the state (national scale) and that contain rather than facilitate their production and reproduction of everyday life. By focusing on the process of scaling the Haram al-Sharif, mostly by the Israeli Islamic Movement, I aim to explore the continuous reorganizing through political struggle of the hierarchical interrelationships among scales (Brenner 2001). To fully comprehend the unique position of the Israeli Islamic Movement in national to global politics, in the following section I contextualize Jerusalem and the Temple Mount/Haram al-Sharif since the early beginnings of the Israeli-Palestinian conflict.[1]

Jerusalem and Its Sacred Center under the Yoke of Nationalism

As early as 1905, Najib Azuri, a Maronite Christian intellectual and Arab nationalist, summed up, rather harshly, the future of the region against the awakening of the Arab and Jewish national movements:

Two important phenomena, of the same nature and yet opposed, which have still not attracted anyone's attention are emerging at this moment in Asiatic Turkey. These are the awakening of the Arab nation and the quiet effort of the Jews to reconstitute the ancient kingdom of Israel on a very large scale. These two movements are destined to fight each other endlessly until one overcomes the other. The fate of the entire world hinges on the final result of this struggle between these two peoples, representing two contrary principles.

(1905: v)

In retrospect, Azuri's ominous prediction was certainly justified, judging by the events that transpired in Jerusalem and its sacred centers since his statement. During the British Mandate (1920–48), the sacred Jewish/Islamic center was mobilized as a religious-national icon by both parties concerned, Palestinians and Zionists. This certainly contributed to the quelling of the lingering concern among European powers, and certainly Christian denominations, regarding the status of the Church of the Holy Sepulcher and other revered Christian places.

Religious encounters in Jerusalem were about to change dramatically in the modern era against what I define as the yoke of nationalism. Since the late nineteenth century, the Temple Mount/Haram al-Sharif transformed into a site of national contestation. To accomplish that, numerous agents produced specific histories of the site's past in order to accommodate views, convictions, and especially goals of the present (Luz 2014b). Invoking the past of places and constructing specific memories about them are precisely what enable them to warrant the building of a desired future (Massey 1995). As both parties were promoting the holy basin in Jerusalem as the nation's "rock of foundation," tensions mounted and shortly after the British assumed control over the region (aka the British Mandate), violence erupted by the Western Wall of the sacred compound in the summer of 1929 and spread across the region (Cohen 2015).

These events became a major watershed in the history of the Israeli-Palestinian conflict and were a rather ominous overture to what the future held in store for both parties. Mandatory rule in Palestine proved to be ill-equipped to suppress the mounting tension. In 1936 the Arabs launched a full-scale revolt, which compelled the Mandate regime to send an inspection committee (the Peel Commission) which was given the task of finding a geopolitical solution for the region (Bartal 2017). The committee met with experts and delegates of all parties concerned, both in public and in camera. The Arab delegates expressed their concern that the Jews—should they become the majority in Palestine—would dismantle the Muslim compounds on the Mount to rebuild their temple. This was a direct outcome of a very successful campaign promoting the centrality of the Haram for the emerging Palestinian national movement, launched by Muhammad Amin al-Husseini, who was appointed by the British as the Grand Mufti of Jerusalem and later the president of the Supreme Muslim Council in Palestine (Kupferschmidt 1989). The Peel Commission published its report in 1937. It proposed a partition of Palestine between a Jewish state and an Arab one. The plan suggested a permanent British mandatory zone, including Jerusalem, Bethlehem, and a corridor to the port of Jaffa. The reason for this was, as stated by the committee, that Jerusalem is "holy to all religions" and it was necessary to guard it as a "sacred trust of civilization" (Bovis 1971). This idea was adopted by the 1947 UN partition plan which treated Jerusalem as a *corpus separatum*, to be governed by an international entity (Yiftachel and Roded 2010). However, all these ideas quickly melted into thin air, as following the 1948 War the city was divided between the State of Israel and the Hashemite Kingdom of Jordan. Hence, from 1948 to 1967 Jerusalem was politically and religiously a divided city. Its western parts were part of the new Jewish state and soon to become its designated capital, while the eastern parts, including the sacred places in the Old City, were under Jordanian rule (Efrat 2000).

As a result of the 1967 War, Israel controls the entire city, including the Old City as part of occupied east Jerusalem. However, as mentioned above, from very early on Israeli authorities realized the problematics of the situation and conceded, albeit informally, the Jordanian Waqf Authorities permission to administer the site while Israel took charge of access and security. Since the arrangement is *de facto*, informal, and pragmatic, there has been little agreement about the specific form, content, or scope of these understandings. The outcome is a tenuous and unstable situation, fueled by a potent mix of religious fervor and misunderstanding, which time and again deteriorates to eruptions of violence and armed conflicts. Over time, a new urban reality began to unfold in Jerusalem as Israel became heavily engaged in changing the existing one to ensure the "Jewish character" of the city (Lustick 2008). The sacred and its spatial manifestations play a pivotal role in this process, which aims to bolster Jerusalem's role as a solely Jewish-Israeli capital. This fetishization process, as Lustick refers to it, is manifested in a frenzied national liturgy all focused on Jerusalem: Jerusalem Day, the Jerusalem Parade, the Jerusalem Covenant, a Jerusalem Ministry, the revival of the cult of the Jerusalem Temple, the Jerusalem 3,000 years celebration extravaganza, and more. One notable spatial outcome of this project was the demolition of a twelfth-century Islamic endowment (*waqf*) due west and adjacent to the Haram al-Sharif, known as the Maghribi neighborhood. This was the first salvo in the national project to make way for the construction of the Western Wall Plaza, just a few days after Israel assumed control over the city (Reiter 2017). Since its construction, this plaza has served as a central gathering place for a plethora of religious and nationalist functions.

Against the Jewish-Israeli mobilization of the sacred place and the construction of a highly semiotic set of rituals that aims to validate Jewish/Israeli ownership, a mirror project of radicalization has been taking place among Islamic Palestinian groups (Zilberman 2001). A case in point is Article 14 in the original charter of Hamas, the Islamic-Palestinian liberation movement, that fuses Palestinian nationalism and Islam through Jerusalem and its Islamic sacred center: "Palestine is an Islamic endowment which is the first of the two *kiblas* (direction of the prayer), the third of the holy (Islamic) sanctuaries, and the point of departure for Muhammad's night journey to the seven heavens" (Hamas 1988). In the current charter of Hamas, Article 7 of the General Principles and Policies section is a slightly more elaborate version, which like its predecessor highlights Jerusalem's pivotal role in the national project:

> Palestine is at the heart of the Arab and Islamic Ummah and enjoys a special status. Within Palestine there exists Jerusalem, whose precincts are blessed by Allah. Palestine is the Holy Land, which Allah has blessed for humanity. It is the Muslims' first Qiblah and the destination of the journey performed at night by Prophet Muhammad, peace be upon him. It is the location from where he ascended to the upper heavens.
>
> (Hamas 2017)

The creation of the Palestinian Authority following the Oslo Accords in 1993 also added to the complexity of the situation, since the Palestinians under the leadership of Arafat constantly strove to better their position and to undermine both Israeli and Jordanian control of the sacred compound and in East Jerusalem at large (Berkovits 2000). A triangle of power was formed in the conflict over the Haram al-Sharif, whose three vertices are the Hashemite Kingdom of Jordan, the Palestinian Authority, and the State of Israel. Another significant player would emerge during the late 1990s, in the shape of the Northern Branch of the Israeli Islamic Movement. This would be achieved, as I argue here, through the glocalization of the Jerusalemite sacred compound and by ceaseless efforts within and outside Israel to promote the movement as the main defender of Palestinian and Islamic rights therein.

The radicalization of religious groups on both sides and their reconceptualization of the site weigh heavily on the daily management of the compound and surely on interreligious encounters within. Innovative, and hitherto forbidden, theological understandings among radical Jewish groups and politicians regarding the construction of a Third Temple atop the mountain is met with parallel radicalization among Islamic-Palestinians that vehemently denies Jewish rights at the site and produces it as a location of political resistance to Israeli occupation (Freas 2017). During the Camp David Summit (July 2000), President Clinton suggested an urban plan which envisages the city as both entities' divided capital, and accordingly, addresses the hotspot of the sacred:

> Regarding the Haram/Temple Mount, I believe that the gaps are not related to practical administration but to the symbolic issues of sovereignty and to finding a way to accord respect to the religious beliefs of both sides. ... 1- Palestinian sovereignty over the Haram, and Israeli sovereignty over a) the Western Wall and the space sacred to Judaism of which it is a part; b) the Western Wall and the Holy of Holies of which it is a part ...
>
> 2- Palestinian sovereignty over the Haram and Israeli sovereignty over the Western Wall and shared functional sovereignty over the issue of excavation under the Haram and behind the Wall such that mutual consent would be requested before any excavation can take place.
>
> (Clinton 2000)

The Clinton parameters, as they came to be known, were yet another unsuccessful attempt in a string of international proposals, aiming to separate the political from the religious in Jerusalem. The two leaders, Barak on the Israeli side and Arafat on the Palestinian, were afraid or ill-equipped to agree to a plan that would imply concessions on their part at the most holy "national" place. The compound proved impervious to any formula of a shared sovereignty. The summit collapsed due to the parties' inability to share the holy or concede to a new power-geometry that would enable "sharing the sacra" (Podeh 2015). Barkan and Barkey's analysis seems to describe the events about to unfold in Jerusalem following the failed summit: "the indivisibility of a site is often raised by politicians and others who focus on the topic with a particular goal ... to explain a political failure, to escalate a conflict or to rally nationalist support" (2015: 16). Indeed, this was exactly the political move which Sharon took when he paid that well-publicized visit to the compound on September 28, 2000. Sharon was exploiting the iconicity of the site among his supporters to gain political cachet. This visit, along with Arafat's recognition that he might restore his international standing through an uprising, paved the way to the bloodiest encounter between the two sides. Between 2001 and 2005 violence in its formal military manifestations and informal daily resistance raged through the land. Since then, time and again the sacred mountain has transformed into a battlefield between Palestinians who want to challenge the Israeli occupation and Israeli security forces. Additionally, a fundamental change regarding the site is occurring among Jewish groups.

Until recently, the general theological understanding among Orthodox Jews was that it is best to avoid the site of the former Temple as it might involve an unlawful transgression of the Holy of Holies. Shortly after the 1967 War, the majority of Jewish religious authorities promoted an understanding along the following lines: Since the sanctity of the site has never ended, it is forbidden to enter the Temple Mount until the Temple is built (Zolti 1967). However, over time and against the lure of the sacred, this understanding gradually eroded. In recent years, voices have increased among Jewish religious leaders and activists who promote a different take and advocate the merit of visiting and praying within the compound (Inbari 2009). This relatively new development adds significantly to an already highly contentious and volatile situation.

One way to challenge these growing Jewish visits to the mountain was the formation of the Murabitun movement.[2] The Murabitun regard themselves as the defenders of al-Aqsa against growing Jewish encroachment on the compound's Islamic character. They began to emerge as a constant factor in the late 2000s and engage in prayers, performing *takbir* (chanting "Allah is great") and actively resist Jewish devotees who try to challenge the status quo by praying on the mountain (Schmitt 2020). Until 2015, Murabitun and Murabitat (male and female members of this semi-official organization) received monthly stipends. These were provided by Islamic charities, mainly the Northern Branch of the Islamic Movement, headed by Shaykh Ra'id Salah, who apparently conceived the idea and jump-started the organization's activities (Eldar 2015). This is but one aspect of the plethora of activities he initiated as the leader and head of a faction of the Israeli Islamic Movement. This is enabled, among other things, by his Israeli citizenship which lends him a status unattainable by Palestinians, who do not enjoy the same freedom of movement. While the Palestinians under Israeli occupation are heavily monitored and at times restricted from visiting the mountain and performing rituals therein, Israeli-Palestinian Muslim citizens are not subjected to the same limitations. This has enabled a unique situation and opportunity for the Israeli Islamic Movement to become a meaningful player in this intricate religio-political situation. This is, as I have narrated up till now, but the last phase in the convoluted modern history of the compound which was transformed under nationalism into the most iconic and sacred landmark of both parties concerned. Against the countless studies of Jerusalem, this analysis may be taken as rudimentary at best, but I rather think it allows a sufficient background to follow my argument regarding the Islamic Movement as an agent of change. In what follows, I focus on the role played by the Movement in the glocalization of the Haram al-Sharif.

The Israeli Islamic Movement and the Glocalization of the Haram al-Sharif

This self-appointed sheikh of al-Aqsa has built his own kingdom within Jerusalem. He is seeking to capture the hearts and minds of Jerusalemites as victory in Jerusalem offers him the greatest platform to Islamic victory in the Arab world.

(A PA official on Ra'id Salah, cited in Larkin and Dumper 2012: 50)

Following the Oslo Accords (1995), the involvement of the Israeli Palestinian minority in the Israeli public sphere has grown. This is due to the realization that the negotiations between Israel and the Palestinian Authority do not contribute to any significant improvement in their civil status or rights. This realization was translated into activities that "localize the national struggle" (Rekhess 2002). Thus, issues that have haunted Palestinian communities for decades, such as the right of return, accessibility to heritage sites, the "opening of the '48 files," refugees, land ownership, and their very definition as a national minority, began to surface in the public media, courts, as well as in the Israeli parliament. This is particularly salient in struggles concerning sacred heritage, as many of the case studies presented hitherto clearly demonstrate. One of the dominant players among the Palestinian minority has been the local organization(s) of the Islamic Movement. This is an ideological offshoot of the transnational Sunni Islamist organization, the Society of the Muslim Brothers (better known simply as the Muslim Brothers). Since its foundation during the 1970s, the movement has become one of the leading social and political powers within the Israeli Palestinian minority. The founder of the Israeli chapter was Shaykh 'Abdullah Nimr Darwish who ideologically was a follower of the writings and teachings of the likes of Hassan al-Bana, Muhammad Abduh, and more (interview with 'Abdullah Nimr Darwish, October 15, 2002). During the 1970s, the movement's activities were mainly involved with *da'wa*, that is, preaching and writing that invite devotees to return and practice their Islamic faith. Darwish saw the return to "pure" Islam as the remedy for internal strife and the solution to the national problem. In the early 1970s he and his followers had a violent phase, which landed them in prison. However, after that period of incarceration Darwish began to express more moderate views and opted for non-violent conduct (Larkin and Nasasra 2021).

In the 1980s, the movement entered a new phase when a generation of young intellectuals, graduates of religious colleges who were a decade junior to Darwish, joined in the ranks of the movement. They became involved in local politics, particularly at the municipal level, and hence became more influential and armed with resources to affect changes in their respective communities (interview with Ibrahim Sarsur, November 29, 2008).[3] Ra'id Salah was a notable figure among these young leaders, who later became the mayor of his hometown of Umm al-Fahm (1989–2001). Eventually, he became the driving force behind the split in the movement and the head of its Northern Branch. This was also the period when the movement became actively involved in defending Islamic sacred heritage such as sacred places, cemeteries, ruined villages, and more. This was achieved through the foundation of the Al-Aqsa Association for the Preservation of Holy Sites by Shaykh Kamal Rayan in 1991. The Association was the first Islamic body to attempt to fill in the lack of religious leadership among Palestinian communities in Israel since 1948, which had rendered Islamic endowments and abandoned Islamic heritage properties, vulnerable to development plans, land confiscations, and neglect (interview with Kamal Rayan, October 14, 2002). During the 1990s, the Islamic movement gained wide popular support, largely because of its effective network of social services and welfare programs in Palestinian communities. This is also connected to the rise of political Islam in the Middle East (Dakwar 2007). In 1996, a disagreement within the movement concerning participation in the national elections to the Israeli Knesset ended in a schism. Since then, the movement has been operating through two factions: the Northern Branch of the Islamic Movement, which opposes participation in national elections on ideological grounds and takes part only in municipal elections, and the Southern Branch of the Islamic Movement, which has become a constant feature in Israeli national politics (Luz 2013a). The names given to these factions were based on a somewhat loose geography of their respective leaders' origins.

Shortly after the split, Salah gained recognition as a tenacious and fearless champion of the Palestinian struggle. Time and again he challenged Israeli policies that he perceived as destined to annihilate Palestinian existence, heritage, and memories. This has landed him on a collision path with the Israeli authorities, which also amounted to repeated periods of incarceration for breaching numerous state laws (Larkin and Dumper 2012). Since 2001, when he resigned from office as mayor, he generally refuses even to meet with Israeli (Jewish) officials, press, or academics. Since 2000, when I began following and studying the Islamic movement's activities, I have met with dozens of leaders and activists from both factions. It is rather telling that all my endeavors to arrange an audience with him were denied. This is part of his unyielding ideology and resistance to the current Israeli hegemonic position, as can be clearly seen in the following concise narration of his manifesto as head of the Islamic Movement:

> The Islamic Movement was established in the mid-1970s and has been concerned with preserving the identity of its followers and with integrating their Islamic, Arab, and Palestinian dimensions. At the same time the movement seeks, through its members and institutions, to protect our existence on our land, defend our rights and sacred sites, and assume our legitimate role in supporting the Palestinian people. We are particularly concerned about the status of Jerusalem and its holy places, especially al-Aqsa Mosque. Currently, the movement enjoys good relations with the entire political and religious spectrum of the Arab Palestinian community within the 1948 borders, and at the same time endeavors to play a positive role with respect to Palestinian society in the West Bank and the Gaza Strip.
>
> (Dakwar 2007)

Salah's ceaseless engagements with Jerusalem, and particularly his ongoing activities concerning al-Aqsa Mosque, have won him the title of Shaykh al-Aqsa along with global recognition. This was achieved through different projects revolving around al-Aqsa, eventually positioning him and his Branch as major players and hardliners against Israel in both internal Palestinian politics and Arab and Islamic international relations (Luz 2014b). His first project in this direction took place in 1996, shortly after the schism in the movement and revolved around the al-Aqsa Mosque. In the summer of that year, the Endowment Authority received the Israeli government's approval to perform maintenance work at the underground halls at the south end of the compound. These halls were originally constructed by King Herod (37–4 BCE) as part of his ambitious project of rebuilding the Jewish Temple (Ritmeyer and Ritmeyer 1989). During the Crusader period, as the al-Aqsa Mosque was identified as the Temple of Solomon, these underground halls were known as Solomon's Stables. They were generally known among Muslim devotees as "ancient al-Aqsa" (Arabic: *al-Aqsa al-atiqa*). The Waqf received Israel's approval to renovate this underground site as the claim was made that since Ramadan would be celebrated that year during the winter (January 21 to February 18), this site would provide for suitable shelter from the rains for the thousands of expected visitors. Under the leadership of Ra'id Salah, the Northern Branch joined hands with this initiative and was responsible for the mobilization of thousands of volunteers from across Israel to collect money and materials which were indispensable for this building project. The movement was thus in charge of the execution of an unprecedented renovation project, ultimately transforming the halls into a huge underground compound of 4,000 m² that could accommodate some 6,000 worshippers and is considered among the largest mosques in the world.

Carpets for its interior were donated by the Arab Republic of Egypt and donations arrived from around the Middle East (Abd al-Rahman 2022). The project was carried out along with fierce and constant clashes with Israeli authorities—both in courts and on the ground with Israeli police (Reiter 2016). It was a great success for the movement and for Salah personally. The fact that he confronted the Israeli authorities directly and prevailed not only won him the title of "Shaykh of al-Aqsa" but also positioned him as the most influential Islamic leader among Israeli-Palestinian Muslims. This was a live demonstration that the power of the place, combined with the organizational skills of the movement, could bring about massive public support among Israeli-Palestinian citizens and beyond. The name given to this underground mosque is *al-Musalla al-Marwani*, that is, the al-Marwani praying area. This is a highly intriguing

Figure 6.1 The Underground Marwani Mosque (courtesy of Mr. Ron Peled).

idea, as it relates the site to the family of 'Abd al-Malik ibn Marwan, the caliph who was responsible for the building project of al-Aqsa and the Dome of the Rock in the late seventh century (Elad 1995). However, it is also totally fictitious, in the sense that there is neither indication nor a valid source that can verify the use of this name at any previous period in history, and certainly no connection to 'Abd al-Malik's project. This is a calculated move, meant to authenticate this new place, not only to local Palestinians who come to pray at the compound, but surely to Muslims across the globe. This invented tradition was quickly accepted, as one of my interviewees rejoined when asked about the name: "If it is called al-Marwani, then surely it was built by the caliph al-Marwan" (interview with L., August 15, 2004).[4] One of the outcomes of the 1996 al-Aqsa campaign was an annual rally conducted under the name "al-Aqsa is in Danger" (Ar.: *al-Aqsa fi Khatar*). The rally was initially organized as a fundraiser for the 1996 renovation campaign but was such an astounding success that it was continued annually until the movement was outlawed in 2015 (Nasasra 2018).

Salah was not the first to come up with the notion of "al-Aqsa is in Danger." This was a well-known slogan, heavily used by the Grand Mufti of Jerusalem Hajj Amin al-Husseini during the Mandate period. As previously mentioned, he promoted the notion among Palestinians that the Jews wanted to demolish the Dome of the Rock and the al-Aqsa Mosque in order to pave the way to building their own temple there (Porat 1977). That being said, Salah certainly took this idea to a higher level and managed to transform it into the cornerstone of his movement's course of action. The yearly rallies attracted tens of thousands of people, during which speeches were made by dignitaries of the movement and funds were allocated for the numerous projects the movement was conducting throughout Israel/Palestine (Luz 2004). These rallies inspired solidarity events across the Arab and the Muslim world which supported the Palestinian cause and called for safeguarding the al-Aqsa Mosque. A case in point is the 2008 rally in Umm al-Fahm, which was attended also by a delegation from South Africa. During his speech, the South African delegate assured the audience that "occupied al-Aqsa" would be freed: "Know that the wheel turns, and that the sun will yet shine. We say to you, be patient, in the end victory will belong to Islam. We hope that soon we will pray together in Jerusalem, in Al-Aqsa." A telegram carrying a message from 'Amru Moussa, the Arab League's Secretary-General, was also read to the crowd: "We are saddened by what is happening in Al-Aqsa and by what the Israeli occupation is doing in Jerusalem. Jerusalem is at the center of the Arab League's agenda, and the Arab media should focus on what is being done in the city and in the mosque" (Roffe-Ofir 2008). Shaykh Salah's speech at this rally was aimed at various audiences, from the Israeli government to Palestinian leaders and to the four corners of the Muslim world:

> I say to the Israeli occupation, and those representing it on behalf of all the people here, that your plan, which we exposed, despite your dream to destroy the mosque, your occupation will not last for long … [to PA president Mahmoud Abbas and Hamas prime minister Ismail Haniyeh—N.L.] What we are asking from you both for this holiday [the upcoming Ramadan–N.L.] is a gift for every Muslim and every free man, is to renew the dialogue and reconcile … [to the Arab world] Where is your manliness? For 40 years the al-Aqsa Mosque calls to you and asks where you are. Do you accept that we, the besieged, must ask permission from the Israeli occupation to enter the mosque? Must ask for permission to pray in the mosque?
>
> (Roffe-Ofir 2008)

Positioning himself as the champion of al-Aqsa and East Jerusalem at large and the defender of endangered Islamic endowments transformed Salah's status, not only into a leading figure of what are commonly called "the Palestinians of 1948," but has placed him on the Islamic world stage. This multi-scalar politics has long been utilized in the Northern Branch's weekly magazine, aptly named *Sawt al-Haqq wal-Huriyya* ("The Voice of Truth and Freedom"). Since its first appearance in 1996, and with growing fervor since 2000 until it was closed following a governmental injunction in 2015, the magazine has dedicated numerous articles, special supplements, and opinion columns to the "al-Aqsa is in Danger" campaign.[5] In what follows, I will only touch upon a fraction of these narratives, through which the Haram is glocalized.

On September 15, 2002, a special supplement to the magazine featured under the title "al-Aqsa in Danger." It was dedicated to the history, religious importance, and contemporary challenges (mostly violations of its sanctity) by Israeli authorities (*Sawt al-Haqq wal-Huriyya*, special supplement 15.9.2002). In an article called "Al-Aqsa is above and beyond any would-be negotiator," Tawfiq Muhammad 'Ari'ar presents us with an uncompromising view of the Islamic character of the Haram ('Ari'ar 2002). The conflict is essentially a religious one, claims 'Ari'ar, and since it is one of the three most important Islamic shrines, it is not to be negotiated nor compromised. The author exploits all the standard religious justifications in order to warn PA officials against concessions when negotiating with Israel over the place. He is particularly averse to the idea that Jews should be allowed to continue to pray at the Western Wall. An even more confrontational and adamant approach is advanced in an article by Ra'id Salah. He vows to defend the Haram with his life and warns against even the smallest concession of any of its parts:

> This is the destination of the nocturnal journey of the Prophet (*isra'*) and from here he ascended to heaven (*mi'raj*). This place witnessed the conquest of Jerusalem by 'Umar ibn al-Khattab and the liberation of Jerusalem from the hands of the Crusaders by Salah al-Din ... and because it is so important it is beyond negotiation and no voice will rise higher than the voice of al-Aqsa. And to those of feeble character that say that America is stronger than them, the blessed al-Aqsa answers and says: God is stronger. And the Western Wall from within and from without is part of al-Aqsa and so are the other buildings and mosques within it, including al-Musalla al-Marwani. This being the true nature of al-Aqsa, we will renew our covenant with God and our covenant with al-Aqsa and we will pin our hopes on our Islamic *umma* and our Arab world and our Palestinian people and reiterate: We shall redeem you in spirit and blood.
>
> (Salah 2002a)

Rhetoric of this nature positions the Israeli-Palestinian Islamic movement as the most hawkish and reluctant Palestinian player regarding any concession over the Haram. Salah also makes a connection among the local, regional, and global scales as part of his strategy to thwart or resist Israeli control over the Temple Mount/Haram al-Sharif. This is even more emphasized in the following excerpt from another op-ed:

> The Mosque of al-Aqsa is an Islamic, Arab, and Palestinian property and no one save them, regardless of their identity and who they are, and particularly the Jews, have any rights over there until the end of days. Whoever accepts their right on even a stone or anything else there is a traitor! It is our duty to confront this person and inform him he is indeed a traitor. It is a treacherous act against God, Muhammad, the believers, the Islamic nation, the Arab world, and the Palestinian people. It is an act of betrayal of the first of the *qiblas*, of the second mosque, and the Prophet's ascension to heaven and it is a betrayal of the mosque in Mecca and the mosque of Medina. It is betrayal of the infant martyrs, of Muhammad Durra[6] and others. We say to whoever tries to undermine these standpoints: You will not succeed; the mosque of al-Aqsa is ours and no one of the Jewish public has any part in it. We firmly believe that no Muslim, Arab, or Palestinian with a shred of pride in his heart will forsake any part, stone, wall, path, monument, dome, or structure in the blessed al-Aqsa within and without, above ground or underground.
>
> (Salah 2002b)

Myth has the task of giving an historical intention a natural justification (Lincoln 1989). The strength of the myth is discovered when contingency and the temporary appear eternal, or in other words, as if it has always been like that. Thus, the act of mythification is exposed and projected as a highly politicized act which aims to answer the contemporary needs of a group. This realization can never be truer than in the current ways the Haram al-Sharif is being produced and promoted. The past of the place, argues Massey, is as open to multiplicity of meanings as is its present (Massey 1995). Claims and counter-claims about the present character of a place depend in almost all cases on rival interpretations of the past. The past of a place is up for grabs, and it is in the present that we may produce a certain understanding of it, such a one that promotes our most urgent needs and political necessities. In the case in point, Salah is promoting a twofold understanding regarding the place. Firstly, its religious and political significance for Palestinians and Muslims worldwide. Secondly, total denial of any Jewish heritage in the compound. Salah's skillful use of the media, and surely his perpetual endeavors in and around the Haram al-Sharif, has enabled him to gain attention from regional and global Islamic organizations and governments. He hosts delegations from around the Muslim world and frequently dialogues with the Islamic international community. Delegations from the Northern Branch are often invited to participate in Islamic conferences around the world and often visit Arab and Islamic countries. In 2005 Salah visited Malaysia, had audiences with officials while there, and lectured at Islamic institutions, during which he declared: "If al-Quds continues to be under occupation, every Muslim in the world is occupied" (Nasasra 2018). This is exactly the kind of rhetoric that enables the glocalization of the Haram and fleshes out a multi-scalar politics that constantly challenges the current power structure in Jerusalem. His meteoric rise to becoming a well-known and admired figure throughout the Muslim world rests mostly on this strategy. When incarcerated (again) in August 2017, a campaign demanding his release was launched in Turkey with the support of Muslim activists from around the Middle East. The late Shaykh Yusuf al-Qaradawi, one of the most renowned Islamic leaders, spoke on his behalf in a rally in Istanbul. The media campaign was conducted under the slogan: We are all Shaykh al-Aqsa. Yunus Abu Jarad, the media coordinator for the campaign, was quoted as saying: "Sheikh Ra'id Salah is the icon of al-Aqsa. Until now, they [Israel] has not found a clear accusation or charge against him—they merely want to shut him down ... his arrest is not just a Palestinian issue, but an Islamic one as well" (al-Tahan 2017). It is pertinent to stress again that these are but a few examples of Salah's relentless campaign. Even though I have stressed his activities as he is the person most identified with this glocalization process, he is surely not the only Palestinian leader engaged with the Haram al-Sharif, but again: he is the most iconic one. The utilization of al-Aqsa's threatened status has enabled him and his movement to challenge the current national power-geometry as a global rallying mechanism, along what I define throughout this chapter as glocalizing the sacred.

* * *

This chapter revolves around scaling the sacred and scalar politics which involve the move from the national to the supranational and global. It centers around the most iconic holy place which serves also as the most conflicted ground in Israel/Palestine, some would surely argue also on a world scale. The nation-state is one of the most effective organizations of domination as far as scaling our lives is concerned. Jumping scale from the national, either upward or downward, allows the subordinate a contested ethnic nationalism, or at least a partial liberation and control of their life. Following this understanding, I highlighted the ways the Islamic movement in Israel is promoting new understandings regarding the Haram al-Sharif as a way to actively produce scale, within a multi-scalar configuration. Promoting the Haram as a national Palestinian symbol effectively challenges prevalent notions about the place within the Jewish majority in Israel. Yet at the same time, it enables the Palestinian minority to play a more active and meaningful role among their compatriots outside Israel. This perfectly explains the active role the Israeli-Palestinian Islamic Movement is playing in opposing various state initiatives regarding the site. A case in point is the demonstrations organized against the police's intentions to allow Jewish groups to pray at the Haram during the Passover of 2009. By advancing the place as a Palestinian national icon and actively defending it as such, the movement is bettering its position within Israel/Palestine, and it is also actively approaching the regional (Arab) and the global (Islamic).

The glocalization of the Haram al-Sharif is first and foremost an emancipatory project of rescaling the local and promoting it to the supranational and the global, while simultaneously introducing a global understanding of the place within the local. The Islamic movement in Israel is actively engaged in a process of multi-scalar configuration of the place as a way to transcend the control of the national state (deterritorialization) on the one hand, and to bring about a new understanding of the place into the national and local scale (reterritorialization) on the other. The interaction between the local and the global is mediated by signs and symbols, images and narratives, and by circulating meanings (Ivakhhiv 2006). Through active engagement with the place (both in tangible and intangible ways) and circulating specific meanings of the Haram, the Islamic movement is engaged in highly affective multi-scalar politics, as it engages with the inherently contested and highly evocative nature of sacred places. This process also introduces the movement as an active player and a glocal agent of the place, thus gaining respectability and agency not only locally and nationally within Israel, but also reaching for the global.

7

Epilogue

The Crown is an historical televised drama series about the reign of Queen Elizabeth II that portrays her life from 1947 to the early twenty-first century. The fourth episode of the first season revolves around the magnificent event of her coronation. While the ceremony is taking place in London, the Queen's uncle, known by his regnal name as Edward VIII, who abdicated the throne, is depicted in his Paris mansion, watching the ceremony on television accompanied by a group of American guests. As the ceremony reaches its culmination with the anointing of the new queen by the Archbishop of Canterbury, the audience back home and around the world are not privy to the ritual, as the screen is deliberately frozen. One of the guests wonders how come the most important part is not shared with the viewers, to which the former king answers: "Because this is the most sacred moment, and we are mere mortals." As we, the audience, are slowly exposed to the televised ritual (to be clear, not the original one), the former king stands in front of his TV screen, as he narrated and translates—vicariously through his guests to us—the enigmatic, indeed holy, aspects of the coronation ceremony:

> Duke of Windsor: And thus, through oils and oaths, orbs and scepter, symbol after symbol. An unfathomable web of arcane mystery and liturgy blurring so many lines no clergyman, or historian, or lawyer could ever untangle any of it.
> Guest: It is crazy.
> Duke of Windsor: On the contrary, it is perfectly sane. Who wants transparency when you can have magic? Who wants prose when you can have poetry? Pull away the veil and what are you left with? An ordinary young woman of modest ability and little imagination, but wrap her like this, anoint her with oil and hey presto, what do you have? A goddess.
> (*The Crown*, season 1, episode 4)

Surely unknowingly, the writers of the series depicted most accurately an enchanted encounter with the holy. Indeed, those meetings with the sacred realm, as the abdicating king perceptively observes, separate regular mundane life from the divine. This encounter was brilliantly, and at least for me rather challengingly, articulated by Rudolph Otto as the encounter with the numinous (1959). By that he meant the outwardly mysterious quality of the divine, which, according to him (and others such as Eliade), is unequivocally separated from the profane. This theoretical approach to the sacred was defined previously in this book as substantial.

The pre-modern understanding of the sacred and its pivotal role in humans' lives, which informed rituals such as coronations of kings and queens, daily encounters with food and other mundane aspects of life, individual and communal events, saw sanctity and magic everywhere. Against the changes brought forth by newly emerging philosophies, most notably the Enlightenment, and their entanglement with the scientific revolution of the nineteenth century, there developed a different understanding of the sacred realm and its role in daily life. Put simply, the sacred, the holy, and surely the magical were deemed to be losing their influence and authority over human life. Schiller defined this process as the de-divinization of the world, and along the same logic, Max Weber referred to it as disenchantment (Jenkins 2012). These theoretical constructions try to encapsulate the historical process that characterizes Western culture of that time, according to which nature and all areas of human experience are becoming less mysterious and more comprehensible and measurable. Classification of the phenomena that surround us, greater understanding of causality in nature and the entire universe through scientific theories and empirical discoveries, entangled with the growing impact of more egalitarian political theories combined and separately were leading to the secularization of modern societies, or so it seemed. As Saler puts it, "wonders and marvels have been demystified by science, spirituality has been supplanted by secularism, spontaneity has been replaced by bureaucratization, and the imagination has been subordinated to instrumental reason" (Saler 2006: 692).

This understanding has loomed large among students of religion for the better part of the twentieth century under what might be loosely termed the secularization theory (Swatos and Christiano 1999). The dominant working hypothesis among scholars was that modernization and all that it brings under its wings would amount to the decline of religion. Be that as it may, along with a growing critique by post-modern and post-colonial theorists of Weber's (and other early modernist theorists) binary approach to modernity versus religion, secularization theory is losing its sway. Surely, modernization has had some secularizing effects and yet scholars have begun to accept that the relations between religion and modernity are far from the binary approach according to which they were previously explained (Berger 1999). The world apparently still holds magic and awe for the majority of humanity, who attest in survey after survey that faith and indeed religion are still vital to their existence (Sherwood 2018). Nurit Stadler and I explored these ideas in our joint project "Enchanted Places on the Margins" (http://sacredplaces.huji.ac.il/). In this multi-sited project, we scrutinized sacred places we identified as enchanted, that is, in their early stages of development and in their charismatic phase before routinization. By availing ourselves of the term "enchanted places," we not only accepted the prevailing criticism of the desecularization theory but took it one step further, as we demonstrated in numerous publications: devotion and magic are currently being reinforced and reincorporated into everyday reality (e.g., Stadler and Luz 2015; Luz and Stadler 2019). Indeed, some of the sites in question and the data harvested therein inform and furnish this current endeavor. Further still, I still pursue some of these ideas by centering this book on the crucial importance that sacred places hold in the socio-political reality of current societies. In that sense, this book should be seen as another brick in the growing structure of desecularization theory and a contribution to a retheorized cultural geography of religion.

In his opus magnum, *Les formes élémentaires de la vie religieuse* (*Elementary Forms of Religious Life*), Durkheim was searching (among other things) for the role and definition of religion within contemporary societies. He suggested focusing on the functional aspects of religion for society by emphasizing the role of the sacred in boundary making, regulating, and constructing attractions (Koenig 2020). Set within a Durkheimian understanding of the importance of the sacred in religious practices, this book focused on contemporary sacred places and their socio-political meanings for minorities within a hegemonic and secularizing state-system. My overarching argument is that sacred places and the manifold socio-religious-political practices they entail provide a space which is less scrutinized by the state, and by hegemonic powers within it. This allows for alternative ideas of the socio-political to be envisioned, contested, and produced. This argument emerges from my growing understanding that these spatialities, which are evolving at the intersection of religion and politics, are lenses and arenas through which we may further explore society-space reflexive relations. The places explored therein were studied under the assumption that they are, due to their inherent spatiality, always in flux, and therefore, constantly being produced, contested, and in a perpetual dynamic process. The study of sacred places was conflated with scalar awareness and scalar analysis ranging from the body to the global scale. This has enabled me to uncover the different forces that shape and contest the sacred. To that end, I divided my analysis into six chapters.

Chapter 1 was of an introductory nature and offered a contextualization of the highly complex and variegated hagio-geography of Israel/Palestine. This was accomplished by marrying together the notion of the Holy Land and the concept of ethnocracy. This follows my firm conviction that one simply cannot understand current events in Israel/Palestine apart from the ethnocratization process of the Holy Land. Chapters 2 to 6 followed sacred places set in a scalar matrix. This construction proved to be highly suggestive to understanding the politics involved with the places, as the very move from one scale to another involves engagement with power and, in many of the sites, challenges to the current power-structure. In Chapter 2, I focused on the body scale and embodied practices within and outside sacred places. I centered my analysis on what I deem highly important, which is the web of significance individuals weave within and outside sacred places and the personal-scale politics which their encounters construct. Embodiment, as explored in its various (but surely not all) manifestations in the realm of the sacred, takes many shapes and narrates the relational dynamics of the spatial and the social. It is in the body and through the body that sacred places are experienced, and other scales (rural, urban, national, and the global) are enacted and surely become more tangible. For many of my interlocutors, healing was very much on their mind. Healing, both physical and spiritual, is arguably one of the most striking embodied practices often associated with sacred places. Religious practitioners, pilgrims, and visitors are often engaged in recreating self and body through rituals enacted on site. And yet, even at the body scale socio-political processes were often very much on the agenda, as the personal indeed is always political. This is also a direct result of the geopolitical changes following the 1948 war, during which the Palestinian majority became the minority and many of its sacred places were either taken over or are currently at risk of being erased from the landscape. Thus, in many of the sites a strong connection was found between body and nation, through what I framed as embodying the nation.

Chapter 3 moves from the body scale to the community scale and looks at two rural sacred places, Maqam Abu al-Hijja and the Shrine of Mariam Bawardy. I was mostly engaged with the current transformations of these sites and explored both the micro and macro politics within and outside their communities' scale.

In doing so I followed Hertz's pioneering ideas of how to study a local cult and thus my analysis of the place at the village/community scale fleshed out various spheres of influence and complex politics which foregrounded the places and enabled us to cross their threshold. The chapter revealed the mythology of the place(s), as well as the changing landscape and materiality as manifestations of the politics of the place. The ways places are constructed, produced, and surely understood among community members, and their evolving landscape and materiality, are nothing short of the spatialization of politics in different scalar settings. Focusing on the community/village scale allowed for an analysis which transcends the individual understanding of the sites and indeed, the embodied practices, lands us squarely within the politics of the place as it is negotiated among different players within and outside the community. My analysis thus entailed both micro and macro politics within and outside their respective communities' scale.

Chapters 4 and 5 focused on the urban scale. In Chapter 4, I explored struggles and conflicts over urban sacred places while engaging with Lefebvre's notion of the right to the city. This is executed here by harnessing his post-Marxist approach into the field of symbolic goods and by exploring the sacred as a resource in the urban sphere. Lefebvre's approach is highly conducive to examining the ways in which different actors are conversing and contesting their right of ownership and control of their past, their heritage, and surely their preferred urban culture. Unpacking Lefebvre's right to the city through the religious factor seems a much-needed theoretical expansion, given the unparalleled urban growth entwined with the (re)emergence of religion in the public sphere. I engaged with the idea of the "right to the city" as a launching pad to explore the struggles over the sacred as ways of executing the right of access as claiming the city. I examined these ideas while engaging with two urban conflicts over sacred sites, in both cases by a marginalized community that seeks way to repossess and gain ownership over its (endangered) heritage. In the conflicts over both the Grand Mosque of Beersheba and the Mosque of Hassan Bek in Tel Aviv-Jaffa, these were exactly the sentiments expressed by members of the subaltern groups, that is, aspiring for greater impact and influence on their city. These two examples demonstrate how in Israeli mixed cities, minority's sacred places are found time and again at the very center of urban conflicts, as they become grounds where subaltern groups compete to share the city. This has to do, as I demonstrated in both cases, with firstly, the intrinsic contested nature of sacred places; and secondly, in that they are replete with meaning which is there to be owned and controlled. Additionally, I followed Göle's construction of visibility as a form of agency in the public domain. Visibility, and the semiotic reading it entails and provokes, is a discursive agency which is articulated through materialities. Following these semiotic interpretations, I was able to take up the mantle of the hidden (hi)stories of the politics of sacred places in the urban landscape. By tapping into the realms of materiality, I also wanted to offer a more expansive understanding of how cultural-political analysis of the sacred and heavy engagement with matters of control and ownership may benefit from introducing the ways in which people experience the landscape, and more specifically, matters of belief and religious objects. This understanding and growing engagement with the non-human and the impacts of materiality have brought me to my *ReligioCity* project, which furnishes Chapter 5.

ReligioCity is a place-based dynamic concept I developed to grapple with the role of religion(s) in cities, rather than a unitary logic to account for faith within global-cities theorizing. As such, *ReligioCity* does not indicate a type or class of cities, nor does it address a certain cityness. It is a concept that opens up a myriad of opportunities to engage in urban-religion encounters and explore these intricate relations. *ReligioCity* needs be seen as a frame of reference, indeed a theoretical model, that allows us to account for urban-religion(s) dynamics and highlights the importance and ample influences of these intricate relations in cities. When coining this concept, I brought together two defined bodies of scholarship: the desecularization of cities and the spatial turn in religious studies. *ReligioCity* emerges directly from my long-time engagement with the sacred, and particularly the conflictual nature of sacred places, and my growing interest in more than human analysis of the cultural landscape. To further explain *ReligioCity* and expand my take on the urban scale, I empirically explored religious infrastructures in Acre, a multi-ethnic and multi-religious city. This facilitated a deeper engagement with the many ways religion and city are interacting, but also the ways the religious subjects experience, envision, and produce their city and are affected by it. My exploration of Acre suggested firmly that one simply cannot understand the prevailing urban logic in Acre (as a case in point of the mixed-ethnocratic city) in disconnect from urban ethnocracy. This situation also informs the ethno-religious urban identity. Following a discussion of the extensive ways religion informs the urban sphere, I concluded the chapter with an analysis of the conflict over the Lababidi Mosque. I framed the discussion and conflict along the lines of decolonization by an indigenous minority within a colonial-settler society. This theoretical lens allowed an analysis of the role of urban religion(s) as a site of converging and conflicting visions and voices, practices, and orientations, which arise out of the complex desires, needs, and fears of many different people in the context of urban ethnocracy.

Chapter 6 addresses the conflict over the sacred as it moves from the national scale to the supra-national and global scales. In this chapter, I focused on the compound of the Haram al-Sharif/Temple Mount in Jerusalem, and especially on the role played by the Israeli Islamic Movement in glocalizing the place. Throughout the chapter I portray an intricate and highly nuanced picture of the ways this place is assuming a unique and unparalleled position in the ethno-national conflict within and outside Israel. Glocalization is a process where the global and local are entangled together and construct a new reality. The very move to the global involves scalar politics, whose main agent in this case is the Israeli Islamic Movement. This upscaling of the sacred is a way to challenge, if not overthrow, Israeli control of what has become the most iconic symbol of both national projects, Jerusalem and its most holy compound. Therefore, the glocalization of the Haram al-Sharif is first and foremost an emancipatory project of rescaling the local and promoting it to the supranational and the global, while simultaneously introducing a global understanding of the place within the local. The Islamic movement in Israel is actively engaged in a process of multi-scalar configuration of the place as a way to transcend the control of the national state (deterritorialization) on the one hand, and to bring about a new understanding of the place into the national and local scale (reterritorialization) on the other.

My intentions in this book were to flesh out the politics of sacred places as they transpire and impact everyday lives in contemporary societies. Further, I wanted to locate them at the very center of socio-political reality while focusing on Israel/Palestine. This was executed, indeed inspired, by following a Durkheimian approach which focuses on the functional role of religion per se and its constitutive function for society. What I find particularly felicitous (for my probes into the sacred) in Durkheim's sociology of religion is surely the importance he assigns to the political aspects of religion. In his sociology of religion, the sacred holds a pivotal position as the "realm of non-ordinary reality" with which humans engage through various forms of religious representations (Bellah 2011). It is through the sacred as a regulatory power, and in tandem with the fascination it holds for devotees, that Durkheim pushes us to explore religion in modernity. Certainly, his definition of the sacred and particularly his universalistic approach, which was heavily criticized as a rather Christianized version of the world, have won ample and justifiable critique. Arguably, one of the most elaborated and sound condemnations coms from Hervieu-Léger (2000). In a chapter she titled "The Elusive Sacred," she argues that Durkheim and his ilk transformed the sacred into a notion that was held to be common to all people, and this is precisely why they played a decisive role as semantic producers regarding the sacra. By addressing the sacred as common to all and turning it into a theoretical concept, they enabled, so claims Hervieu-Léger, the sacred to become a tangible reality, a subject that can be identified by its property to be found in every religion. The "sacred," she claims, was perfected by Durkheim to facilitate and to posit a universal approach to religious expression in humanity. The problem, she argues, is that this understanding of the sacred is bound to reintroduce surreptitiously the very thing it was supposed to eliminate, namely the superiority of the Christian model in thinking about religion. Ultimately, she holds that the prevailing understanding of the sacred brings more confusion than clarity in current debates on religious modernity. To furnish her argument, she cites Isambert's discussion on contemporary religions: "the right to a faith that holds something to be sacred becomes the basis for recognizing the existence of the sacred" (Isambert 1982: 155, cited in Hervieu-Léger 2000: 49). Disillusioned with Durkheim's universalistic approach, she suggests a definition of religion as a distinctive mode of believing which is legitimized by an authoritative tradition, thus leaving the category of the sacred outside her purview of religious life (Hervieu-Léger 2000: 50). At the risk of being branded as oblivious to the genealogy of the sacred in sociological thought, I focused on the sacred as an essential part of the religious schools that are shaping the contested region I am exploring. I chose a rather simplistic approach which put Isambert's critique on its head, basically relying on my interlocutors' reading of their own world and thus calling a spade a spade. That is, I referred to the places explored herewith as sacred simply because this is the way they are regarded by the very individuals and groups struggling over them.

The sacred is a central currency in contemporary societies due to two intertwined processes: desecularization and the emergence of religious nationalism. As Weber himself lamented the things we lose by the disenchantment of the world which he himself so astutely observed, so did Durkheim acknowledge the possibility of the lingering or reappearance of the importance of the sacred as dovetailing the (possible) reemergence of religion in future (and contemporary) societies:

> In short, the former gods are growing old or dying, and others have not been born. That is what voided Compte's attempt to organize a religion using old historical memories, artificially revived. It is life itself, and not a dead past that

can produce a living cult. But that state of uncertainty and confused anxiety cannot last forever. A day will come when our societies once again will know hours of creative effervescence during which new ideals will again spring forth and new formulas emerge to guide humanity for a time. And when those hours have been lived through, men will spontaneously feel the need to relive them in thought from time to time—that is, to preserve their memory by means of celebrations and regularly recreate their fruits.

(Durkheim 1995: 429–30)

Regardless of our own personal approach to the role and presence of religion in contemporary societies, it is incumbent upon us to concur with Peter Berger's thought-provoking remark: "those who neglect religion in their analysis of contemporary affairs do so at great peril" (Berger 1999: 18). I will avoid the temptation of delving into one of the more contentious issues among students of the field, which is secularization versus desecularization theories. This has already furnished volumes upon volumes and a plethora of studies, and for some the jury is still out. However, I will not shy from stating my firm understanding that the paradigmatic core of secularization theory, namely the assumption that modernity entailed the functional differentiation of religion from other social systems, simply cannot be validated in my ongoing exploration of the field. It is certainly the case in Israel/Palestine, in which religion plays a pivotal role in the national claims of all parties involved. This brings me to the second process heavily affecting the politics of sacred places, the emergence of religious nationalism.

Nation and religion are both conceptual authoritative categories, indeed ideologies, which demand submission to a certain political and social order. Against earlier theoretical notions (e.g., Gellner 1983), which depicted them as diametrically opposed, it would seem today that purely secular nationalism is far from being the only political machination in existence. Further, secular nation-states can no longer be understood as the only or natural outcome of the two intertwined projects of modernization and secularization. Nationalism and religion, argues van der Veer, are better seen as valid products of a multiplicity of modernities in different parts of the world. While commonly an opposition between the secular and the religious is assumed, these categories, in certain situations, are simultaneously produced and complement each other (van der Veer 2013). Contrary to previous predictions, neither nationalism nor religion is disappearing, and the often-assumed dialectic relations between the secular state and religion are paving the way to new possibilities (Juergensmeyer

2010). One form which is emerging in numerous countries around the world is religious nationalism. This intriguing marriage between formerly competing ideologies is heavily influencing the national political realm. Apparently, religious nationalism is not alien to the formation of the modern nation-state. In fact, it was an essential part of the formation of many modern national identities. Nationalist movements were (and are) often suffused with religious narrative and myth, symbolism, and ritual. Religious nationalism requires an institutional approach to the project of collective representation. It offers a particular ontology of power, an ontology revealed and affirmed through its politicized practices and the central object of its political concern, practices that locate collective solidarity in religious faith shared by communities of belief and conceivably among nations (Friedland 2001). This may be found today in numerous nation-states around the world and Iran, Sri Lanka, India, Pakistan, Saudi Arabia, Estonia, and Bosnia-Herzegovina are but notable examples that come to mind.

Israel makes for an extreme case of religious nationalism. While initially based on modernist-secularists ideas of the nation (Zionism, to state the obvious) the desired Enlightenment conception of separation of state authority from religion is increasingly challenged. This is manifested in daily lives in the region on many fronts and informs, as previously and repeatedly demonstrated in my empirical cases, the developments, and surely the politics, of sacred places therein. Religion becomes much more than a doctrine, a set of myths, or a spiritual reading of the world and our role in it; it is an institutional space according to whose logic religious nationalists wish to remake the world. Effectively, religion becomes a network of sacred places and ritual spaces, it dictates, and shapes encounters among groups, and is certainly to be found in many aspects of contemporary life in the region. In the Israeli case, one simply cannot fathom the nation in disconnect from religion, which also heavily influences, as I have shown throughout this book, the ethnocratic logic of the state.

The current foray into the realm of the sacred confronted us with the limitations of ethnocratic logic. In the Israeli case, complementing the ethnocratic logic with the transcendental and cosmic dimension and giving growing legitimation to the latter have surely proved to be a double-edged sword. Time and again, and increasingly in recent years, the State of Israel finds itself involved in conflicts and contestations over the ownership and control of sacred sites. As the religious component is heavily enmeshed into the Israeli ethnocratic logic, it is more often than not impossible to exclude religious justifications and logic from allegedly mundane-political issues. The right of ownership of a deserted mosque, obtaining a permit to renovate a dilapidated church, the infiltration of a Jewish group into a ruined Muslim pilgrimage site, and, in particular, the ongoing contestations in Jerusalem's holy basin have become a constant threat to the very legitimation of the Israeli ethnocratic regime. The cosmic-transcendental-religious logic challenges and ruptures the ethnocratic-national one. The centrality of Israel in the region while operating under a religio-ethnocratic logic affected changes in the spatialities of sacred places of all religious groups. Further, against the ongoing process of the Judaization of the region, we witness a plethora of socio-political processes within sacred places framed as land-claiming, anti-hegemonic rhetoric, and actions, and surely resistance, by minority groups. The fusion of religion into this process proved a highly effective mechanism in the short and medium terms for sustaining the Israeli ethnocratic regime. It allowed the construction of legal mechanisms, disproportional allocations of resources for religious activities and indeed for sacred places, and general neglect of minorities' religious affairs. Sanctity and claims for sanctity are heavily used to buttress the Jewish hegemonic position, which is responded to, time and again, by counterclaims and contestations from subaltern groups.

As I draw toward the end of this book, I am reminded of Veronica della Dora's warning that treating the sacred merely through the prism of the political downplays overwhelming aspects of the spiritual experience of the sacred (2011). Indeed, my own encounters in the field have taught me that the sacred cannot be reduced to the merely political. Thus, in addition to feelings, emotions, and personal narratives (discussed at length in Chapter 2), I also engaged with phenomenological experimentation, such as what I referred to as materiality, which also informs my *ReligioCity* project. This "more than representational approach" is gaining more currency in the field, which has already borne fruits in the material turn in religious studies (Hazard 2013). It also allowed for an analysis that engages with aspects of the sacred and that challenges both sociological determinism and structuralist narratives. This was facilitated also through the theoretical tools arriving from new paradigmatic understandings to be found among cultural geographers and geographers of religion since the 1990s. Particularly, the way post-modern places have been emancipated from their previous Cartesian shackles enables us to open the door to a more dynamic understanding of places. And yet, it is mostly with this understanding and frame of reference, that considers power, power-structure, and changing power-geometries, that I narrated sacred places in this multi-sited and prolonged, and surely still wanting, project which I now leave for the readers.

Notes

Introduction

1. It was only later on that I discovered the identity of the inscriber. On him and the Beersheba Mosque Conflict, see Chapter 4.
2. Inquiries with the regional archaeologist revealed no such excavation plans.
3. Like place, culture is always in the process of becoming and may not be reified or understood as a rigid and specific setting of human ideals, norms, etc.
4. This intangible quality is what Rudolf Otto defined as "numinous." R. Otto (1959) *The Idea of the Holy:* [an inquiry into the non-rational factor in the idea of the divine and its relation to the natural], (Trs. J. W. Harvey) (Harmondsworth, Middlesex, Pelican Books).
5. Profane here should be understood as turning Eliade's concept of the nature of the sacred on its head.
6. This will be further discussed as glocalization.

Chapter 1

1. Unless otherwise specified all interviews were conducted by the author. The implementation of the Charitable Trust Law is discussed regarding the Hassan Bek Mosque conflict in Chapter 4.

Chapter 2

1. As a rule, throughout the book, I use only initials of the interviewees' first names. However, in specific cases where permission was granted, such as with Umm Ahmad, the full name was used.
2. Special thanks are due to Ms. Haya Abu-Sa'di for this interview and for the two years of ethnographies, participant observations, and interviews with members of the group. This proved to be a rather difficult task as the members never warmed up to the idea of the project team following them. In addition to the "regular" obstacles of entering the field, there were also the ramifications of the Covid-19

pandemic, which among other things altered the nature of the group's activities and at times halted their meetings.
3   The hijab is the Islamic head scarf, and the jilbab refers to a garment, usually ankle length and long sleeved, which loosely covers the body.
4   Data collected from fieldnotes, January–May 2013, during which time I met with M. six times.
5   Sufism is a general term for the mystical path in Islam. Since our meeting, which took place in 2013, the shaykh has passed away and the group of followers disbanded.
6   *Dhikr* (sometime to be found as *zikr*) is the ritual conducted by Sufi groups for the purpose of glorifying God and achieving spiritual perfection.
7   Area B regions are under Palestinian civic jurisdiction, but joint Israeli-Palestinian security control.
8   I wish to thank Mr. Chen Reuveni for conducting this part of the research while participating as an RA in Stadler and Luz's joint project on enchanted sacred places. See further on that http://sacredplaces.huji.ac.il/.

Chapter 3

1   Mahmood is referring here to Salafism, or the Salafiyyah movement, which is a reform movement in Sunni Islam originating in the nineteenth century. The name derives from the *salaf*, that is, the pious predecessors; see Esposito (2004). Salafi groups are often involved in waging war against folk Islam and, in particular, pilgrimage to sites other than Mecca and are more commonly known for their onslaught against sacred places and grave visitations. This is considered *bid'a*, that is, a wrongful novelty that was banned by the Prophet Muhammad. Notoriously infamous are the acts of aggression performed by both ISIS and the Taliban against world heritage sites such as the Bamiyan Buddhas, as well as against Islamic holy sites such as the Raqqa Mosque.
2   http://en.radiovaticana.va/news/2015/02/14/consistory_three_new_canonisations_approved/1123441.
3   More on this later, but suffice it to say at this point that Assad Daoud is an architect specializing in conservation, who launched an almost one-man project of renovation at the birthplace of Mariam Bawardy, which is located, literally, in his family's backyard.
4   This will be discussed at length in Chapter 6.
5   Ironically, it was I who suggested my former student Mr. Assad Daoud, who is an architect and an experienced restorer to the council. And thus, as I joked about it later, it was the Jew who suggested the Christian to renovate a Muslim site.

6   Our fruitful and enriching discussions yielded a grant proposal that was funded by the Israel Science Foundation (131/12). This has enabled us to launch an exhaustive comparative study of enchanted places of all Abrahamic religions, as well as to design a website that still holds many of our findings: http://sacredplaces.huji.ac.il/.
7   This is the accepted mythology among most biographers and surely among the people of I'bbelin. However, in recent years the miniscule Christian community of the predominantly Druze settlement of Hurfeish has cultivated a different narrative, according to which her birthplace is in their village.
8   The following video from 2016 provides a visual introduction to the shrine and of the village: https://youtu.be/d3ZI8p5-vW0.
9   Which is where we met, Assad in the capacity of a student and me as a teacher. Since then, it is usually he who serves as my teacher and an invaluable source of information about his work in I'bbelin, about the village, and of course regarding his unique understanding in Palestinian history and material culture.

Chapter 4

1   Indeed, the settling of immigrants in marginal locations occurred first, and the construction of mosques therein to answer the needs of those communities happened only later.
2   In 2004 the Hebrew version was no longer visible.
3   I am indebted to my friend and colleague Prof. Yitzhak Reiter for sharing with me his vast knowledge of the mosque conflict and for his good advice over many a year.
4   It is difficult to arrive at an accurate number, as many of the Muslim residents of Beersheba are undocumented. There are several reasons for that, among them the residents' wish to keep their formal address in their city/village of origin and receive several benefits from the state (such as refunding their transportation to work). Another reason suggested to me during talks and interviews was that by keeping their original address, they maintain the right to vote in their city/village of origin and thus support their own clan's (Arabic: *hamule*) political interests. According to Israel's Central Bureau of Statistics, the current official number of Arab citizens in Beersheba is 6,185 (see https://www.cbs.gov.il/he/Settlements/Pages/עשבע%20בארשבע/ישובים.aspx; last accessed October 24, 2022). Unofficial estimates set the number somewhere between ten to twenty thousand.
5   Attorney Shchada ibn Bari is a Muslim resident of Beersheba and a longtime activist in the mosque struggle.

6 Attorney Ilan Sharqon specializes in real estate transactions and serves as counsel for the Jaffa Muslim Charitable Trust.
7 Attorney Victor Herzberg served as the legal counsel to the Jaffa community at the early stages of the Hassan Bek conflict.
8 Engineer and real estate appraiser Shmuel Penn is a former Tel Aviv-Yafo city engineer.
9 Attorney Nissim Shaqar was one of the founders of the Rabita. At the time of the interview, he served as Jaffa's elected representative on the municipal council.
10 Samih Tuhi is the Imam of the Mahmudiyya Mosque and served as the chair of the Islamic Council of Jaffa. Yusuf Reyhan is a contractor and served as the chair of the Islamic Council of Jaffa in 1988–96, when most of the renovations of the mosque were underway.
11 Shamai Assif was the city engineer when the unofficial oral agreement between the mayor and the delegates of the Rabita was made.
12 Since 2015, the faction headed by Raid Salah has been outlawed by the government. In Chapter 6, I discuss their impact and activities in regard to sacred places at length.

Chapter 5

1 The survey was conducted over two years by Mr. Idan Edut as part of the *ReligioCity* project funded by the Israel Science Foundation (ISF 1242/17). I am indebted to Idan for his meticulous and elaborate survey.
2 Jewish halachic rules require at least ten adult males (a *minyan*) for public prayers.
3 The voting pattern in the [add precise date—LC] general elections indicates high rates of voters for the only Arab party in the Israeli parliament in the central parts of the city.
4 Courtesy of the authors.
5 N. is a former Muslim student of mine. She and her family resided in the eastern side of town and felt compelled to move due to daily harassment, stone throwing, and intimidation by Jewish neighbors.
6 N. is a Muslim woman who left the Old City in recent years for a modern housing solution in the Mandatory Quarter. In her professional capacity, she is in daily contact with residents of the Old City.
7 I am indebted to Dr. Mori Ram for pointing me in this direction, and indeed for our ongoing dialogue on religions in Acre.
8 Yaacov Salama is the former head of the Branch of Religious Communities at the Ministry of the Interior. Oral communication, December 6, 2013.
9 The Trusts were discussed at length in Chapter 4.

Chapter 6

1. An historical analysis of the region and the emergence of a religious narrative which centers around Jerusalem to the modern period is provided in Chapter 1.
2. This movement was previously discussed in the latter parts of Chapter 2.
3. Ibrahim Sarsur was the head of the Islamic party named United Arab List (the umbrella party aiming at all Arab voters in national elections) and a member of the Knesset when interviewed.
4. L. is an activist in the Northern Branch.
5. I surveyed the magazine publications from 2000 to 2015. I cannot recall one time when the Haram al-Sharif did not appear in the weekly edition! I wish to thank Ms. Hila Raz for her much-appreciated work assisting me with this time-consuming task.
6. Muhammad al-Durra was a twelve-year-old boy killed during an IDF operation in Gaza in September 2000. He became an iconic martyr in the Arab world and a symbol of Palestinian grievances against Israel.

References

Abbasi, M. (2010), "The Fall of Acre in the 1948 Palestine War," *Journal of Palestine Studies*, 39 (4): 6–27.

Abd Al-rahman, M. (2022), "The Marwani Praying Place. From Stables for Horses to Lighthouse of Learning," Al-Arabi 21, April 14. Available online: https://arabi21.com/story/1431519/المصلى-المرواني-من-إسطبلات-للخيل-إلى-منارات-للعلم (accessed August 30, 2022). [Arabic]

Abed, S. (2022), "The Politics of Provocation: Islamic and Feminine Ribat in al-Aqsa Mosque in Jerusalem," in L. Chen, O. Hacker and N. Stadler (eds), *Sacred Places in the Holy Land. An Ethnographic Perspective*, 200–30, Rannana: Open University Press. [Hebrew]

Abu 'Amar, A., S. Al-Hudaliyya and J. Mansur (2014), *Encyclopedia of Sacred Places in Palestine*, 4 vols. Umm al-Fahm: Al-Aqsa Association for Endowments and Heritage. [Arabic]

Abulof, A. (2009), "Small Peoples: The Existential Uncertainty of Ethnonational Communities," *International Studies Quarterly*, 53 (1): 227–48.

Abulof, A. (2014), "The Role of Religion in National Legitimation: Judaism and Zionism's Elusive Quest for Legitimacy," *Journal for the Scientific Studies of Religion*, 53 (3): 515–33.

Aburaiya, I. (2004), "The 1996 Split of the Islamic Movement in Israel: Between the Holy Text and Israeli-Palestinian Context," *International Journal of Politics, Culture, and Society*, 17: 439–55.

ACNS (2017), "Jerusalem Archbishop Rededicates Israeli Church Closed for Nearly 80 Years," *Anglican News*, February 23. Available online: https://www.anglicannews.org/news/2017/02/anglican-archbishop-in-jerusalem-rededicates-a-church-in-northern-israel,-closed-for-nearly-80-years.aspx (accessed August 26, 2022).

Adallah (2002), "Petition 02/7311 Submitted to HCJ," August.

Agnew, J. A. (1987), *Place and Politics. The Geographical Mediation of State and Society*, London: Routledge.

Agnew, J. A. (2006), "Religion and Geopolitics," *Geopolitics*, 11 (2): 183–91.

Agnew, J. A. and J. S. Duncan (1989), *The Power of Place: Bringing Together Geographical and Social Imagination*, Boston: Unwin Hyman.

Akenson, D. (1992), *God's People: Covenant and Land in South Africa, Israel, and Ulster*, Ithaca: Cornell University Press.

Akkonet (2011), "Inauguration Ceremony of the Yeshiva New Campus." Available online: http://www.akkonet.co.il/forums/viewtopic.php?f=8&t=66 (accessed October 6, 2012). [Hebrew]

Al-Aref, A. (1999), *Tarikh Bi'r al-Sabʻ wa-qabaʾiluha*, Cairo: Maktabat Madbouli.

Alexandrowicz, O. (2013), "Civilian Demolition: The Premeditated Destruction of Manshiya Neighborhood in Jaffa 1948–1949," *Studies in Zionism, the Yishuv and the State of Israel. Iyyunim Bitkumat Israel*, 23: 274–314.

AlSayyad, N. and M. Massoumi, eds. (2010), *The Fundamentalist City? Religiosity and the Remaking of Urban Space*, New York: Routledge.

Amitai, R. (2017), "Post-Crusader Acre in Light of a Mamluk Inscription and a Fatwā Document from Damascus," in Y. Ben-Bassat (ed.), *Developing Perspectives in Mamluk History Essays in Honor of Amalia Levanoni*, 335–51, Leiden and London: Brill.

Anderson, B. (1991), *Imagined Communities: Reflections on the Origin and Spread of Nationalism*, London and New York: Verso.

Antonius, G. (1938), *The Arab Awakening: The Story of the Arab National Movement*, London: Hamish Hamilton.

Arafat, W. (2013), "Bilāl b. Rabāḥ," *Encyclopedia of Islam*, second edition, Leiden: Brill. Available online: http://dx.doi.org/10.1163/1573-3912_islam_SIM_1412 (accessed March 15, 2022).

ʻAriʾar, T. M. (2002), "Al-Aqsa Is above and beyond Any Would-Be Negotiator," *Sawt al-Haqq wal-Huriyya* (special supplement), September 15: A 9. [Arabic]

Arraf, S. (1993), *Tabaqat al-anbiyaʾ wal-salihin fi al-ard al-muqaddasa*. Tarshiha: Matbaʻat al-Ikhwan Makhul.

Arraf, S. (1996), *al-Qarya al-ʻarabiyya al-filastiniyya*, Tarshiha: Matbaʻat al-Ikhwan Makhul.

Arraf, S. (2008), *Kawkab Abu al-Hijja*, Tarshiha: Kawkab Abu al-Hijja local council. [Arabic]

Asad, T. (1999), "Religion, Nation-State, Secularism," in P. van der Veer and H. Lehmann (eds), *Nation and Religion. Perspectives on Europe and Asia*, 176–96, Princeton NJ: Princeton University Press.

Ash, J. and P. Simpson (2016), "Geography and Post-Phenomenology," *Progress in Human Geography*, 40 (1): 48–66.

Ashkenazy, J. (2009), *The Mother of All Churches: The Church of Jerusalem from Its Onset to the Muslim Conquest*, Jerusalem: Yad Izhak Ben-Zvi Publications. [Hebrew]

Ashkenazi, J. (forthcoming), "Eudocia, Pulcheria and Juvenal: The Competition in the Field of Religion and the Built Environment of Jerusalem in the Fifth Century CE," in M. Goodman and B. Bitton-Ashkelony (eds), *Ode for Oded: Essays on Jews and Christians in Late Antiquity in Honor of Oded Irshai* (Cultural Encounters in Late Antiquity and the Middle Ages, 40), Brepols: Turnhout.

Associated Press (2015), "Pope Francis Canonizes 2 Saints from 19th Century Palestine," May 17. Available online: https://www.cbc.ca/news/world/pope-francis-canonizes-2-saints-from-19th-century-palestine-1.3077416#:~:text=Pope%20

Francis%20canonized%20two%20nuns,of%20persecution%20from%20Islamic%20 extremists (accessed July 16, 2022).

Avci, Y. (2009), "The Application of Tanzimat in the Desert: The Bedouins and the Creation of a New Town in Southern Palestine (1860–1914)," *Middle Eastern Studies*, 45: 969–83.

El-Azhari, T. (2016), *Zengi and the Muslim Response to the Crusades: The Politics of Jihad*, London and New York: Routledge.

Azuri, N. (1905), *Le reveil de la nation Arabe dans l'Asie Turque*, Paris: n. p.

Bahat, D. (1991) "Topography and Archeology of Crusader and Ayyubid Jerusalem," in J. Prawer (ed.), *The History of Jerusalem. Crusaders and Ayyubids (1099–1250)*, 68–134, Jerusalem: Yad Yitzhak Ben Zvi Publications. [Hebrew]

Bakshi, A. (2011), "Memory and Place in Divided Nicosia," *Spectrum: Journal of Global Studies*, 3 (4): 27–40.

Bar, D. (2007), *Sanctifying a Land: The Jewish Holy Places in the State of Israel: 1948–1968*, Jerusalem: Ben-Gurion Institute in the Negev and Yad Ben Zvi. [Hebrew]

Baranes, Y. (2020), "Acre: The Municipality Stopped Infrastructures Maintenance at the Muslim Cemetery," *Yediot Hatzafon*, January 3, 10. [Hebrew]

Bard, M. G. (2003), *The Founding of the State of Israel*, Farmington Hills: Greenhaven Press.

Barkan, E. and K. Barkey, eds (2014), *Choreographies of Shared Sacred Sites: Religion, Politics and Conflict Resolution*, New York: Columbia University Press.

Barkey, K. and G. Gavrilis (2016), "The Ottoman Millet System: Non-Territorial Autonomy and Its Contemporary Legacy," *Ethnopolitics*, 15 (1): 24–42.

Bar-Tal, D. (2013), *Intractable Conflicts: Socio-Psychological Foundations and Dynamics*, New York: Verso.

Bartal, S. (2017), "The Peel Commission Report of 1937 and the Origins of the Partition Concept," *Jewish Political Studies Review*, 28 (1/2): 51–70.

Barthes, R. (1981), "Semiology and the Urban," in M. Gottdiener and A. P. Lagopoulos (eds), *The City and the Sign: An Introduction to Urban Semiotics*, 87–98, New York: Columbia University Press.

Beaumont, J. and C. Baker, eds (2011), *Post-Secular Cities: Space, Theory and Practice*, London and New York: Continuum.

Becci, I., J. Casanova, and M. Burckhardt, eds (2013), *Topographies of Faith: Religion in Urban Spaces*, Leiden: Brill.

Becci, I., M. Burchardt, and M. Giorda (2017), "Religious Super-Diversity and Spatial Strategies in Two European Cities," *Current Sociology*, 65 (1): 73–91.

Beck, U. (2000), *What Is Globalization?*, Oxford: Polity.

Beckford, J. A. (2012), "SSSR Presidential Address Public Religions and the Postsecular: Critical Reflections," *Journal for the Scientific Study of Religion*, 51 (1): 1–19.

Bellah, R. N. (2011), *Religion in Human Evolution: From the Paleolithic to the Axial Age*, Cambridge MA: Harvard University Press.

Ben-Bassat, Y. and Y. Ben-Artzi (2016), "Cartographical Evidence of Efforts to Develop Acre during the Last Decades of Ottoman Rule: Did the Ottomans Neglect the City?," *Mediterranean Historical Review*, 31 (1): 65–87.

Benvenisti, M. (2000), *Sacred Landscape: The Buried History of the Holy Land since 1948*, Berkeley: University of California Press.

Berkovits, S. (2000), *The Battle for the Holy Places. The Struggle over Jerusalem and the Holy Sites in Israel, Judea, Samaria, and the Gaza Districts*, Or Yehuda: Hed Arzi Publishing House. [Hebrew]

Berger, P. L. (1967), *The Sacred Canopy: Elements of a Sociological Theory of Religion*, Garden City: Doubleday.

Berger, P. L. (1999), "The Desecularization of the World: A Global Overview," in P. L. Berger (ed.), *The Desecularization of the World: Resurgent Religion and World Politics*, 1–19, Grand Rapids MI: William B. Eerdmans Publishing Company.

Berger, M. (2017), "What's the Issue with Metal Detectors in Jerusalem?," *Reuters*, July 24. Available online: https://ca.news.yahoo.com/whats-issue-metal-detectors-jerusalem-110414794.html (accessed July 20, 2022).

Berman, M. (1965), "The Evolution of Beersheba as an Urban Center," *Annals of the American Association of Geographers*, 55: 308–26.

Berretta, D. (2015), "Holy Land Christians Celebrate Sainthood of Arab Nuns," Associated Press, May 13. Available online: https://apnews.com/article/b5306214853f45db84dcdcf4751d063a (accessed July 16, 2022).

Bigger, G. (2004), *The Boundaries of Modern Palestine 1840–1947*, London and New York: Routledge Curzon.

Bitton-Ashkelony, A. (2005), *Encountering the Sacred. The Debate on Christian Pilgrimage in Late Antiquity*, Berkeley, Los Angeles and London: University of California Press.

Blakey, J. (2021), "The Politics of Scale through Ranciere," *Progress in Human Geography*, 45 (4): 620–47.

Boas, A. (2001), *Jerusalem in the Time of the Crusades*, London and New York: Routledge.

Booth, W. and R. Eglash (2017), "Abbas to 'Freeze Contact' with Israel until Metal Detectors at al-Aqsa Mosque Are Removed," *The Washington Post*, July 21. Available online: https://www.washingtonpost.com/world/clashes-expected-in-jerusalem-as-government-moves-to-keep-metal-detectors-in-place-at-holy-site/2017/07/21/00cea916-6d8e-11e7-abbc-a53480672286_story.html (accessed August 28, 2022).

Bourdieu, P. (1980), "The Production of Belief: Contribution to an Economy of Symbolic Goods," in R. Collins (ed.), *Media, Culture, and Society: A Critical Reader*, 261–93, London: Routledge and Kegan Paul.

Bourdieu, P. (1985), "The Market of Symbolic Goods," *Poetics*, 14: 13–44.

Bourdieu, P. (1991), "Genesis and Structure of the Religious Field," *Comparative Social Research*, 13 (1): 1–44.

Bovis, H. E. (1971), *The Jerusalem Question, 1917–1968*, Stanford: Stanford University Press.

Brenner, B. (2001), "The Limits to Scale? Methodological Reflections on Scalar Structuration," *Progress in Human Geography*, 25 (4): 591–614.

Brenner, N. (1999a), "Globalisation as Reterritorialisation: The Re-scaling of Urban Governance in the European Union," *Urban Studies*, 36 (3): 431–51.

Brenner, N. (1999b), "Beyond State-Centrism? Space, Territoriality and Geographical Scale in Globalization Studies," *Theory and Society*, 28 (2): 39–78.

Brunot, A. (1981), *Mariam: The Little Arab, Sister Mary of Jesus Crucified*, Bethlehem: Carmel du Saint Enfant Jesus.

Buck, D. C. (2004), "Louis Massignon and Mariam Baouardy (Blessed Mary of Jesus Crucified) A Palestinian Saint for Our Time." Available online: http://www.dcbuck.com/Articles/Baouardy/Baouardy.html (accessed July 15, 2022).

Burchardt, M. and S. Hönne (2015), "The Infrastructure of Diversity: Materiality and Culture in Urban Space—an Introduction," *New Diversities*, 17 (2): 1–13.

Busse, H. (1968), "The Sanctity of Jerusalem in Islam," *Judaism*, 17 (4): 441–80.

Butler, J. (1990), *Gender Trouble: Feminism and the Subversion of Identity*, New York: Routledge.

Butler, J. (1993), *Bodies that Matter: On the Discursive Limits of "Sex"*, New York: Routledge.

Butler, A. and P. Burns (1995), *Butler's Lives of the Saints*, Collegeville: The Liturgical Press.

Buzy, D. (1921), *Life of Sister Mary of Jesus Crucified*, Paris: Carmel of Bethlehem.

Canaan, T. (1927), *Mohammedan Saints and Sanctuaries in Palestine*, London: Luzac.

Canard, M. (1965), "Da'wa," in *Encyclopedia of Islam*, second edition, Leiden: Brill. Available online: http://dx.doi.org/10.1163/1573-3912_islam_SIM_1738 (accessed November 9, 2022).

Casanova, J. (1994), *Public Religion in the Modern World*, Chicago: University of Chicago Press.

CBS (2019), *Central Bureau of Statistics, Demography and Censuses of Population: Acre*, Jerusalem: Prime Minister Office.

Chidester, D. and E. D. Linenthal (1995), *American Sacred Places*, Bloomington: Indiana University Press.

Chivallon, C. (2001), "Religion as Space for the Expression of Caribbean Identity in the United Kingdom," *Environment and Planning D: Society and Space*, 19 (4): 461–83.

Clinton, W. J. (2000), *The Clinton Parameters. Clinton Proposal on Israeli-Palestinian Peace*. Available online: https://ecf.org.il/media_items/568 (accessed July 15, 2020).

Cloke, P. and J. Beaumont (2013), "Geographies of Postsecular Rapprochement in the City," *Progress in Human Geography*, 37 (1): 27–51.

Cobb, P. M. (2014), *The Race for Paradise: An Islamic History of the Crusades*, Oxford: Oxford University Press.

Cohen, H. (2015), *Year Zero of the Arab-Israeli Conflict 1929*, Waltham: Brandeis University Press.
Cohen, H. (2017), "The Temple Mount/al-Aqsa in Zionist and Palestinian National Consciousness: A Comparative View," *Israel Studies Review*, 32 (1): 1–19.
Cohen, R. (2021), "Riots Shatter Veneer of Coexistence in Israel's Mixed Towns," *The New York Times*, August 1. Available online: https://www.nytimes.com/2021/08/01/world/middleeast/israel-arabs-jews-palestinians-riots.html (accessed September 15, 2021).
Cooper, J. E. (2016), "The Turn to Tradition in the Study of Jewish Politics," *Annual Review of Political Science*, 19: 67–87.
Cortellessa, E. (2017), "US 'Applauds' Israel for Nixing Temple Mount Metal Detectors," *The Times of Israel*, July 26. Available online: https://www.timesofisrael.com/us-applauds-israel-for-removing-metal-detectors-from-temple-mount/ (accessed September 3, 2022).
Crawford, S. J. (2006), "Teaching Religion and Embodiment in Global Context," in L. Barnes and I. Talamantez (eds), *Teaching Religion and Healing*, 29–46, Oxford: Oxford University Press.
Creswell, K. A. C. (1969), *Early Islamic Architecture*, Oxford: Clarendon Press.
Creswell, T. (2004), *Place: A Short Introduction*, Oxford: Blackwell.
Creswell, T. (2014), *Place: An Introduction*, Malden: Willey Blackwell.
Cust, L. G. A. (1929), *The Status Quo in the Holy Places*, London: n.p.
Dabagh, M. M. (1972), *Biladuna Filastin*, Beirut: Matba'at al-Hukuma. [Arabic]
Dakwar, J. (2007), "The Islamic Movement inside Israel: An Interview with Shaykh Ra'id Salah," *Journal of Palestinian Studies*, 36 (2): 66–76.
Dallaire, G. (2016), "Saint Mariam Baouardy. The Lily of Palestine." Available online: https://www.mysticsofthechurch.com/2010/07/blessed-mariam-baouardy-little-arab-and.html (accessed July 16, 2022).
Daoud, E. (2008), *Al-Sira al-Qadisiyya al-Jaliliyya al-Filastiniyya Mariam Yasua' al-Maslub (Mariam Bauardy)*, Ibbelin: Monaleza Press. [Arabic]
De Certeau, M. (1984), *The Practice of Everyday Life*, Berkeley: University of California Press.
Deleuze, G. and F. Guattari (1987), *A Thousand Plateaus: Capitalism and Schizophrenia*, Minneapolis: University of Minnesota Press.
Della Dora, V. (2011), "Engaging Sacred Space: Experiments in the Field," *Journal of Geography in Higher Education*, 35 (2): 163–84.
Della Dora, V. (2016), "Infrasecular Geographies. Making, Unmaking and Remaking Sacred Space," *Progress in Human Geography*, 42 (1): 44–71.
Dikec, M. (2012), "Space as a Mode of Political Thinking," *Geoforum*, 43 (4): 669–76.
Donner, H. (1992), *The Madaba Mosaic: An Introductory Guide*, Kampen: Kok Pharos.
Douglas, M. (1970), *Natural Symbol*, London: Routledge.
Dumper, M. (2014), *Jerusalem Unbound: Geography, History, and the Future of the Holy City*, New York: Columbia University Press.

Durkheim, E. (1995), *The Elementary Forms of Religious Life*, New York: Free Press.
Dwyer, C. (2016), "Why Does Religion Matter for Cultural Geographers?," *Social and Cultural Geography*, 29: 1–5.
Dwyer, C., D. Gilbert and S. Bindi (2013), "Faith and Suburbia: Secularisation, Modernity, and the Changing Geographies of Religion in London's Suburbs," *Transactions of the Institute of British Geographers*, 38 (3): 403–19.
Eade, J. (1992), "Pilgrimage and Tourism at Lourdes, France," *Annals of Tourism Research*, 19 (1): 18–32.
Eade, J. (2011), "From Race to Religion: Multiculturalism and Contested Urban Space," in J. Beaumont and C. Baker (eds), *Postsecular Cities: Space, Theory and Practice*, 154–67, London: Continuum.
Eade, J. and J. M. Sallnow, eds (1991), *Contesting the Sacred*, London: Routledge.
Eade, J. and D. Garbin (2006), "Competing Visions of Identity and Space: Bangladeshi Muslims in Britain," *Contemporary South Asia*, 15 (2): 181–93.
Efe-EPA (2017), "Erdogan Condemns Metal Detectors at Jerusalem Mosque, Urges Muslims to Visit," July 25. Available online: https://www.efe.com/efe/english/world/erdogan-condemns-metal-detectors-at-jerusalem-mosque-urges-muslims-to-visit/50000262-3335235 (accessed September 7, 2022).
Efrat, E. (2000), "Jerusalem: Partition Plans for a Holy City," *Israel Affairs*, 6 (34): 238–55.
Elad, A. (1995), *Medieval Jerusalem and Islamic Worship: Holy Places, Ceremonies. Pilgrimage*, Leiden-New York-Köln: Brill.
Eldar, S. (2015-), "Who Are Temple Mount's Mourabitoun?," *Monitor*, September 18. Available online: https://www.al-monitor.com/originals/2015/09/israel-mourabitun-temple-mount-compound-settlers-islamists.html#ixzz7dtUqY480 (accessed August 26, 2022).
Eliade, M. (1959), *The Sacred and the Profane: The Nature of Religion*, New York: Harcourt, Brace.
Eliav, Y. (2005), *God's Mountain: The Temple Mount in Time, Space, and Memory*, Baltimore: Johns Hopkins University Press.
Eliav, Y. (2008), "The Temple Mount in Jewish and Early Christian Traditions: A New Look," in T. Mayer and S. Mourad (eds), *Jerusalem: Idea and Reality*, 47–66, London and New York: Routledge.
Eliaz, Y. (2008), *Land/Text: The Christian Roots of Zionism*, Tel Aviv: Resling. [Hebrew]
Ellenblum, R. (2003), *Frankish Rural Settlement in the Latin Kingdom of Jerusalem*, Cambridge: Cambridge University Press.
Entwistle, J. (2000), *The Fashioned Body: Fashion, Dress and Modern Social Theory*, Cambridge: Cambridge Polity Press.
Escobar, A. (2001), "Culture Sits in Place: Reflections on Globalism and Subaltern Strategies of Localization," *Political Geography*, 20: 139–74.
Esposito, J. L. (2004), *The Islamic World Past and Present*, New York: Oxford University Press.

Express Tribune (2017), "Anti-Israel Protest at Istanbul Synagogue: Report," *The Express Tribune*, July 21. Available online: https://tribune.com.pk/story/1462972/anti-israel-protest-istanbul-synagogue-report (accessed August 10, 2022).

Fabian, R. (1999), "Jaffa—A Narrative of Politics and Architecture/Urbanism," MA thesis, Harvard University, Cambridge MA.

Finkelstein, I. and N. A. Silberman (2001), *The Bible Unearthed: Archeology's New Vision of Ancient Israel and the Origin of Its Sacred Texts*, New York: Free Press.

Fischbach, M. R. (2003), *Records of Dispossession: Palestinian Refugee Property and the Arab-Israeli Conflict*, New York: Columbia University Press.

Forman, J. and A. Kedar (2004), "From Arab Land to 'Israel Lands': The Legal Dispossession of the Palestinians Displaced by Israel in the Wake of 1948," *Environment and Planning D: Society and Space*, 22: 809–30.

Foucault, M. (1980), *Power/Knowledge: Selected Interviews and Other Writings, 1972–1977*, New York: Pantheon Books.

Frantzaman, S. and D. Bar (2013), "Mapping Muslim Sacred Tombs in Palestine during the Mandate Period," *Levant*, 45 (1): 96–111.

Freas, E. (2017), *Nationalism and the Haram al-Sharif/Temple Mount*, Cham: Palgrave Macmillan.

Frenkel, Y. (1999), "Political and Social Aspects of Islamic Religious Endowments (*awqāf*): Saladin in Cairo (1169–73) and Jerusalem (1187–93)," *Bulletin of the School of Oriental and African Studies*, 62 (1): 1–20.

Frenkel, Y. (2001), "Baybars and the Sacred Geography of Bilad al-Sham: A Chapter in the Islamization of Syria's Landscape," *Jerusalem Studies in Arabic and Islam*, 25: 153–70.

Friedland, R. (2001), "Religious Nationalism and the Problem of Collective Representation," *Annual Review of Sociology*, 27: 125–52.

Gal, S. (2000), "The Arab Minority Has Not Radicalized. It Has Reached the Limits of Its Endurance," *Haaretz*, October 3: A3.

Gale, T., A. Maddrell, and A. Terry, eds (2015), *Sacred Mobilities: Journeys of Belief and Belonging*, London: Ashgate Publishing.

Galili, E., B. Rosen, D. Zvieli, N. Silbersten, and G. Finkelstein (2010), "The Evolution of Akko Harbor and Its Mediterranean Maritime Trade Links," *Journal of Island and Coastal Archeology*, 5: 191–211.

Gans, H. (2008), *A Just Zionism: On the Morality of the Jewish State*, New York: Oxford University Press.

Garbin, D. (2012), "Introduction: Believing in the City," *Culture and Religion*, 13: 401–4.

Geertz, C. (1966), "Religion as a Cultural System," in M. Banton (ed.), *Anthropological Approaches to the Study of Religion*, 1–46, London: Tavistock Publications.

Gellner, E. (1983), *Nation and Nationalism*, Ithaca: Cornell University Press.

Gerber, H. (1986), "A New Look at the Tanzimat: The Case of the Province of Jerusalem," in D. Kushner (ed.), *Palestine in the Late Ottoman Period: Political, Social and Economic Transformation*, 30–45, Leiden: Brill.

Gesler, W. M. (1993), "Therapeutic Landscapes: Medical Issues in the Light of the New Cultural Geography," *Social Science and Medicine*, 34 (7): 735–46.

Gesler, W. M. (1996), "Lourdes: Healing in a Place of Pilgrimage," *Health and Place*, 2 (2): 95–105.

Gil, M. (1987), "Political History of Jerusalem in the Early Islamic Period," in J. Prawer (ed.), *The History of Jerusalem. The Early Islamic Period*, 1–31, Jerusalem: Yad Izhak Ben-Zvi Publications. [Hebrew]

Goitein, S. D. (1950),"The Historical Background of the Erection of the Dome of the Rock," *Journal of the American Oriental Society*, 70: 104–8.

Gökarıksel, B. (2009), "Beyond the Officially Sacred: Religion, Secularism and the Body in the Production of Subjectivity," *Social and Cultural Geography*, 10: 657–74.

Gökarıksel, B. and A. J. Secor (2015), "Postsecular Geographies and the Problem of Pluralism: Religion and Everyday Life in Istanbul, Turkey," *Political Geography*, 46: 21–30.

Golan, A. (1995), "The Demarcation of Tel Aviv-Jaffa's Municipal Boundaries Following the 1948 War: Political Conflicts and Spatial Outcome," *Planning Perspectives*, 10: 383–95.

Golan, A. (2001), *Wartime Spatial Changes. Former Arab Territories within the State of Israel, 1948–1950*, Beer Sheva: Ben-Gurion University of the Negev Press. [Hebrew]

Goldziher, I. (1967), *Muslim Studies*, London: Allen & Unwin.

Göle, N. (2011), "The Public Visibility of Islam and European Politics of Resentment: The Minarets-Mosques Debate," *Philosophy and Social Criticism*, 37 (4): 383–92.

Gonen, R. (2003), *Contested Holiness: Jewish, Muslim, and Christian Perspectives on the Temple Mount in Jerusalem*, Jersey City: KTAV Publishing House.

Habermas, J. (2006), "Religion in the Public Sphere," *European Journal of Philosophy*, 14 (1): 1–25.

Habermas, J. (2008), "Notes on a Post-Secular Society," *New Perspectives Quarterly*, 25 (4): 17–29.

Haggett, P. (1965), *Location Analysis in Human Geography*, London: E. Arnold.

Hamas (1988), "The Covenant of the Islamic Resistance Movement HAMAS," *Oxford Islamic Studies Online*. Available online: http://www.oxfordislamicstudies.com/article/book/islam-9780195174304/islam9780195174304-chapter-66 (accessed June 20, 2020).

Hamas (2017), "Hamas General Principles and Policies." Available online: https://www.middleeasteye.net/news/hamas-2017-document-full (accessed September 15, 2022).

Hamilton, B. (1994), "The Impact of Crusader Jerusalem on Western Christendom," *The Catholic Historical Review*, 80 (4): 695–713.

Hamuda, S. (1985), *Masjid Hassan Bek*, Bayt Safafa: Hassan Abu Daw. [Arabic]

Al-Harawi, 'Ali (1953), *Kitab al-Isharat ila ma'rifat al-ziyarat*, Damascus: Institute Français de Damas. [Arabic]

Harris, A. (2013), "Lourdes and Holistic Spirituality: Contemporary Catholicism, the Therapeutic and Religious Thermalism," *Culture and Religion Advances in Research*, 14 (1): 23–43.

Harvey, D. (1990), "Between Space and Time: Reflections on the Geographical Imagination," *Annals of the Association of American Geographers*, 80 (3): 414–34.

Harvey, D. (1993), "From Space to Place and Back Again," in J. Bird, B. Curtis, T. Putnam, G. Robertson, and L. Tickner (eds), *Mapping the Futures*, 3–29, London: Routledge.

Harvey, D. (2003), "The Right to the City," *International Journal of Urban and Regional Research*, 27: 939–94.

Harvey, D. (2008), "The Right to the City," *New Left Review*, 53: 23–40.

Hashimshoni, Z. (1968), *Tel Aviv Yafo Master Plan*, Tel Aviv: n.d. [Hebrew]

Hasson, N. (2015), "Pope to Canonize Two Palestinian Nuns," *Haaretz Online*, May 11. https://www.haaretz.com/2015-05-11/ty-article/.premium/pope-to-canonize-2-palestinian-nuns/0000017f-dc2e-df62-a9ff-dcffbfd70000 (accessed July 20, 2022). [Hebrew]

Hatuka, T. and R. Kallus (2006), "Loose Ends: The Role of Architecture in Constructing Urban Borders in Tel Aviv–Jaffa since the 1920s," *Planning Perspectives*, 21 (1): 23–44.

Hazard, S. (2013), "The Material Turn in the Study of Religion," *Religion and Society: Advances in Research*, 4 (1): 58–78.

HCJ (2011), "Decision in Response to a Petition Filed by Adallah 7311-02," June 22.

Heidecker, N. (2022), "The Making of a Mixed Municipality in Israel: The Case of Acre," *Middle Eastern Studies*, 58 (4): 649–67.

Herod, A. (2011), *Scale*, London and New York: Routledge.

Hertz, R. (1985), "St. Besse: A Study of an Alpine Cult," in S. Wilson (ed.), *Saints and their Cults. Studies in Religious Sociology, Folklore and History*, 55–109, Cambridge: Cambridge University Press.

Hertzberg, A. (1997), *The Zionist Idea: A Historical Analysis and Reader*, Philadelphia: The Jewish Publication Society.

Hervieu-Léger, D. (2000), *Religion as a Chain of Memory*, New Brunswick: Rutgers University Press.

Hirsch, S. R. (1951), *Responsa Shemesh Umarpe*, New York: Feldheim.

Holloway, J. (2003), "Make-Believe: Spiritual Practice, Embodiment and Sacred Space," *Environment and Planning A*, 35 (11): 1961–74.

Holloway, J. and O. Valins (2002), "Placing Religion and Spirituality in Geography," *Social and Cultural Geography*, 3 (1): 5–9.

Home, R. (2003), "An 'Irreversible Conquest'? Colonial and Postcolonial Land Law in Israel/Palestine," *Social and Legal Studies*, 12 (3): 291–310.

Howitt, R. (2002), "Scale and the Other: Levinas and Geography," *Geoforum*, 33 (3): 299–313.

Ibn Al-athir, Muhammad (1982), *Al-Kamil fi tarikh*, Beirut: Dar al-Fikr. [Arabic]

Ibrahim, M. E. (2021), "Who Are the Murabitat? The Palestinian Women Guarding Al-Aqsa Mosque," *Al-Jazeera*, July 14. Available online: https://english.alaraby.co.uk/analysis/who-are-murabitat-women-guarding-al-aqsa-mosque (accessed May 11, 2022).

Ihmoud, S. (2019), "*Murabata:* The Politics of Staying in Place," *Feminist Studies*, 45 (2–3): 512–40.

Inbari, M. (2009), *Jewish Fundamentalism and the Temple Mount: Who Will Build the Third Temple?*, Albany: State University of New York Press.

Al-isfahani, Muhammad al-Katib (1888), *Kitab al-Fath al-qasi fi fath al-qudsi*, Leiden: Brill. [Arabic]

Isambert, F. A. (1982), *Le Sens du Sacré. Féte et religion populaire*, Paris: Ed. de Minuit.

Isnart, C. (2009), "Recent Papers about Robert Hertz and St. Besse," *Etnográfica. Revista do Centro em Rede de Investigação em Antropologia*, 13 (1): 215–22.

Ivakhiv, A. (2006), "Toward a Geography of 'Religion': Mapping the Distribution of an Unstable Signifier," *Annals of the Association of American Geographers*, 96 (1): 169–75.

Izenberg, D. (2008), "Poverty and Jewish-to-Arab Population Ratios Underlie the Eruption of Riots on Yom Kippur," *The Jerusalem Post*, October 23. Available online: https://www.jpost.com/features/front-lines/acre-affairs-a-microcosm-called-acre (accessed November 5, 2016).

Jenkins, R. (2012), "Disenchantment, Enchantment and Re-enchantment: Max Weber at the Millennium," *Mind and Matter*, 10 (2): 149–68.

Jolti, B. (1967), "The Prohibition on Entering the Temple Mount in These Times," *The Oral Law*, 10: 39–45. [Arabic]

Jonas, A. E. G. (1994), "The Scale Politics of Spatiality," *Environment and Planning D: Society and Space*, 12 (3): 257–64.

Jonas, A. E. G. (2007), "Pro Scale: Further Reflections on the 'Scale Debate' in Human Geography," *Transactions of the Institute of British Geographers*, 31 (3): 399–406.

Jones, J. P. (2017), "Scale and Anti-Scale," in D. Richardson, N. Castree, A. K. Goodchild, W. Liu, A. Kobayashi and R. A. Marston (eds), *International Encyclopedia of Geography: People, the Earth, Environment and Technology*, 1–9, Hoboken: Wiley.

Jones, J. P. III, H. Leitner, S. A. Marston and E. Sheppard (2017), "Neil Smith's Scale," *Antipode*, 49 (1): 138–52.

Jones, K. (1998), "Scale as Epistemology," *Political Geography*, 17: 25–8.

Juergensmeyer, M. (2010), "The Global Rise of Religious Nationalism," *Australian Journal of International Affairs*, 64 (3): 262–73.

Kais, R. (2022), "Arabs Protest Wine Festival Near Mosque," *Ynet*, July 4. Available online: https://www.ynetnews.com/articles/0,7340,L-4276987,00.html (accessed July 20, 2022). [Hebrew]

Kalimi, I. (1990), "The Land of Moriah, Mount Moriah, and The Site of Solomon's Temple in Biblical Historiography," *Harvard Theological Review*, 83: 345–62.

Karamustafa, A. T. (2018), "Shi'is, Sufis, and Popular Saints," in A. Salvatore (ed.), *The Wiley Blackwell History of Islam*, 159–75, Hoboken: John Wiley & Sons.

Karsh, E. (2010), *Palestine Betrayed*, New Haven: Yale University Press.

Keane, W. (2008), "The Evidence of the Senses and the Materiality of Religion," *Journal of the Royal Anthropological Institute*, 14: 110–27.

Kedar, A. (2000), "The Legal Transformation of Ethnic Geography: Israeli Law and Palestinian Landholders 1948–1967," *New York University Journal of International Law and Politics*, 33 (4): 923–1000.

Kedar, S. (1998), "Minority Time, Majority Time: Land, Nation and the Law of Adverse Possession in Israel," *Iyunnei Mishpat*, 21 (3): 665–746. [Hebrew]

Keith, M. and S. Pile, eds (1993), *Place and the Politics of Identity*, London: Routledge.

Khalidi, R., ed. (1992), *All that Remains: The Palestinians Villages Occupied and Depopulated by Israel in 1948*, Washington: Institute for Palestinian Studies.

Khondker, H. H. (2004), "Glocalization as Globalization: Evolution of a Sociological Concept," *Bangladesh. e-journal of Sociology*, 1 (2): 1–9.

Khoury, L. (2022). Available online: https://m.facebook.com/lafe.khoury (accessed July 15, 2022).

Kimmerling, B. (2001), *The Invention and Decline of Israeliness: State, Society, and the Military*, Berkeley, Los Angeles and New York: University of California Press.

Kipnis, B. A. and I. Schnell (1978), "Changes in the Distribution of Arabs in Mixed Jewish-Arab Cities in Israel," *Economic Geography*, 54: 168–80.

Knott, K. (2005), *The Location of Religion. A Spatial Analysis*, Durham: Acumen.

Knott, K. (2008), "Spatial Theory and the Study of Religion," *Religion Compass*, 2 (6): 1102–16.

Knott, K. (2010), "Religion, Space, and Place: The Spatial Turn in Research on Religion," *Religion and Society: Advances in Research*, 1 (1): 29–43.

Knott, K., V. Krech, and B. Meyer (2016), "Iconic Religion in Urban Space," *Material Religion*, 12 (2): 123–36.

Koenig, M. (2020), "Emile Durkheim and the Sociology of Religion," in H. Joas and A. Pettenkofer (eds), *The Oxford Handbook of Emile Durkheim*, online edition, Oxford Academic. https://doi.org/10.1093/oxfordhb/9780190679354.013.18 (accessed October 10, 2022).

Komarova, M. and L. O'Dowd (2013), "Territorialities of Capital and Place in 'Post-Conflict' Belfast," in W. Pullan and B. Baillie (eds), *Locating Urban Conflicts: Nationalism, Ethnicity, and the Everyday*, 233–51, London: Palgrave Macmillan.

Kong, L. (1993a), "Ideological Hegemony and the Political Symbolism of Religious Buildings in Singapore," *Southern Asian Journal of Social Sciences*, 20 (1): 18–42.

Kong, L. (1993b), "Negotiating Conception of Sacred Space: A Case Study of Religious Building in Singapore," *Transactions of the Institute of British Geographers*, 18: 342–58.

Kong, L. (2001), 'Mapping "New"' Geographies of Religion: Politics and Poetics in Modernity', *Progress in Human Geography*, 25: 211–33.

Kong, L. (2005), "Religious Processions: Urban Politics and Poetics," *Temenos: Finnish Journal of Religion*, 41 (2): 225–49.

Kong, L. (2010), "Global Shifts, Theoretical Shifts: Changing Geographies of Religion," *Progress in Human Geography*, 34 (6): 755–76.

Korff, R. (2003), "Local Enclosures of Globalization. The Power of Locality," *Dialectical Anthropology*, 27 (1): 1–18.

Kupferschmidt, U. M. (1989), *The Supreme Muslim Council: Islam under the British Mandate for Palestine*, Leiden: E. J. Brill.

Lanz, S. (2013), "Assembling Global Prayers in the City: An Attempt to Repopulate Urban Theory with Religion," in J. Becker, K. Klingan and S. Lanz (eds), *Global Prayers: Contemporary Manifestations of the Religious in the City*, 17–43, Zürich: Lars Müller Publishers.

Larkin, C. (2010), "Remaking Beirut: Contesting Memory, Space, and the Urban Imaginary of Lebanese Youth," *City and Community*, 9 (4): 414–42.

Larkin, C. and M. Dumper (2012), "In Defense of Al-Aqsa: The Islamic Movement Inside Israel and the Battle for Jerusalem," *The Middle East Journal*, 66 (1): 30–51.

Larkin, C. and M. Nasasra (2021), "The 'Inclusion-Moderation' Illusion: Re-Framing the Islamic Movement inside Israel," *Democratization*, 28 (4): 742–61.

Latour, B. (1993), *We Have Never Been Modern*, Cambridge MA: Harvard University Press.

Latour, B. (1996), "On Actor-Network Theory: A Few Clarifications," *Soziale Welt*, 1: 369–81.

Lay, D. and K. Olds (1988), "Landscape as Spectacle: World's Fairs and the Culture of Heroic Consumption," *Environment and Planning D: Society and Space*, 6: 191–212.

Lecoquierre, M. (2019), *The Maqamat as Place of Popular Practice: Evolution and Diversity*. Available online: EU-funded project: My Heritage! My Identity! www.myheritage.ps (accessed September 9, 2021).

Leeuw, van der G. (1933/1963), *Religion in Essence and Manifestations*, New York: Harper and Row.

Lefebvre, H. (1991), *The Production of Place*, Oxford: Blackwell.

Lefebvre, H. (1996), *Writings on the City*, New York: Wiley-Blackwell.

LeVine, M. (2005), *Overthrowing Geography: Jaffa, Tel Aviv, and the Struggle for Palestine 1880–1948*, Berkeley, Los Angeles, and London: University of California Press.

Lewis, B. (1961), *The Emergence of the Modern Turkey*, London: E. Benn.

Lincoln, B. (1989), *Discourse and the Construction of Society: Comparative Studies of Myth, Ritual, and Classification*, Oxford: Oxford University Press.

Lustick, I. S. (1997), "Has Israel Annexed East Jerusalem?," *Middle East Policy*, 5 (1): 34–45.

Lustick, I. (2008), "Yerushalayim, al-Quds, and the Wizard of Oz: The Problem of 'Jerusalem' after Camp David II and the Aqsa Intifada," in T. Mayer and S. A. Mourad (eds), *Jerusalem. Idea and Reality*, 283–302, London and New York: Routledge.

Luz, N. (2002), "Aspects of Islamization of Space and Society in Mamluk Jerusalem and Its Hinterland," *Mamluk Studies Review*, 6: 135–55.

Luz, N. (2004), *Al-Haram Al-Sharif in the Arab-Palestinian Public Discourse in Israel: Identity, Collective Memory and Social Construction*, Floersheimer Institute for Policy Study, Jerusalem: Achva Press. [Hebrew]

Luz, N. (2005a), *The Arab Community of Jaffa and the Hassan Bey Mosque. Collective Identity and Empowerment of the Arabs in Israel via Holy Places*, Floersheimer Institute for Policy Study, Jerusalem: Achva Press. [Hebrew]

Luz, N. (2005b), "The Re-Making of Beersheba: Winds of Modernization in the Late Ottoman Sultanate," in I. Weismann and F. Zachs (eds), *Ottoman Reform and Muslim Regeneration. Studies in Honour of Butrus Abu-Manneh*, 187–209, London: I. B. Tauris.

Luz, N. (2007), *On Land and Planning: Majority-Minority Narrative in Israel: The Misgav-Sakhnin Conflict as Parable*, Floersheimer Institute for Policy Study, Jerusalem: Achva Press. [Hebrew]

Luz, N. (2008a), "The Politics of Sacred Places. Palestinian Identity, Collective Memory, and Resistance in the Hassan Bek Mosque Conflict," *Environment and Planning D: Society and Space*, 26 (6): 1036–52.

Luz, N. (2008b), "The Creation of Modern Beersheba—An Imperial(istic) Ottoman Project," in Y. Gardus and E. Meir-Glitzenstein (eds), *Beer Sheva. Metropolis in the Making*, 163–78, Beersheba: Ben Gurion University Press.

Luz, N. (2013a), "The Islamic Movement and the Seduction of Sanctified Landscapes: Using Sacred Places to Conduct the Struggle for Land," in E. Rekhess and A. Rudnitzky (eds), *Muslim Minorities in Non-Muslim Majority Countries: The Test Case of the Islamic Movement in Israel*, 67–77, Tel Aviv University: The Konrad Adenauer Program for Jewish-Arab Cooperation, Tel Aviv: ART Press.

Luz, N. (2013b), "Metaphors to Live By: Identity Formation and Resistance among Minority Muslims in Israel," in P. Hopkins, L. Kong, and E. Olson (eds), *Religion and Place: Landscape, Politics and Piety*, 57–74, Dordrecht: Springer.

Luz, N. (2013c), "Islam, Culture and the 'Others': Landscape of Religious (in) Tolerance in Jerusalem, 638–1517," *Jerusalem Studies in Arabic and Islam*, 40: 301–40.

Luz, N. (2014a), *The Mamluk City in the Middle East. History, Culture, and the Urban Landscape*, Cambridge: Cambridge University Press.

Luz, N. (2014b), "The Glocalization of al-Haram al-Sharif. Landscape of Islamic Resurgence and National Revival: Designing Memory, Mystification of Place," in U. Martensson, I. Weismman and M. Sedgwick (eds), *Islamic Myths and Memories: Mediators of Globalization*, 99–120, London: Ashgate.

Luz, N. (2015), "Planning with Resurgent Religion: Informality and Gray Spacing of the Urban Landscape," *Planning Theory and Practice*, 16 (2): 278–84.

Luz, N. (2020), "Materiality as an Agency of Knowledge. Competing Forms of Knowledge Concerning Rachel's Tomb in Tiberias," *Journeys. The International Journal of Travel and Travel Writing*, 21 (1): 63–84. Available online: https://doi.org/10.3167/jys.2020.210104 (accessed November 12, 2022).

Luz, N. (2021a), "Unholy Religious Encounters and the Development of Jerusalem's Urban Landscape. Between Particularism and Exceptionalism," in M. Giora and M. Burchardt (eds), *Geographies of Encounter: The Rise and Fall of Multi-Religious Spaces*, 29–54, London: Palgrave Macmillan.

Luz, N. (2021b), "Spatial Sanctity Transformation in Israel/Palestine," in L. Chen, O. Hacker and N. Stadler (eds), *Sacred Places in the Holy Land: An Ethnographic Perspective*, 126–53, Rannana: Lamda Scholarship, The Open University of Israel Press.

Luz, N. (2022a), "ReligioCity in Acre. Religious Processions, Parades, and Festivities in a Multi-Religious City," *Cities*: 127. Available online: https://doi.org/10.1016/j.cities.2022.103765 (accessed November 12, 2022).

Luz, N. (2022b), "Gentrification and Hierarchies of Urban Planning. Reflections on the Religious Neighborhood in Acre," *Numen, International Review for the History of Religions*, 69 (2–3): 212–35.

Luz, N. and N. Collins-Kreiner (2015), "Studying Jewish Pilgrimage in Israel," in J. Eade and D. Albera (eds), *International Perspectives on Pilgrimage Studies Itineraries, Gaps and Obstacles*, 134–51, New York and London: Routledge.

Luz, N and N. Stadler (2019), "Religious Urban Decolonization: New Mosques/Antique Cities," *Colonial Settler Society*, 9: 284–300.

MacCormack, S. (1990), "Loca Sancta: The Organization of Sacred Topography in Late Antiquity," in R. G. Ousterhout (ed.), *The Blessings of Pilgrimage*, 7–40, Urbana: University of Illinois Press.

Maeir, A. (2000), "Jerusalem before King David: An Archeological Survey from Protohistoric Times to End of the Iron Age," in S. Achituv and A. Mazar (eds), *The History of Jerusalem. The Biblical Period*, 33–65, Jerusalem: Yad Izhak Ben-Zvi Publications. [Hebrew]

Mahmood, S. (2004), *Politics of Piety: The Islamic Revival and the Feminist Subject*, Princeton: Princeton University Press.

Mansfield, B. (2005), "Beyond Rescaling: Reintegrating the 'National' as a Dimension of Scalar Relations," *Progress in Human Geography*, 29 (4): 158–73.

Mara'i, T. and U. Halabi (1992), "Life under Occupation in the Golan Heights," *Journal of Palestine Studies*, 22 (1): 78–93.

Marcuse, P. (2009), "From Critical Urban Theory to the Right to the City," *City* 13 (2–3): 185–97.

Markus, R. A. (1994), "How on Earth Could Places Become Holy? Origins of the Christian Idea of Holy Places," *Journal of Early Christian Studies*, 2 (3): 257–71.

Marston, S. A. (2000), "The Social Construction of Scale," *Progress in Human Geography*, 24 (2): 219–44.

Marston, S. A., P. J. Jones III and K. Woodward (2005), "Human Geography without Scale," *Transactions of the Institute of British Geographers*, 30: 416–32.

Mashiach, A. (2021), "The Heralds of Zionism as Theological Revolutionaries," *Religions*, 12 (12): 1100. Available online: https://doi.org/10.3390/rel12121100 (accessed August 5, 2022).

Massey, D. (1993), "Power-Geometry and a Progressive Sense of Place," in J. Bird, B. Curtis, T. Putnam, G. Robertson, G. and L. Tickner (eds), *Mapping the Futures*, 60–70, London: Routledge.
Massey, D. (1995), "Places and Their Pasts," *History Workshop Journal*, 39: 182–92.
Massey, D. (1999), "Space-Time, 'Science' and the Relationship between Physical Geography and Human Geography," *Transactions of the Institute of British Geographers*, 24 (3): 261–76.
Massey, D. (2004), "The Responsibilities of Place," *Local Economy*, 19 (2): 91–101.
Massey, D. (2005), *For Space*, London: Sage.
Mayer, J. (2011), "A Country without Minarets: Analysis of the Background and Meaning of the Swiss Vote of 29 November 2009," *Religion*, 41 (1): 11–28.
McGuire, M. B. (1990), "Religion and the Body: Rematerializing the Human Body in the Social Sciences of Religion," *Journal for the Scientific Study of Religion*, 29 (3): 283–96.
Mitchell, D. (1995), "There's No Such Thing as Culture: Towards a Reconceptualization of the Idea of Culture in Geography," *Transactions of the Institute of British Geographers*, 20 (1): 102–16.
Mitchell, D. (2001), *Cultural Geography. A Critical Introduction*, Oxford: Blackwell Publishers.
Molendijk, A. L., J. Beaumont and C. Jedan, eds (2010), *Exploring the Postsecular: The Religious, the Political and the Urban*, Leiden and Boston: Brill.
Monterescu, D. (2009), "The Bridled Bride of Palestine: Orientalism, Zionism and the Troubled Urban Imagination," *Identities: Global Studies in Culture and Power*, 16 (6): 643–77.
Monterescu, D. (2015), *Jaffa Shared and Shattered: Contrived Coexistence in Israel/Palestine*, Bloomington: Indiana University Press.
Monterescu, D. and D. Rabinowitz, eds (2007), *Mixed Towns, Trapped Communities: Historical Narratives, Spatial Dynamics, Gender Relations, and Cultural Encounters in Palestinian-Israeli Towns*, London: Ashgate Publishing, Ltd.
Moore, A. (2008), "Rethinking Scale as a Geographical Category: From Analysis to Practice," *Progress in Human Geography*, 32 (2): 205–25.
Moor, A. (2016), "Ethno-Territoriality and Ethnic Conflict," *Geographical Review*, 106 (1): 92–108.
Morgan, D., ed. (2010), *Religion and Material Culture: The Matter of Belief*, London: Routledge.
Morgan, D. (2016), "Material Analysis and the Study of Religion," in T. Hutchings and J. McKenzie (eds), *Materiality and the Study of Religion. The Stuff of the Sacred*, 14–32, London: Routledge.
Morris, B. (1987), *The Birth of the Palestinian Refugee Problem, 1947–1949*, Cambridge: Cambridge University Press.
Mujir, Al-din, 'Abd al-Rahman b. Muhammad al-Hanbali al-'Ulaymi (1995), *Al-Uns al-jalil bi-ta'rikh al-Quds wal-Khalil*, 2 vols. Baghdad: Matba'at al-Nahda.

Murre-van den Berg, H. (2021), "The Christians of the Middle East. From Arab Christians to Marginalized Minorities," in R. Meijer, J. N. Sater and Z. R. Babar (eds), *Routledge Handbook of Citizenship in the Middle East and North Africa*, 364–77, London: Routledge.

Naamnih, H. (2018), "Palestinian Refugees' Property in Their Own Land: Politics of Absence and Alienation," in N. N. Rouhana and A. Sabbagh-Khoury (eds), *The Palestinians in Israel: Readings in History, Politics and Society*, vol. 2, 42–58, Haifa: Mada al-Carmel. Arab Center for Applied Social Research.

Nabulsi, G. (2015), "The Vatican Announces the Sainthood of Two Palestinian Nuns," May 17. Available online: http://www.arab48.com (accessed April 12, 2022).

Nakhleh, K. (2011), "Yawm al-Ard (Land Day)," in N. N. Rouhana and A. Sabbagh-Khoury (eds), *The Palestinians in Israel: Readings in History, Politics and Society*, vol. 1, 83–9, Haifa: Mada al-Carmel. Arab Center for Applied Social Research.

Nasasra, M. (2015), "Ruling the Desert: Ottoman and British Policies towards the Bedouin of the Naqab and Transjordan Region, 1900–1948," *British Journal of Middle Eastern Studies*, 42 (3): 261–83.

Nasasra, M. (2017), *The Naqab Bedouins: A Century of Politics and Resistance*, New York: Columbia University Press.

Nasasra, M. (2018), "The Politics of Claiming and Representation: The Islamic Movement in Israel," *Journal of Islamic Studies*, 29 (1): 48–78.

Navaro-Yashin, Y. (2012), *The Make-Believe Space: Affective Geography in a Postwar Polity*, Durham NC and London: Duke University Press.

Naylor, S. and J. R. Ryan (2002), "The Mosque in the Suburbs: Negotiating Religion and Ethnicity in South London," *Social and Cultural Geography*, 3 (1): 39–59.

Negev, A. and S. Gibson (2001), "Akko (Tel)," in *Archaeological Encyclopaedia of the Holy Land*, 26–8, New York: Continuum.

Neuman, B. (2015), *Land and Desire in Early Zionism*, Waltham: Brandeis University Press.

Nir, O. (2001), "The Muslims Demand a House of Prayer, the Municipality Insists on a Museum," *Haaretz*, March 29. Available online: https://www.haaretz.co.il/misc/2001-03-29/ty-article/0000017f-da79-d718-a5ff-fafd1d650000 (accessed July 22, 2022). [Hebrew]

Ohana, D. (2008), *Neither Canaanites nor Crusaders*, Ramat Gan, Israel: Bar-Ilan University Press. [Hebrew]

Ombudsman (2020), *The State Comptroller Annual Report 70A*. Available online: https://www.mevaker.gov.il/sites/DigitalLibrary/Documents/2020/70a/2020-70A-EN.pdf (accessed August 10, 2022). [Hebrew]

Orsi, R. A. (1985), *The Madonna of 115th Street: Faith and Community in Italian Harlem, 1880–1950*, New Haven: Yale University Press.

Orsi, R. A. (1999), *Gods of the City: Religion and the American Urban Landscape*, Bloomington: Indiana University Press.

O'Toole, M. (2016), "Inside al-Aqsa: Who Are the Guardians of al-Aqsa," *Al-Jazeera*. Available online: https://interactive.aljazeera.com/aje/2016/al-aqsa-mosque-jerusalem-360-degrees-tour-4k-video/the-protectors-of-al-aqsa-jerusalem.html (accessed March 17, 2022).

Otto, R. (1959), *The Idea of the Holy*, Harmondsworth: Penguin Books.

Parnell, S. and S. Oldfield (2014), "Introduction," in S. Oldfield and S. Parnell (eds), *Handbook on Cities in the Global South*, 1–5, London: Routledge.

Passi, P. (2004), "Place and Region: Looking through the Prism of Scale," *Progress in Human Geography*, 28 (4): 536–46.

Peck, J. (1998), "Geographies of Governance: TECs and the Neo-Liberalisation of 'Local Interests,'" *Space and Polity*, 2: 5–31.

Peck, J. (2015), "Cities beyond Compare?," *Regional Studies: The Journal of the Regional Studies Association*, 49 (1–2): 160–82.

Peled, K. (2019), "History, Memory and the Meaning of Place: The Renovation of Sidnā 'Alī Mosque as a Nexus of Palestinian, Arab and Islamic Identity in Israel," *Journal of Israeli History*, 37 (1): 61–85.

Peters, E. E. (1985), *The Typology of the Holy City in the Near East: Jerusalem and Mecca*, New York: New York University Press.

Petersen, A. (2018), *Bones of Contention: Muslim Shrines in Palestine*, Singapore: Palgrave Macmillan.

Philipp, T. (2001), *Acre: The Rise and Fall of a Palestinian City, 1730–1831*, New York: Columbia University Press.

Podeh, E. (2015), *Chances for Peace: Missed Opportunities in the Arab-Israeli Conflict*, Austin: University of Texas Press.

Porath, Y. (1974), *The Emergence of the Palestinian-Arab National Movement 1918–1929*, London: Frank Cass.

Porath, Y. (1977), *The Palestinian Arab National Movement*, London: F. Cass.

Prawer, J. (1987), "Jerusalem in the Christian Perspective of the Early Middle Ages," in J. Prawer (ed.), *The History of Jerusalem. The Early Islamic Period*, 242–82, Jerusalem: Yad Izhak Ben-Zvi Publications. [Hebrew]

Pred, A. (1984), "Place as Historically Contingent Process: Structuration and the Time-Geography of Becoming Places," *Annals of the Association of American Geographers*, 79 (2): 279–97.

Pullan, W., M. Sternberg and L. Kyriacou, eds (2013), *The Struggle for Jerusalem's Holy Places: Radicalisation and Conflict*, London: Routledge.

Purcell, M. (2002), "Excavating Lefebvre: The Right to the City and Its Urban Politics of the Inhabitant," *GeoJournal*, 58 (2): 99–108.

Purcell, M. (2003), "Islands of Practice and the Marston/Brenner Debate: Toward a More Synthetic Critical Human Geography," *Progress in Human Geography*, 27 (3): 317–32.

Al-Qalaqashandi, Ahmad (1987), *Subh al-a'sha fi sina'at al-inshā*, 14 vols. Beirut: Dar al-Kutub al-'Ilmiyya. [Arabic]

Qian, J. and L. Kong (2017), "Buddhism Co. Ltd? Epistemology of Religiosity, and the Reinvention of a Buddhist Monastery in Hong Kong," *Environment and Planning D: Society and Space*, 36 (1): 159–77.

Rabinowitz, D. and K. Abu Bakr (2005), *Coffins on Our Shoulders: The Experience of the Palestinian Citizens of Israel*, Berkeley: The University of California Press.

Ram, M. and M. Aharon-Gutmann (2017), "Strongholding the Synagogue to Stronghold the City: Urban-Religious Configurations in a Mixed Israeli Town," *Tijdschrift voor Economische en Sociale Geografie*, 108 (5): 641–55.

Raz-Karkotzkin, A. (2002), "A National Colonial Theology: Religion, Orientalism and the Construction of the Secular in Zionist Discourse," *Tel Aviver Jahrbuch für Deutsche Geschichte*, 30: 304–18.

Raz-Karkotzkin, A. (2005), "There Is No God but He Promised Us This Land," *Mitaam*, 3: 71–6. [Hebrew]

Raz-Karkotzkin, A. (2007), "Jewish Memory between Exile and History," *The Jewish Quarterly Review*, 97 (4): 530–43.

Reader, I. (2007), "Pilgrimage Growth in the Modern World: Meanings and Implications," *Religion*, 37 (3): 210–29.

Reiner, E. (2014), "Jewish Pilgrimage to Jerusalem in Late Antiquity and the Middle Ages," in O. Limor, E. Reiner and M. Frenkel (eds), *Pilgrimage: Jews, Christians, Muslims*, 45–130, Rananna: The Open University of Israel Press.

Reiter, Y. (2008), *Jerusalem and Its Role in Islamic Solidarity*, New York: Palgrave Macmillan.

Reiter, Y. (2009), "The Waqf in Israel since 1965: The Case of Acre Reconsidered," in M. J. Berger, Y. Reiter and L. Hammer (eds), *Holy Places in the Israeli-Palestinian Conflict. Confrontation and Co-Existance*, 116–39, London and New York: Routledge.

Reiter, Y. (2016), *Status Quo in Change: The Struggles for Control on the Temple Mount*, Jerusalem: Jerusalem Institute for Israel Studies. [Hebrew]

Reiter, Y. (2017), *Contested Holy Places in Israel-Palestine. Sharing and Conflict Resolution*, London and New York: Routledge.

Reiter, Y. and L. Lehrs (2013), *A City with a Mosque in Its Heart. Conflict Resolution at Holy Places: The Case of the Beer-Sheva Grand Mosque*, Jerusalem: Jerusalem Institute for the Study of Israel. [Hebrew]

Rekhess, E. (2002), "The Arabs of Israel after Oslo: Localization of the National Struggle," *Israel Studies*, 7 (3): 1–44.

Relph, E. (1976), *Place and Placelessness*, London: Pion.

Reuveni, C. (2022), "From the Tomb of Rachel to the Mosque of Bilal ibn Rabah: The Development of a Palestinian Sacred Place," in L. Chen, O. Hacker, and N. Stadler (eds), *Sacred Places in the Holy Land. An Ethnographic Perspective*, 231–58, Rananna: Open University Press. [Hebrew]

Riley-Smith, J. (2003), *The First Crusade and the Idea of Crusading*, London, New York: Continuum.

Ritmeyer, K. and L. Ritmeyer (1989), "Reconstructing Herod's Temple Mount in Jerusalem," *Biblical Archaeology Review*, 15 (6): 23–42.

Robertson, R. (1995), "Glocalization: Time-Space and Homogeneity-Heterogeneity," in M. Featherstone, R. Robertson and S. Lash (eds), *Global Modernities*, 25–44, London: Sage.

Robinson, J. (2006), *Ordinary Cities. Between Modernity and Development*, London: Routledge.

Roffe-Ofir, S. (2008),"Israel Defiled Al-Aqsa," *Ynet News*, August 22, 2008, http://www.ynetnews.com/articles/0,7340,L-3586354,00.html (accessed August 20, 2022).

Rogers, S. S. (2011), *Inventing the Holy Land: American Protestant Pilgrimage to Palestine, 1865–1941*, Lanham, Boulder, New York: Lexington Books.

Rose, G. (1993), *Feminism and Geography: The Limits of Geographical Knowledge*, Cambridge: Polity.

Rotbard, S. (2005), *White City, Black City*, Tel Aviv: Bavel. [Hebrew]

Roudometof, V. (2016), "Theorizing Glocalization: Three Interpretations," *European Journal of Social Theory*, 19 (3): 391–408.

Rouhana, N. N. (2001), "Outsiders' Identity: Are the Realities of 'Inside Palestinians' Reconcilable?," *Palestine-Israel Journal*, 8 (4): 61–70.

Roy, A. (2014), "Worlding the South: Towards a Postcolonial Urban Theory," in S. Parnell and S. Oldfield (eds), *The Routledge Handbook on Cities of the Global South*, 9–20, New York: Routledge.

Rubin, U. (2008), "Between Arabia and the Holy Land: A Mecca-Jerusalem Axis of Sanctity," *Jerusalem Studies in Arabic and Islam*, 34: 345–62.

Sack, R. D. (1980), *Homo Geographicus: A Framework for Action, Awareness, and Moral Concern*, Baltimore: Johns Hopkins University Press.

Said, E. (1993), *Culture and Imperialism*, New York: Vintage Books.

Salaama, Y. (2004), *A Letter to Mr. Kamal Jayyushi, Director of the Al-Jazzar Charitable Trust*, November 23.

Salah, R. (2002a), "Jerusalem Is above and beyond Negotiation," in *Sawt al-Haqq wal-Huriyya* (special supplement) September 15: A 5. [Arabic]

Salah, R. (2002b), "Al-Aqsa Is Muslim, Arab and Palestinian," *Sawt al-Haqq wal-Huriyya*, January 25: 3. [Arabic]

Saler, M. (2006), "Modernity and Enchantment: A Historiographic Review," *The American Historical Review*, 111 (3): 692–716.

Sand, S. (2014), *The Invention of the Jewish People*, London and New York: Verso.

Sandercock, L. (1998), *Towards Cosmopolis: Planning for Multicultural Cities*, London: John Wiley.

Saposnik, A. (2021), *Zionism's Redemptions: Images of the Past and Visions of the Future in Jewish Nationalism*, Cambridge: Cambridge University Press.

Schmit, K. (2020), "Murabitat al-Aqsa: The New Virgins of Palestinian Resistance," *Contemporary Islam*, 14: 289–308.

Scholem, G. (1971), *The Messianic Idea in Judaism, and Other Essays on Jewish Spirituality*, New York: Schocken Books.

Secor, A. J. (2002), "The Veil and Urban Space in Istanbul: Women's Dress, Mobility and Islamic Knowledge," *Gender, Place and Culture: A Journal of Feminist Geography*, 9 (1): 5–22.

Sedgwick, E. K. (1993), *Tendencies*, Durham: Duke University Press.

Selwyn, T. (2009), "Ghettoizing a Matriarch and a City: An Everyday Story from the Palestinian/Israeli Borderlands," *Journal of Borderlands Studies*, 24 (3): 39–55.

Shahak, I. and N. Mezvinsky (1999), *Jewish Fundamentalism in Israel*, London: Pluto Press.

Sherwood, H. (2018), "Religion: Why Faith Is Becoming More and More Popular?," *The Guardian*, August 25. Available online: https://www.theguardian.com/news/2018/aug/27/religion-why-is-faith-growing-and-what-happens-next (accessed October 10, 2022).

Shimoni, Y. (1947), *The Arabs of Palestine*, Tel-Aviv: Am Oved. [Hebrew]

Shlay, B. A. and G. Rosen (2015), *Jerusalem: The Spatial Politics of a Divided Metropolis*, Cambridge: Polity Press.

Shmaryahu-Yeshurun, Y. (2022), "Retheorizing State-Led Gentrification and Minority Displacement in the Global South-East," *Cities*, 130. Available online: https://doi.org/10.1016/j.cities.2022.103881 (accessed November 12, 2022).

Shmaryahu-Yeshurun, Y. and G. Ben-Porat (2020), "For the Benefit of All? State-Led Gentrification in a Contested City," *Urban Studies*, 58 (13): 2605–22.

Shoham, H. (2014), *Carnival in Tel Aviv: Purim and the Celebration of Urban Zionism*, Boston: Academic Studies Press.

Shragai, N. (2002), "Rachel's Tomb to be Annexed—de Facto," *Haaretz*, September 12. Available online: http://www.haaretz.com/print-edition/news/rachel-s-tomb-to-be-annexed-de-facto-1.34418 (accessed April 23, 2022). [Hebrew]

Simmel, G. (1903), "The Metropolis and Mental Life," in D. Levine (ed.), *Individuality and Social Forms*, 324–39, Chicago: University of Chicago Press.

Smith, J. Z. (1987), *To Take Place: Towards a Theory of Ritual*, Chicago: Chicago University Press.

Smith, N. (1984), *Uneven Development. Nature, Capital, and the Production of Space*, Oxford: Blackwell.

Smith, N. (1992), "Geography, Difference, and the Politics of Scale," in J. Doherty, E. Graham and M. Malek (eds), *Postmodernism and the Social Sciences*, 57–79, London: Macmillan.

Smith, N. (1993), "Homeless/Global: Scaling Places," in J. Bird, B. Curtis, T. Putman, G. Robertson, and L. Tickner (eds), *Mapping the Future—Local Cultures, Global Change*, 81–119, London: Routledge.

Smith, N. (1997), "Commentary on Peter Taylor's Materialist Framework," *Progress in Human Geography*, 21 (4): 555–62.

Squires, J. A., J. Donald and E. Carter (1993), *Space and Place: Theories of Identity and Location*, London: Lawrence and Wishart.

Stadler, N. and N. Luz (2015), "Two Venerated Mothers Separated by a Fence: Iconic Spaces and Borders in Israel/Palestine," *Journal of Religion & Society Advances in Research*, 6: 127–41.

Stern, Y. (2007) "Letter to Yeshiva Students." Available online: http://yakko.co.il/eng/maamar.asp?id=33661&cat=2577 (accessed October 6, 2012). [Hebrew]

Strickert, F. M. (2007), *Rachel Weeping: Jews, Christians, and Muslims at the Fortress Tomb*, Collegeville: Liturgical Press.

Swatos, W. H. and K. J. Christiano (1999), "Secularization Theory: The Course of a Concept," *Sociology of Religion*, 60 (3): 209–28.

Swyngedouw, E. (1997), "Neither Global nor Local: 'Glocalization' and the Politics of Scale," in K. R. Cox (ed.), *Spaces of Globalization. Reasserting the Power of the Local*, 137–66, New York and London: The Guilford Press.

Swyngedouw, E. (2003), "Globalisation or 'Glocalisation'? Networks, Territories and Rescaling," *Cambridge Review of International Affairs*, 17 (1): 25–48.

Tadmor-Shimony, T. (2013), "Yearning for Zion in Israeli Education: Creating a Common National Identity," *Journal of Jewish Identities*, 6 (1): 1–21.

Al-Tahan, Z. (2017), "Campaign to Free Palestinian Leader Launched in Turkey," *Al-Jazeera*, November 6. Available online: https://www.aljazeera.com/news/2017/11/6/campaign-to-free-palestinian-leader-launched-in-turkey (accessed August 8, 2022).

Talmon-Heller, D. (2006), "Graves, Relics and Sanctuaries: The Evolution of Syrian Sacred Topography (Eleventh-Thirteenth Centuries)," *Aram*, 18–19: 601–20.

Tamimi Arab, P. (2013), "Mosques in the Netherlands: Transforming the Meaning of Marginal Spaces," *Journal of Muslim Minority Affairs*, 33 (4): 477–94.

Taylor, P. J. (1982), "A Materialist Framework for Political Geography," *Transactions, Institute of British Geographers*, 7: 15–34.

Al-Tihi, S. (2022), "One Does Not Drink Alcohol in a Mosque. Even If in Beersheba It Was Turned into a Mosque," *Sicha Mekomit*, July 4. Available online: https://www.mekomit.co.il/ (accessed July 20, 2022). [Hebrew]

Tong, C. K. and L. Kong (2000), "Religion and Modernity: Ritual Transformations and the Reconstruction of Space and Time," *Social and Cultural Geography*, 1: 29–44.

Torstrick, R. L. (2000), *The Limits of Coexistence: Identity Politics in Israel*, Ann Arbor: University of Michigan Press.

Tuan, Y. (1977), *Space and Place: The Perspective of Experience*, Minneapolis: University of Minnesota Press.

Tubul, S. (2022), "Vice Mayor of Beersheba Municipality: There Will Be No Mosque Here! Beersheba Is a Jewish City," July 5. Available online: https://www.radiodarom.co.il/item?id=14344 (accessed July 21, 2022).

Tweed, T. A. (1997), *Our Lady of the Exile: Diasporic Religion at a Cuban Catholic Shrine in Miami*, New York and Oxford: Oxford University Press.

Tweed, T. A. (2006), *Crossing and Dwelling: A Theory of Religion*, Cambridge, London: Harvard University Press.

Van Teeffelen, T. (2021), "Rachel's Tomb Narrative Counterspaces in a Military Geography of Oppression," *Jerusalem Quarterly*, 87: 55–72.

Veer van der, P. (2013), "Nationalism and Religion," in J. Breilly (ed.), *The Oxford Handbook of the History of Nationalism*, online edition. Oxford Academic (accessed October 20, 2022).

Veracini, L. (2010), *Settler Colonialism: A Theoretical Overview*, New York: Palgrave Macmillan.

Vetrovec, S. (2007), "Super-Diversity and Its Implications," *Ethnic and Racial Studies*, 30 (6): 1024–54.

Wallach, Y. (2021), "The Violence that Began at Jerusalem's Ancient Holy Sites Is Driven by a Distinctly Modern Zeal," *The Guardian*, May 13. Available online: https://www.theguardian.com/commentisfree/2021/may/13/violence-jerusalemholy-sites-israeli-right-templemount?fbclid=IwAR0bonPRnJHOVbsCrJfN3q3LxcqXHP7Tca0KIF1rPJHIszVdB68DK02zVdY (accessed June 12, 2021).

Waqid, A. and Y. Pais (2001), "Severe Riots by the Hassan Bek Mosque," *Ynet*, June 3. Available online: https://www.ynet.co.il/articles/0,7340,L-783369,00.html (accessed August 14, 2022). [Hebrew]

Warf, B. and S. Arias, eds (2009), *The Spatial Turn: Interdisciplinary Perspectives*, London: Routledge.

Waterman, S. (1971), "Pre-Israeli Planning in Palestine: The Example of Acre," *The Town Planning Review*, 42 (1): 85–99.

Wehr, H. (1994), *Arabic-English Dictionary*, Ithaca: Spoken Language Services.

Weiler, G. (1976), *Jewish Theocracy*, Tel Aviv: Am Oved. [Hebrew]

Weismann, I. (2001), *Taste of Modernity: Sufism, Salafiyya, and Arabism in Late Ottoman Damascus*, Leiden: Brill.

Wilford, J. (2010), "Sacred Archipelagos: Geographies of Secularization," *Progress in Human Geography*, 34 (3): 328–48.

Wilken, R. L. (1986), "Early Christian Chiliasm, Jewish Messianism, and the Idea of the Holy Land," *Harvard Theological Review*, 79 (1–3): 298–307.

Wilken, R. L. (1992), *The Land Called Holy: Palestine in Christian History and Thought*, New Haven: Yale University Press.

Wilson, S. (1985), "Introduction," in S. Wilson (ed.), *Saints and Their Cults. Studies in Religious Sociology, Folklore and History*, 1–54, Cambridge: Cambridge University Press.

Wirth, L. (1938), "Urbanism as a Way of Life," *American Journal of Sociology*, 44 (1): 1–24.

Wolfe, P. (2006), "Settler Colonialism and the Elimination of the Native," *Journal of Genocide Research*, 8 (4): 387–409.

Woods, O. (2019), "Religious Urbanism in Singapore: Competition, Commercialism and Compromise in the Search for Space," *Social Compass*, 66 (1): 24–34.

Wright, J. K. (1966), *Human Nature in Geography: Fourteen Papers, 1925–1965*, Cambridge MA: Harvard University Press.

Yacobi, H (2003), "The Architecture of Ethnic Logic: Exploring the Meaning of the Built Environment in the 'Mixed' City of Lod—Israel," *Geografiska Annaler*, 84: 171–87.

Yagne, Y. and J. Khoury (2001), "Muslims in the Negev Erected a Protest Tent against a Wine Festival in the Mosque of Beersheba," *Haaretz*, September 3. Available online: https://www.haaretz.co.il/news/education/2012-09-03/ty-article/0000017f-e395-df7c-a5ff-e3ff35ed0000 (accessed July 21, 2022). [Hebrew]

Yashar, Y. (2017), "Inauguration Speech of the Religious Neighborhood," August 30. Available online: www.facebook.com/watch/?v=1389040691217597 (accessed January 19, 2021). [Hebrew]

Yiftachel, O. (2002), "Territory as the Kernel of Nationalism," *Geopolitics*, 7 (3): 215–48.

Yiftachel, O. (2006), *Ethnocracy: Land and Identity Politics in Israel/Palestine*, Philadelphia: University of Pennsylvania Press.

Yiftachel, O. (2016), "The Aleph—Jerusalem as Critical Learning," *City*, 20 (3): 483–94.

Yiftachel, O. and S. Kedar (2000), "Landed Power: The Emergence of an Ethnocratic Land Regime in Israel," *Theory and Critique*, 19 (1): 67–100. [Hebrew]

Yiftachel, O. and B. Roded (2010), "Abraham's Urban Footsteps: Political Geography and Religious Radicalism in Israel/Palestine," in N. AlSayyad and M. Massoumi (eds), *The Fundamentalist City? Religiosity and the Remaking of Urban Space*, 187–203, New York: Routledge.

Yiftachel, O. and H. Yacobi (2003), "Urban Ethnocracy: Ethnicity and the Production of Space in an Israeli Mixed City," *Environment and Planning D: Society and Space*, 21: 673–93.

Zaban, H. and N. Luz (2021), "The Acre Riots as a Display of Rage," *Theory and Critique* (special volume: Spreading like a Wildfire), 1–6. (online publication). [Hebrew]

Zatari, F. (2018) "Palestinian Culture of Sumud," *Daily Sabah*, April 4. Available online: https://www.dailysabah.com/feature/2018/04/04/palestinian-culture-of-sumud (accessed August 31, 2022).

Zilberman, I. (2001), "The Conflict over Mosque/Temple in Jerusalem and Ayhodya," in Y. Reiter (ed.), *Sovereignty of God and Man: Sanctity and Political Centrality on the Temple Mount*, 241–68, Jerusalem: The Jerusalem Institute for the Study of Israel. [Hebrew]

Index

Abbasi, M. 129–30
Abbas, M. 86, 90, 94, 156, 171
Abd Al-rahman, M. 169
Absentee Property Act 38–9, 112
Abu 'Amar, A. 41
Abu Bakr, K. 148
Abu Jarad, Y. 173
Abulof, A. 41
Abu-Zayd, B. 119
Acre 15–16, 18, 51–4, 72, 74, 100, 124–5, 128, 182
    Lababidi Mosque 146–52
    ReligioCity in 136–46
    religion into urban ethnocracy 129–36
Adallah 106
Agnew, J. A. 7, 9, 98
Aharon-Gutmann, M. 133
Ahmad, U. 51, 66
Akenson, D. 38
'*Akka* Baladi ("Acre My Town") 130
Akko 139–40
Akkonet 140, 147–50
Al-Aqsa Association for the Upkeep of Sacred Places 41
al-Aqsa Intifada 119
al-ard al-muqaddasa 33
Alexandrowicz, O. 113
Al-Jazzar Charitable Trust 136, 147–8
al-Marwani Mosque 169–70
al-Nakba 36
al-Qalqashandi 33
Amer, A. 135
Amitai, R. 129
Anderson, B. 40
Antonius, G. 22
Arab national awakening 22
Arafat, W. 62, 163–4
Arculfus 28
al-'Aref, A. 104
'Ari'ar, Tawfiq Muhammad 171
'Ari'ar, T. M. 171
Arias, S. 10

Arraf, S. 61, 72, 74–6
Asad, T. 98
Aṣfur, A. 40, 117, 120–1
Ash, J. 127
Ashkenazi, J. 27–8
Assif, S. 117, 191 n.11
Auda, A. 137
Avci, Y. 103
Azuri, N. 160–1

Bahat, D. 154
Baker, C. 97, 126
Bakshi, A. 98
Baranes, Y. 137
Bar, D. 29, 41
Bard, M. G. 58
Barkan, E. 34, 164
Barkey, K. 22, 34, 164
Bar-Tal, D. 41
Bartal, S. 161
Barthes, R. 98
Bawardy, M. 16, 18, 56–7, 70, 72–3, 84
    birthplace 86–90, 189 n.3
    complex 88–9
    history and mythology 84–6
    politics of the shrine 90–5
Beaumont, J. 97, 126
Becci, I. 123–4, 126
Beckford, J. A. 126
Beck, U. 158
Beersheba Mosque 3–5, 15, 18, 43, 97, 102–9, 118, 120, 181, 190 n.4
Bellah, R. N. 183
Ben-Artzi, Y. 129
Ben-Bassat, Y. 129
Ben-Porat, G. 132, 135
Benvenisti, M. 37
Berger, P. L. 11, 98, 123, 127, 155, 179, 185
Berkovits, S. 163
Berman, M. 104
Berretta, D. 90
Bindi, S. 123, 127

Bi'r al-Sab' 103–5
al-Bishtawi, F. 130
Bitton-Ashkelony, B. 28
Blakey, J. 13–14
body and embodiment 47–54, 66
Boker, E. 106–7
Booth, W. 156
Bourdieu, P. 50, 128
Bovis, H. E. 162
Brenner, N. 157–8, 160
British Mandate 22, 34, 41, 91, 104, 129, 161
Brunot, A. 85
Buck, D. C. 86
Burchardt, M. 123–4, 126, 128
Burckhardt, M. 124
Burns, P. 85
Busse, H. 153
Butler, J. 47–8, 85
Buzy, D. 85

Camp David Summit 158, 164
Canaan, T. 34, 41, 76
Canard, M. 52
Carter, E. 8
Casanova, J. 11, 98, 123–4, 126
Chidester, D. 9–11
Christianity 23, 27, 32, 90, 94, 100, 153–4
Christiano, K. J. 178
City of David 25
Clinton, W. J. 164
Cobb, P. M. 154
Cohen, N. 22, 135, 142–4, 161
Collins-Kreiner, N. 29
colonialism 124, 133
Cooper, J. E. 30
corpus separatum 162
Cortellessa, E. 156
Crawford, S. J. 60
Creswell, K. A. C. 7, 10, 28, 101
critical urban theories (CUT) 123
The Crown 177

Dabagh, M. M. 111
Dahamshe, 'Abd al-Malik 158–60
Dakwar, J. 167–8
Dallaire, G. 72
Daoud, A. 71, 79, 84–9, 91, 189 n.3, 189 n.5
Darwish, Shaykh 'Abdullah Nimr 166–7

Dawani, S. 138
de Certeau, M. 1, 8, 127
decolonization 18, 122, 124–5, 146–8, 152, 182
Deleuze, G. 12
della Dora, V. 8, 126, 187
desecularization theory 179, 185
Development Authority 112
dhikr 59, 189 n.6
Diabes, I. 138
Dikec, M. 12
Donald, J. 8
Donner, H. 28
Douglas, M. 47, 67
Dumper, M. 3, 166–7
Duncan, J. S. 9
Durkheim, E. 9–10, 25, 179, 183–5
al-Durra, M. 172, 192 n.6
Dwyer, C. 123, 127

Eade, J. 10, 95, 123, 127
Efe-epa 156
Efrat, E. 162
Eglash, R. 156
Elad, A. 15, 29, 170
El-Azhari, T. 154
Eldar, S. 165
Eliade, M. 9–10
Eliav, Y. 26
Eliaz, Y. 31–2
Elijah 5–6
Eliyahu, R. S. 142, 145
Ellenblum, R. 154
embodiment 66, 180
   body and 47–54
enchanted places 5, 84, 179
Entwistle, J. 53
Escobar, A. 9
Essallam Mosque 99
ethnocracy 16, 21, 23, 34, 36–44, 102, 122, 125, 128, 131, 133, 135, 137, 145–6, 148, 151–2
Eudocia, A. 28
Eusebius 27
Express Tribune 156

Fabian, R. 112
Fares, H. 138
Fazl Mosque 97–9
fetishization process 162

fin de siècle Palestine 22
Finkelstein, I. 24, 26
Fischbach, M. R. 38
Foucault, M. 8, 10, 47–8
Francis, Pope 57, 84, 86, 94
Freas, E. 164
Frenkel, Y. 77, 154
Friedland, R. 186

Gale, T. 92, 159
Galili, E. 129
Gans, H. 41
Garbin, D. 97, 123, 127
Gavrilis, G. 22
Geertz, C. 55
Gelber, Y. 104
Gellner, E. 185
gender 47–8
Gesler, W. M. 60
Gibson, S. 129
Gilbert, D. 123, 127
Giorda, M. 126
glocalization 157–60, 163, 166, 173–4, 183
Goitein, S. D. 33
Gökarıksel, B. 97
Golan, A. 112
Golan Heights 5–6
Goldziher, I. 73
Göle, N. 110, 122, 181–2
Gonen, R. 153
Gordon, A. G. 42
Grand Mosque 102–5, 181
Guattari, F. 12

Habermas, J. 126
Hagget, P. 11
Haifa 99–100, 129–30, 132, 138
Hajj, Ahmad 61, 77, 81–2
Halabi, U. 6
Hamas 3, 135, 163, 171
Hamilton, B. 154
Hamuda, S. 112, 117
Hamza, H. 83–4
Haram al-Sharif/Temple Mount 2–3, 9, 13, 15–16, 18, 26–8, 64–5, 78, 94, 135, 153–8, 160–74, 183, 192 n.5
Al-Harawi, ʿAli 62
Harris, A. 60
Harvey, D. 8, 10
Hashimshoni, Z. 113

Hassan Bek Mosque 15, 43, 97, 100, 109–20, 181
Hasson, N. 86
Hatuka, T. 113
Hazard, S. 101, 127, 187
Heidecker, N. 131, 133
Herod, A. 11
Herod, King 168
Hertzberg, A. 42
Hertzberg, V. 114
Hertz, R. 72–3, 95, 181
Hervieu-Léger, D. 140, 183–4
Herzberg, V. 113, 191 n.7
hijab 53, 66, 189 n.3
Hirsch, S. R. 31
Holloway, J. 49–51
Holy Land 21, 23–34, 37, 44, 90, 93, 96, 140, 145
Holy Sepulcher 27, 32, 153–4, 161
Home, R. 40
Hönne, S. 128
Howitt, R. 49
Husam al-Din Abu al-Hijja 59–61, 72–3
al-Husayni, A. 3

Iʿbbelin 16, 56–7, 70–2, 84–6, 88–95, 190 n.7, 190 n.9
ibn Bari, S. 4, 107, 190 n.5
Ibrahim, M. E. 65
Ihmoud, S. 64
Inbari, M. 165
Isambert, F. A. 184
Islamic movement 3, 13, 15, 19, 34, 41, 43, 52, 65, 118, 156–7, 159–60, 163, 165–75, 183
Isnart, C. 72
Israel Defense Forces (IDF) 36, 105, 192 n.6
Israeli Absentee Property Act (1950) 38
Israeli-Palestinian 2–3, 16, 34, 62, 95, 102–3, 107, 109, 155, 157, 160–1, 165, 169, 172, 174
Israel Science Foundation 190 n.6, 191 n.1
Izenberg, D. 132

Jaffa Charitable Trust (1967) 113–14, 117
Jedan, C. 126
Jenkins, R. 178
Jeroboam 25
Jerome 28

Jerusalem 153–7
Jerusalem Day 2
Jerusalem Temple 26, 30, 162
Jewish-Israeli mobilization 163
Jones, J. P. 13
Judaization of the Galilee 82
Juergensmeyer, M. 185

Kabub, 'Abd Badawi 114–16, 120
Kadduri, Y. 16
Kais, R. 107
Kalimi, I. 25
Kallus, R. 113
Kamal Rayan, S. 167
karamat 75
Karsh, E. 130
Kaukab Abu al-Hijja 59, 61, 69, 72–4, 76–7, 79–83
Keane, W. 101–2
Kedar, A. 36–7, 40, 112
Keith, M. 8
Khalidi, R. 22, 36
Khoury, J. 107
Khoury, L. 93, 107
Kimmerling, B. 23
Kipnis, B. A. 133
Knott, K. 10, 48, 72, 92, 101, 127–8
Koenig, M. 179
Komarova, M. 98
Kong, L. 10, 92, 97–8, 123, 126
Korff, R. 157
Kupferschmidt, U. M. 162

Lababidi Mosque 18, 122, 125, 146–52, 182
Lahat, S. 112, 116–17
Lankri, S. 135, 145
Lanz, S. 127
Larkin, C. 3, 98, 166–7
Latour, B. 98, 127, 160
Lay, D. 8
Lecoquierre, M. 40, 81
Leeuw, van der G. 11
Lefebvre, H. 1, 8, 10, 18, 47–8, 54–6, 97–8, 121, 127, 181
Lehrs, L. 4, 106
LeVine, M. 111–13, 120
Lewis, B. 103, 126
Lincoln, B. 173
Linenthal, E. D. 9–11

Lustick, I. S. 155, 162
Luz, N. 2–4, 6, 9, 29, 33–4, 43, 56, 63–4, 77, 82, 97, 104, 114, 116, 125, 132–3, 135, 153–4, 161, 167–8, 170, 179
Luzon, R. 137, 146–7

MacCormack, S. 32
Maddrell, A. 92
Maeir, A. 24
Maghribi neighborhood 162
Mahmood Qasim 69–70, 79, 189 n.1
Mahmood, S. 50, 66–7
Mahmud 'Abd al-Fattah 76
Majid, U. 64
Mamluk 34, 77, 129
Mandatory Palestine 22
Mandatory Quarter 129, 133–4, 138–40, 146, 149, 191 n.6
Mansfield, B. 13
Manshiyya 109–13, 116–18
maqām 73, 75
Maqam abu al-Hijja 15–16, 18, 59–60, 73–84, 95, 180
Mara'i, T. 6
Marcuse, P. 98
Markus, R. A. 32
Marston, S. A. 12–13
Massey, D. 5, 8, 10, 49, 52, 58, 161, 173
Massoumi, M. 97, 126
materiality 26–9, 48, 73, 76, 81, 86, 92, 99–102, 110–11, 114, 116, 120–2, 124, 127–8, 142, 150, 181–2, 187
Mayer, T. 99
McGuire, M. B. 51
Mezvinsky, N. 30
Millet system 21
minarets 99, 101, 104, 109–12, 116–18, 120, 148, 150
Mi'raj 10
Mitchell, D. 58, 101
Molendijk, A. L. 126
Monterescu, D. 39, 109–11
Moore, A. 13, 134
Morgan, D. 101, 127
Morris, B. 22, 36, 105, 112
mu'adhdhin 62
Muhammad, Prophet 2, 10, 33, 62, 75, 81, 163, 189 n.1
mujahid 60, 74–5
Mujir, Al-din 155

mukarsakh 75
Murabitat 65–6
Murabitat al-Aqsa 64
Murre-van den Berg, H. 91
Muslim Charitable Trust 39, 113, 191 n.6
Muslim-Palestinian community 105–9
Mustafa 'Abd al-Fattah 75

Naamnih, H. 112
Nabi Illiya 5
Nabulsi, G. 57, 94
Najami, S. 148–51
Nakhleh, K. 103
Nasasra, M. 104–5, 167, 170, 173
nationalism 40, 155, 160–6, 184–6
Navaro-Yashin, Y. 101, 128
Naylor, S. 10, 97, 99
Negev 103–5, 107, 129, 141
Negev, A. 129
Neuman, B. 42
Nir, O. 103
Northern Wind Yeshiva 139
Nuri al-Ukbi 103, 106

O'Dowd, L. 98
Ohana, D. 30
Oldfield, S. 126
Olds, K. 8
Ombudsman 136
Ometz 142–3
Orsi, R. A. 101, 126
Oslo Accords 62, 163, 166
O'Toole, M. 66
Otto, R. 10, 178, 188 n.4

Pais, Y. 120
Parnell, S. 126
Passi, P. 12
Paul II, J. 57, 86
Peck, J. 118, 126
Peel Commission 161–2
Peled, K. 102
Penn, S. 113, 116, 191 n.8
Peres, G. 113–14, 120
Petersen, A. 34
Philipp, T. 129
Pile, S. 8
places 7–11, 32, 49
Podeh, E. 164
politics of the sacred 2–5, 151–2

Porat, Y. 170
Porter, J. L. 62
Prawer, J. 27
Pred, A. 9
profane space 9–11, 178, 188 n.5
promised land 22, 29–30, 32, 36
Pullan, W. 98
Purcell, M. 98, 118, 123

Qever Rachel 62
Qian, J. 126
qibla (prayers) 28, 33, 154, 172
Qubbat Rahil 62–4
Qur'an 33, 69, 78

Rabinowitz, D. 39, 109, 114, 148
Rabita 115–21
Ram, M. 133, 191 n.7
Raz-Karkotzkin, A. 31
Reader, I. 95
Reiner, E. 29
Reiter, Y. 4, 43, 64, 106–7, 147, 155, 163, 169
Rekhess, E. 83, 166
ReligioCity project 16, 18, 51, 96, 100, 122, 124–8, 130–3, 136–46, 151–2, 182, 187, 191 n.1
Relph, E. 8
Reuveni, C. 64, 189 n.8
Reyhan, Y. 116, 118, 191 n.10
Riley-Smith, J. 153
Rimawi, M. 53
Ritmeyer, K. 168
Ritmeyer, L. 168
Robertson, R. 157
Robinson, J. 126
Roded, B. 40, 133, 162
Roffe-Ofir, S. 171
Rogers, S. S. 33
Rose, G. 8, 49–50
Rosen, G. 3
Rotbard, S. 111
Roudometof, V. 157
Rouhana, N. 99–100
Roy, A. 126
Rubin, U. 28, 33
Rubin, Y. 142–4
Ryan, J. R. 10, 97, 99

Sack, R. D. 7
Said, E. 58

Salaama, Y. 147
Salah al-Din (Saladin) 34, 74, 154, 172
Salah, R. 3, 34, 118–19, 156–7, 165, 167–74, 191 n.12
Salama, Y. 147, 191 n.8
Saler, M. 178
Sallnow, J. M. 10
Sandercock, L. 108, 121–2
Sand, S. 30–1
Sarsur, I. 167, 192 n.3
Satil, 'Abd al-Qadir 109–10, 115
Al-Sayyad, N. 97, 126
scale 11–14
   community 72, 91, 93, 95, 180–1
   jumping 13–14, 53, 160, 174
   politics of 12–13
   urban 18, 39, 56, 96–100, 118, 120, 122–4, 151–2, 181–2
Schmit, K. 65, 165
Schnell, I. 133
Scholem, G. 30
Second Intifada 78–9, 81, 119, 158–9
Secor, A. 50, 54, 67, 97
secularization theory 178–9, 185
Sedgwick, M. 48
Selwyn, T. 62
settler-colonialism 124, 133, 151
settler colonialism 124, 151
Shahak, I. 30
Shakur, E. 92
Shaqar, N. 114, 116, 118, 191 n.9
Sharon, A. 6, 144, 158, 164
Sharqon, I. 113, 191 n.6
Shaykh Hassan 5–7
Shlay, B. A. 3
Shmaryahu-Yeshurun, Y. 132, 135, 142
Shoham, H. 42
Shragai, N. 63
Silberman, N. A. 24, 26
Simmel, G. 39, 98
Simpson, P. 128
situational approach 9–11
Smith, N. 12, 25–7, 29
socio-spatial analysis 76–81, 86–90
Solomon, King 26
Solomon Temple 25–6, 154, 168
space 48–9
   construction of 54–5
spatial turn 1, 7, 10, 12, 99, 101, 127, 182
Squires, J. A. 8

Stadler, N. 5, 63, 84, 92, 133, 179
State of Israel 4, 21–2, 34, 36, 40, 43–5, 53, 58, 100, 105, 112, 115, 150, 162–3, 186
Stern, Y. 132, 140–1
Strhan, A. 123
Strickert, F. M. 62
substantial 9, 11, 113, 178
Sufism 189 n.5
Suna' al-Haya 51
Swatos, W. H. 178
Swyngedouw, E. 14, 157–8, 160

Tadmor-Shimony, T. 30
al-Tahan, Z. 173
Talmon-Heller, D. 34
Tamimi Arab, P. 99
Taylor, P. J. 12
Tel Aviv-Yafo 43, 97, 109–14, 116–18, 121, 181
terra repromissionis 28
Terry, A. 92
al-Tihi, S. 107
Tong, C. K. 97
Torstrick, R. L. 130
Tuan, Y. 7–8, 58
Tubul, S. 108
Tuhi, S. 116, 191 n.10
Tweed, T. A. 126

al-Ukbi, N. 103, 106
Umayyads 28–9
Umm al-Fahm 167, 170
urban
   ethnocracy 102, 122, 125, 128–37, 145–6, 148, 151–2, 182–3
   religion 123–7, 130, 151–2, 182
   sphere 97, 102, 108, 111, 118, 123, 125–6, 150, 181–2

Valins, O. 51
Van Teeffelen, T. 62
Veer van der, P. 185
Veracini, L. 124

Wallach, Y. 3
Waqf 34, 65, 104, 136–7, 150, 162, 168
Waqid, A. 120
War Bi'r al-Sab' 105

Warf, B. 10
Waterman, S. 129
Weber, M. 5, 127, 178, 184
Wehr, H. 65
Weiler, G. 30
Weismann, I. 41
Western Wall 76, 161, 163–4, 171–2
Wilford, J. 126
Wilken, R. L. 27–8, 32–3
Wilson, S. 72
Wirth, L. 126
Wolfe, P. 124
Woods, O. 126
Wright, J. K. 10

Yacobi, H. 39, 102, 125, 131
Yagne, Y. 107
Yashar, Y. 125, 143
yawm al-ard 103
Yiftachel, O. 23, 37–8, 40, 102, 125–6, 130–1, 133, 162

Zahra, M. 147, 150
Zatari, F. 102
Zechariah 24, 29
Zilberman, I. 163
Zionism 30–1, 41–2
Zionist 16, 30–1, 36, 41–3, 53, 130, 139–40, 142, 159, 161